fluent tarot: matters of the heart

READ LOVE & RELATIONSHIPS WITH
CONFIDENCE

THE DIVINATION ACADEMY

LORELAI HAMILTON

RAINBOW QUARTZ PUBLISHING

contents

Also by Lorelai Hamilton — ix

1. Introduction: Tarot & the Language of Love — 1

PART ONE
FOUNDATIONS OF LOVE READINGS

1. How Love Readings Differ from General Spreads — 7
2. Setting the Right Tone — 9
3. Blunt vs. Compassionate Language — 12
4. Handling Client Sensitivity & Expectations — 16
5. Karma in Love Readings — 20
6. Soul Contracts in Love Readings — 24
7. Signs of Karmic or Soul-Contract Love in Readings — 27
8. Tarot Cards That Often Signal Karma & Soul Contracts in Love — 30
9. Love Reading Foundations: Reader's Checklist — 32
10. Client Bill of Rights in Love Readings — 34
11. Foundations of Love Readings: Recap & Practice — 36

PART TWO
TYPES OF ROMANCE

12. Introduction — 43
13. Single & Searching — Attracting Love with Tarot — 45
    "What do I need to know about attracting love?"
14. Action Steps for Singles — 49
15. Dating / Complicated — 55
    "Where is this connection headed?"
16. How to Speak to Querents in "It's Complicated" Love — 57
17. Long-Term / Commitment — 61
    "How do we deepen our bond?"
18. Cautions for Long-Term Readings — 63
19. The Seasons of Long-Term Love — 66
20. Intimacy Beyond Romance — 69
21. Legacy & Shared Dreams — 72
22. Healing Old Wounds Together — 75
23. Long-Term Relationship Card Guide — 79
24. Self-Love — 82
    "How do I love myself the way I deserve?"

25. Tips for Reading Self-Love Spreads	85
26. Self-Love Affirmation Builder	89
27. The Court Cards as Self-Love Voices	91

PART THREE
TIMING IN LOVE

28. Why "When Will I Meet Them?" Is Tricky	97
29. How to Phrase Timing Questions with Care	100
30. A Reader's Role in Redirection	103
31. Redirect Script Library for Common Love Questions	105
32. Tarot Tools for Timing	108
33. Timing Quick Reference in Tarot	111
34. Right Timing vs. Exact Dates	113
35. Reading Right Timing *Case Study*	115
36. Redirecting Timing Questions in Practice	118

PART FOUR
RED FLAG & GREEN FLAG CARDS

37. What Red & Green Flags Mean in Tarot	123
38. Common Red Flag Cards	125
39. The Red Flag Spread	130
40. Common Green Flag Cards	132
41. The Green Flag Spread	137
42. The Red + Green Flag Spread	139
43. Reader's Script for the Red + Green Flag Spread	142

PART FIVE
SENSITIVE TOPICS IN LOVE READINGS

44. Why Sensitive Topics Matter	145
45. Infidelity *The Big Four Sensitive Topics*	147
46. How to Frame Infidelity Readings with Compassion	151
47. Infidelity Check-In Spread	160
48. Breakups *The Big Four Sensitive Topics*	163
49. Breakup Spread	166
50. "Will They Come Back?" *The Big Four Sensitive Topics*	168
51. Example Spread *The Return Question*	171
52. What to Look For *Will They Come Back*	173

53. The Return or Release Spread (6 Cards)	174
54. Unrequited Love	177
The Big Four Sensitive Topics	
55. Example Spread: One-Sided Love	180
56. How to Hold Space in an Unrequited Love Reading	182
57. The Unrequited to Empowered Spread	184
58. Reading Honestly Without Crushing Hope	187
59. Ethics & Empowerment	189
60. Practice Prompts	191

PART SIX
SHIFTING INTO THE LOVE LETTER VOICE

61. What Is the Love Letter Voice?	197
62. Boundaries & Ethics	200
The Guardrails of the Love Letter Voice	
63. The anatomy of a love-letter reading	207
64. Converting third-person to Love Letter	209
Mini Walk-through	
65. Choosing the Narrator: Four Beautiful Options	212
66. Introducing the Narrator Archetypes	215
67. Structuring Full Love-Letter Spreads	217
68. Three-Card "Past–Present–Invitation"	218
69. Five-Card Soul Letter	220
70. Seven-Card "The Whole Love Story"	222
71. Nine-Card "Letter of Reckoning"	224
72. Delivering Love-Letter Readings	227
73. Practice Assignments (Fast and Potent)	229
74. Deep Practice: The Full Love Letter	231
75. Why This Style Works	233
76. When Not to Use This Style	236
77. How and When to Use Love-Letter Style	238

PART SEVEN
WRITING POETIC YET CLEAR READINGS

78. Why Balance Matters	243
79. Tips for Balancing Beauty with Accuracy	245
80. Archetype Voices in Love-Letter Style	247
Majors	
81. Archetype Voices in Love-Letter Style	253
Swords	
82. Archetype Voices in Love-Letter Style	257
Wands	

83. Archetype Voices in Love-Letter Style — 261
    Cups
84. Archetype Voices in Love-Letter Style — 265
    Pentacles
85. Practice: The Love Letter Voice Lab — 269

PART EIGHT
EXAMPLES OF LOVE LETTER READINGS

86. Single Card Love Note — 273
    Examples
87. 3-Card Love Letter — 275
    Examples
88. 5-Card Soul Letter — 280
89. Tones & Variations — 284
    One Spread, Many Voices
90. Practice Prompts — 288
91. Reflection — 290
92. Reflection Exercise — 292
    Writing a Love Letter to Yourself

PART NINE
TAROT & MUSIC IN LOVE READINGS

93. Why Music Works in Love Readings — 297
94. Practical Ways to Weave Music Into Readings — 299
    1. Assign Songs to Cards
95. Tarot Playlist Starter Kit: The Majors — 301
96. Practical Ways to Weave Music Into Readings — 303
    2. Build Playlists for Spreads
97. The Love Story Playlist Spread 🎵 — 305
98. Practical Ways to Weave Music Into Readings — 307
    3. Invite the Querent's Song
99. Music Prompts for Tarot Readings — 309
100. Practical Ways to Weave Music Into Readings — 311
    4. Use Lyrics as Anchors
101. Lyric Bank for Love Readings — 313
102. The Song Deck — 317
103. Create Your Own Song Deck 🎵 — 320
    Practice Assignment

PART TEN
TAROT + ORACLES IN LOVE

104. Why Use Oracles with Tarot in Romance Readings — 325
105. How to Use Oracle Decks With Tarot in Love Readings — 327
106. Why Oracles Work So Well in Love Readings — 329

| 107. Cautions & Ethics — Using Oracle Cards with Integrity | 332 |
| 108. Blending Tarot and Oracle Cards | 336 |

PART ELEVEN
TAROT & STORYTELLING — ARCHETYPES IN ROMANCE

109. Why Storytelling Matters in Love Readings	343
110. Major Arcana as Romance Archetypes	347
111. Minor Arcana As Romance Archetypes	351
112. Tarot as Character Casting Practice	354
113. Linking Tarot to Tropes	357

PART TWELVE
ETHICS OF THIRD-PARTY LOVE READINGS

114. Why This Matters	363
115. Why Third-Party Readings Are Problematic	366
116. How to Communicate Boundaries with Kindness	369

PART THIRTEEN
HEALING AFTER HEARTBREAK

117. Why Healing Readings Matter	377
118. How to Deliver Healing Readings	381
119. Practice Prompts	384
120. The Art of Reading Romance Goodbye	387

PART FOURTEEN
INTERACTION SYSTEM

121. How cards modify and deepen each other	391
122. Major Arcana Interaction Systems	396
123. Minor Arcana - Swords Interaction Systems	408
124. Minor Arcana - Wands Interaction Systems	415
125. Minor Arcana - Cups Interaction Systems	423
126. Minor Arcana - Pentacles Interaction Systems	430

Acknowledgments 437
About the Author 439

also by lorelai hamilton

Encyclopedia of Divination
Encyclopedia of Cryptids
Encyclopedia of Faeries
Tarot Tales and Magic Spells
Teenage Tarot
Arcane In Verse
The Eclectic Witch's Grimoire
Teenage Witch's Grimoire
Find Your Bliss
Tarot Reflection Journal
Tarot Refection Journal Coloring The Tarot
Dream Journal
Fluent Tarot
Fluent Tarot Workbook
Fluent Tarot: Reading Romance & Love Letters

ADDITIONAL BOOKS BY RAINBOW QUARTZ PUBLISHING

Jax Wilder
Coral Cove Series
Sleighed by Love
Harvesting Love
Dawning Desire
Knead You Now
Love Rewound
Perfect Lover Spell
Haunted by Her
Red, White, and Ravished
Frosted Sugar Charms

Tarot Fantasies Series
The Devil's Temptations
Strength of the Beast

Hanged Passions
Six of Cups
Death's Embrace
Queen of Pentacles
Seven of Pentacles
Ace of Wands
Three of Swords
Lovers In The Veil
<u>Two of Swords</u>
Seven of Wands

Coastal Cupid Series
HeartBound Souls

Witches of Coral Cove
From Hell With Love

Fae Ring Series
Alice and Her Mad Hatters
Bound By The Glass Slipper

Stand Alone Titles
Pride and Prejudice and Witches

Miranda Levi
From A Youth A Fountain Did Flow
The Sea Withdrew
A Tear In Time
Mo(ther) Na(ture)
In Orion's Hands

Jackson Anhalt
From The 911 Files

Isla Watts
A Fairy Bad Day

Surprise! You're a Vampire
Gorgeous, Gorgeous, Gorgons
Mork The Handsome Orc
Adopted By Werewolves
Bite Me If You Can
That's The Spirit!

Rose Dawson's Book Journals
My Time With The Fairies
Enchanted Escapades
Enchanted Escapades
Dewey Decimal Diaries
Siren's Songbook
Pride and Prejudice
Bibliophile's Bounty
Book of Books Journal
Pages & Passages Reading Journal
Bookworm's Companion Reading Journal & Tracker

Illiana Barret
Prompted: 2,339 Romance Prompts: A Writer's Essential Resource
Prompted 1,700 Fantasy Prompts: A Writer's Essential Resource
Prompted 1,605 Science Fiction Writing Prompts: A Writer's Essential Resource
Prompted 1,902 Horror Writing Prompts : A Writer's Essential Resource
Prompted 1,290 Mystery Writing Prompts : A Writer's Essential Resource
Prompted 1,582 Children's Book Writing Prompts: A Writer's Essential Resource
Prompted: 2,265 Historical Fiction Writing Prompts : A Writer's Essential Resource
Prompted 1,500 Steampunk Writing Prompts
Prompted: 1,600 Dystopian Prompts: A Writer's Essential Resource

Fluent Tarot: Matters of the Heart © 2025 by Lorelai Hamilton

All rights reserved. No part of this publication may be reproduced, distributed, or transmitted in any form or by any means, including photocopying, recording, or other electronic or mechanical methods, without the prior written permission of the publisher, except in the case of brief quotations embodied in critical reviews and certain other noncommercial uses permitted by copyright law.

Published by Rainbow Quartz Publishing

RQPublishing.com

RainbowQuartzPublishing@gmail.com

Edmonds, WA 98026

Cover design by Miranda Townsend

Edited by Miranda Townsend

First Edition: September 2025

Disclaimer: The information contained in this book is for educational and informational purposes only and is not intended as health or professional advice. The author and publisher are not liable for any damages or negative consequences from any action, application, or preparation to any person reading or following the information in this book. References are provided for informational purposes only and do not constitute endorsement of any websites or other sources. Readers should be aware that the websites listed in this book may change.

CHAPTER 1

introduction: tarot & the language of love

If you've ever picked up a tarot deck for someone else, chances are the very first question they asked was about love.

"Does he still think about me?"

"Will she come back?"

"Am I going to find my person?"

"Is this the one?"

Love is where we ache, where we hope, and where we dream the loudest. It's no wonder it's the most common type of tarot reading—it's the part of life where we feel the most vulnerable and where we long for clarity the most. Tarot provides a kind of comfort we can't always find elsewhere. It doesn't just hand out answers; it listens. It reflects. It gives shape to the tangled feelings and hidden questions we already carry in our hearts.

This book is designed as a companion to *Fluent Tarot*. If you're new to tarot and still learning the meanings of the cards, I encourage you to begin with that book first. *Fluent Tarot* will teach you the foundations—the 78 cards, their symbols, and how to build a personal relationship with them. Here, we assume you already know the deck. We won't be re-teaching every meaning card by card. Instead, this book takes those foundations and expands them, showing you how to apply your knowledge to the realm of love and relationships in all their complexity.

Tarot can't promise that "the One" will text back on Tuesday, but it can show us patterns of connection, lessons of the heart, and energies at play. It gives language to the things we feel but struggle to articulate. It whispers, you are not crazy for wanting this, you are not alone in feeling this, and yes, love is written in the fabric of your story.

When someone comes to the cards about love, it's rarely just about the surface question. It's about needing reassurance, wanting to be seen, craving hope, or bracing for truth. Tarot gives people a way to hold the intangible—desire, heartbreak, uncertainty—and see it reflected in something real, something they can touch and turn over in their hands.

Tarot can't promise that "the One" will text back on Tuesday, but it can show us *patterns of connection, lessons of the heart, and energies at play*. It gives language to the things we feel but struggle to articulate. It whispers, *you are not crazy for wanting this, you are not alone in feeling this, and yes, love is written in the fabric of your story.*

Because love readings carry so much weight, they also carry great responsibility. When someone opens their heart in a reading, they are giving us their trust. That means it's our job to approach romance spreads with compassion, clarity, and strong boundaries.

Compassion means remembering that love is tender ground. Behind every question about romance, there's vulnerability: the ache of longing, the sting of heartbreak, the hope of connection. Even when the message is difficult—like seeing red flags in a relationship or the cards pointing to an ending—it can always be spoken with empathy. A compassionate reader doesn't dismiss pain or sugarcoat it, but instead says: *"I see where you are, and here's how the cards are guiding you through it."*

Clarity means avoiding vagueness or false hope—love deserves truth, not confusion. If a querent walks away more muddled than before, the reading hasn't served them. Clarity doesn't always mean bluntness; it means being direct and grounded in your interpretation, while still leaving space for nuance. Instead of saying "He'll never come back," you might say, *"The cards show closure and healing here, and encourage you to open to new possibilities."* Clarity is about illuminating a path, not casting shadows.

Boundaries mean knowing where tarot ends. We are readers, not fate-makers. Tarot can illuminate energies, patterns, and lessons, but it does not override free will. People always have the right to choose, change, and surprise us. Boundaries also mean respecting ethical lines—avoiding spying on someone else's private choices or reducing complex relationships to a single card flip. As readers, we hold space for insight and guidance, not control.

We'll talk openly in this book about how to handle sensitive topics—infidelity, breakups, red flag patterns, and timing questions—so that you can navigate them with both honesty and grace.

FLUENT TAROT: MATTERS OF THE HEART

This book explores two complementary approaches to reading love with tarot:

1. Practical Romance Readings

Here, we'll work with structured spreads for different situations: being single, dating, long-term partnerships, or self-love. You'll learn how to frame questions, recognize "green flag" and "red flag" cards, and interpret dynamics between people with sensitivity.

2. Love Letter Readings

In this style, we shift into a more poetic, first-person perspective. The cards become the voice of a soul connection or romantic partner, speaking directly to the querent in the form of a love letter. These readings don't just analyze —they *feel*. They bring intimacy, empathy, and sweetness to the reading experience, giving the querent something to hold close, like a whispered secret.

Together, these two approaches give us balance: clarity for the mind, and tenderness for the heart.

Over the course of this book, we'll dive into:

- Romantic spreads for singles, dating, long-term partnerships, and self-love.
- Timing questions and how to handle them ethically.
- Red flag cards and what they might mean in love readings.
- The ethics of love readings: how to be compassionate without creating false hope, how to handle questions about other people's consent or choices, and how to encourage empowerment.
- How to channel readings as love letters, transforming archetypes into soulful, first-person messages.
- Creative practices that bring romance readings to life—poetry, journaling, dialogue, even music and storytelling.

By the end of this journey, you'll feel confident offering love readings that are both grounded and deeply romantic. You'll know how to navigate sensitive topics with care. You'll be able to read spreads that give clear guidance while also delivering messages that feel like love letters from the soul.

Most importantly, you'll discover that tarot isn't just about predicting the future of relationships—it's about helping people fall in love with themselves, too.

Love is universal. It's the question that brings people to tarot again and again because it matters more than almost anything else. And that's why this book exists: to honor love, to explore it with reverence, and to give you tools to read it with both truth and tenderness.

Your heart-led tarot journey begins here. Let's shuffle.

PART ONE

foundations of love readings

CHAPTER 1

how love readings differ from general spreads

Love changes everything. When someone comes to you with a career question, the energy often feels practical, curious, and goal-oriented. "Should I take this new job?" or "How can I improve my work environment?"—these are important questions, but they tend to sit in the realm of logistics, strategy, and choice. Love questions, though, carry the weight of the heart. They arrive charged with vulnerability, longing, and sometimes even fear.

When someone asks, *"Is this my soulmate?"* or *"Will they come back to me?"* they aren't just looking for information. They are handing you their tenderest hope, their rawest wound, or their deepest secret desire. This is why love readings feel so different from general tarot spreads. The querent isn't just curious—they're exposed. They've brought you into their most intimate story.

Because of that, the stakes of love readings are heightened. In a career spread, even difficult news—like "this path may not be sustainable"—often motivates rather than devastates. But in romance, the same message—"this connection may not last"—can feel like the collapse of an entire dream. As a reader, it is essential to honor this difference. Love readings require a gentler touch, a slower pace, and an awareness that your words carry tremendous weight.

Symbolically, love spreads also move differently than general ones. In career or life path readings, the cards tend to reflect progress, goals, and external circumstances. In romance, the symbolism weaves more deeply into emotional nuance, intimacy, and even soul contracts. Cards like *The Lovers* or *Two of Cups* might surface to show mutual attraction, but in love readings they can also whisper of karmic echoes—connections that feel bigger than one lifetime, entanglements that carry lessons, or dynamics that mirror back what the soul needs to learn. Even ordinary cards shift in tone: the *Four of Pentacles* may talk about finances in a career reading, but in romance it may reveal clinging too tightly to a partner, or the fear of letting love flow.

For you as the reader, this means slowing down. It means pausing before rushing into interpretation, listening not only to the cards but also to the heartbeat beneath the question. Love readings invite you to be intentional with your language, to hold the space with compassion, and to resist the urge to "deliver fast answers." Here, more than anywhere else in tarot, the how is just as important as the what.

PRACTICE PROMPT

Lay out two simple three-card spreads side by side.

> The first, ask: "What do I need to know right now?"
>
> The second, ask: "What do I need to know about my relationship?"

Notice the difference in how you approach them.

> Does your body feel different?
>
> Does your tone shift?
>
> Does one feel more serious, more tender, more emotionally charged?

Journal your reflections on how the same spread structure can change in meaning when the subject turns to love.

CHAPTER 2

Setting the right tone

When you're reading about love, the words you choose matter just as much as the cards themselves. A querent might forget the exact prediction you gave, but they will remember how you made them feel in the moment they were most vulnerable. Love questions ask us to step into sacred territory—the beating heart of another human being. And that requires care.

A safe reading is one where the querent feels held, not judged. It's tempting as readers to be blunt, especially if we see difficult cards, but bluntness can cut too deep when the topic is love. Instead, imagine your words as a soft place for the querent to land. Even if you have to say something hard—like "this connection isn't lasting"—it can be framed in a way that preserves dignity. Safety doesn't mean sugarcoating, but it does mean remembering that your querent's heart may already be raw.

Compassion is the balm that allows truth to be heard. Tarot doesn't shy away from hard messages: the *Tower* collapses, the *Devil* binds, the *Three of Swords* breaks hearts. But even these cards carry gifts. Instead of saying, "They don't love you," you might say, "The cards suggest this connection is pulling away, but they also show your healing and new love ahead." The meaning is the same, but the delivery changes everything. A compassionate reading doesn't deny the pain—it acknowledges it while also pointing toward hope.

Empowerment is the final key. The best love readings give people their power back. If a querent leaves feeling dependent on you or the cards to make every romantic decision, something has gone wrong. Tarot should never strip someone of agency. Instead, it should illuminate choices, highlight patterns, and show possibilities. When someone leaves your table knowing they have the strength to walk away, open their heart, or call in a new chapter, that is empowerment in action.

The truth is, the tone you set in a love reading is often remembered far longer than the specific prediction. Ten years from now, your querent may not recall what card was on the table, but they will remember how your words made them feel: crushed or comforted, judged or encouraged, broken or brave.

PRACTICE PROMPT

Pull one of the so-called "difficult" cards—the *Three of Swords*, the *Tower*, or the *Devil*. Write two versions of your interpretation.

> Blunt: deliver the truth without softening.
>
> Compassionate and empowering: deliver the same message in a way that acknowledges pain but also honors healing and choice.

Read them both aloud. Which one would you want to hear if it were your own heart on the table? Journal your reflections on the difference.

EXAMPLE: THREE OF SWORDS

Blunt Interpretation (harsh tone):

"The three of swords is heartbreak. They don't love you anymore, and the relationship is over."

This might technically be accurate—but it lands like a dagger. It shuts the querent down instead of guiding them forward.

Compassionate & Empowering Interpretation (gentle tone):

"This card reflects deep pain, the kind that feels like a break in the heart. It tells me this connection may be pulling apart, but it also shows me you are ready to heal. The storm clouds here always clear—the dawn is rising in the background, reminding you that even in heartbreak, love hasn't left you. It is transforming, making space for the love that will meet you fully."

Notice the difference? The first version delivers only loss. The second acknowledges pain while holding space for healing and future love.

The second version still honors the truth—the relationship is in trouble—but it also validates the pain and empowers the querent with hope and perspective. That's the power of tone.

EXAMPLE: THE TOWER

Blunt Interpretation (harsh tone):

"This relationship is collapsing. Everything you built together is falling apart, and there's no saving it."

Direct, yes—but it leaves the querent with nothing to hold onto except devastation.

Compassionate & Empowering Interpretation (gentle tone):

"The Tower shows a sudden shake-up in this relationship—something unstable is being revealed. While it may feel shocking, this card isn't here to punish you. It's here to clear away what was never solid so that you can rebuild on truth. In love, The Tower often means the foundation wasn't as steady as it seemed, but it also promises freedom. What falls away now creates the space for real, lasting love to rise."

The blunt reading sounds like doom. The compassionate reading acknowledges the pain but frames it as necessary transformation—helping the querent see hope and agency.

CHAPTER 3

blunt vs. compassionate language

Difficult Love Card Examples

THE DEVIL

✖ **Blunt:** "This relationship is toxic and you're trapped."

☑ **Compassionate:** "This card suggests there may be unhealthy patterns—obsession, control, or fear—that are keeping you stuck. The good news is, awareness brings freedom. You have the power to break these chains and choose love that nourishes rather than drains."

THE TOWER

✖ **Blunt:** "It's over. Everything is falling apart."

☑ **Compassionate:** "This card shows a sudden upheaval. Something unstable is being shaken loose, and though it may feel painful, this is also a release. The Tower clears what cannot stand so you can rebuild on truth and love that lasts."

DEATH

✖ **Blunt:** "This relationship is dead."

☑ **Compassionate:** "This card marks an ending, yes, but also a profound transformation. The love in this form may be closing, but you are stepping into a new chapter. Death reminds us that when one cycle ends, it makes way for something more aligned."

THREE OF SWORDS

✗ **Blunt:** "You've been betrayed—this is heartbreak, plain and simple."

✓ **Compassionate:** "This card speaks of heartbreak, the kind that pierces deeply. It acknowledges your pain while also reminding you that storms pass. Healing and new love are already on the horizon, waiting for you when you are ready."

FIVE OF CUPS

✗ **Blunt:** "You're stuck in sadness. You'll never move on if you keep looking back."

✓ **Compassionate:** "This card shows grief and longing for what's been lost. It's natural to feel sorrow here. But notice—the two full cups still standing. When you are ready, love and connection remain available to you. Healing doesn't erase loss, but it does open the heart again."

EIGHT OF SWORDS

✗ **Blunt:** "You're trapped, and you can't get out of this relationship."

✓ **Compassionate:** "This card reflects feeling trapped or powerless, but look closer: the ropes are loose, the swords form a path. This isn't a prison, it's fear clouding your vision. You have choices, and you're stronger than you realize."

TEN OF SWORDS

✗ **Blunt:** "This is the ultimate betrayal. It's the end."

✓ **Compassionate:** "This card shows a painful ending, yes—but also the dawn rising beyond it. The worst is behind you, and the light ahead is beginning to break. This chapter has closed, but it is not the end of your story."

Green Flag Cards in Love

Even with the most beautiful cards, the goal is not to promise fate but to *highlight possibility*. Green flag phrasing celebrates love's potential without locking the querent into an outcome.

TWO OF CUPS

✓ **Encouraging:** "This card shows mutual attraction and emotional reciprocity. You see each other clearly, and the connection feels equal. This is the kind of bond where love flows both ways."

✗ **Avoid:** *"This is your soulmate forever."*

TEN OF PENTACLES

✓ **Encouraging:** *"This card suggests long-term stability and shared goals. It's the energy of building a legacy together—love that weaves family, home, and future into one vision."*

✗ **Avoid:** *"You're guaranteed marriage and happily-ever-after."*

THE STAR

✓ **Encouraging:** *"This card shines with healing and renewal. It suggests that love brings you hope, gentleness, and a sense of emotional restoration. This is love that feels like light after the storm."*

✗ **Avoid:** *"This person will save you."*

THE SUN

✓ **Encouraging:** *"This card radiates joy, authenticity, and warmth. It's a connection where you can be your truest self and feel celebrated in love."*

✗ **Avoid:** *"This is perfect, nothing could go wrong."*

ACE OF CUPS

✓ **Encouraging:** *"This card is the overflowing heart—the beginning of new love, fresh emotion, and open-hearted connection. It's an invitation to let your feelings bloom."*

✗ **Avoid:** *"This person is The One."*

FOUR OF WANDS

✓ **Encouraging:** *"This card reflects celebration, harmony, and stability. It's often seen in milestones—like moving in together, engagements, or joyfully deepening a bond."*

✗ **Avoid:** *"You'll definitely be engaged soon."*

KNIGHT OF CUPS

✓ **Encouraging:** *"This energy feels romantic, dreamy, and emotionally open. It shows someone expressing love with heart-on-sleeve sincerity."*

✗ **Avoid:** *"They're perfect and will never let you down."*

TEN OF CUPS

☑ **Encouraging:** *"This is the card of emotional fulfillment and shared joy. It reflects a vision of love where you feel at home, surrounded by connection and belonging."*

✗ **Avoid:** "This guarantees your fairytale ending."

THE EMPRESS

☑ **Encouraging:** *"This card represents nurturing, sensuality, and abundant love. It's love that grows and sustains, where care and affection flow freely."*

✗ **Avoid:** "You'll definitely have children with this person."

THE WORLD

☑ **Encouraging:** *"This card speaks to fulfillment, wholeness, and completion. It shows love that feels aligned, like a cycle coming full circle in harmony."*

✗ **Avoid:** "You've found your one true forever love and nothing will change it."

CHAPTER 4
handling client sensitivity & expectations

If you read tarot for love, sooner or later you'll hear the "big" questions:

- *"Tell me if they're the One."*
- *"When will I meet my soulmate?"*
- *"Are they cheating?"*
- *"Will they come back?"*

These questions are powerful because they're not really about facts—they're about hope, fear, and longing. When someone asks, *"Will they come back?"* what they're really saying is, *"I'm afraid of being abandoned. Please tell me love isn't over for me."* When they ask, *"Is this my soulmate?"* they're revealing a desire for certainty, safety, and forever.

This is why romance readings carry such weight — people come with heightened emotions and expectations. The heart doesn't want probabilities—it wants guarantees. And yet, as tarot readers, we know love doesn't work that way.

THE WEIGHT OF THESE QUESTIONS

"Tell me if they're the One" is heavy because it assumes love has only one outcome, one perfect person, one destiny.

"When will I meet my soulmate?" is heavy because it asks for timing, which tarot can only gesture toward through seasons, cycles, and readiness—not a calendar date.

"Are they cheating?" is heavy because the wrong answer could shatter a relationship or validate suspicion unfairly.

"Will they come back?" is heavy because it risks keeping someone stuck in longing instead of helping them move forward.

Each of these questions puts the querent's heart on the line. That's why we, as readers, must tread carefully.

SETTING BOUNDARIES IN SESSION

When love is on the table, it's easy for clients to slip into wanting certainties: *"Tell me if he's the one." "Tell me when she'll come back."* In those moments, you may feel the pressure to give them the black-and-white answer they crave. But tarot isn't a crystal ball—it's a mirror. It doesn't hand out guarantees; it illuminates the path, the patterns, the choices, and the lessons that shape our journey.

Part of your responsibility as a love reader is to set clear boundaries about what tarot can and cannot do. And this isn't about limitation—it's about empowerment.

Tarot can absolutely shine a light on:

- **Patterns in the relationship.** Is there a cycle of chasing and withdrawing? Are they repeating a story they've lived before? The cards reveal dynamics that might not be visible day-to-day.
- **Lessons the querent is being asked to learn.** Love is the greatest teacher, and tarot can show whether a connection is helping them find self-worth, practice boundaries, or open to trust.
- **Energies surrounding a connection.** Is the relationship expansive, heavy, playful, stagnant? Tarot captures the emotional weather of love in the moment.
- **Possibilities that lie ahead.** The cards can show where the energy is flowing—toward deepening intimacy, toward lessons of release, or toward preparing for someone new.

But tarot cannot (and should not) be used to promise absolutes. Ethical love readings require honesty about those limits.

Tarot cannot ethically guarantee:

- **Who someone's "One" is.** Soulmates are many, not one, and "the One" is as much a choice as it is destiny.

- **Exact timing of meeting a soulmate.** The cards can hint at seasons, cycles, or readiness, but pinning love to a calendar date strips away free will.
- **Another person's private thoughts or actions.** Reading someone's mind without their consent crosses ethical lines, and it often leads to projection and confusion.
- **An absolute "yes/no" on the return of an ex.** Relationships are made of two free-willed people. Tarot can show the energy between them, but it cannot override choice.

By setting this boundary gently but firmly, you actually build *trust*. Most querents don't want fantasy—they want clarity. When you explain what you can give them (insight, perspective, empowerment) instead of what you can't (guarantees, certainties), they leave knowing you are a guide they can rely on, not someone who feeds them answers just to soothe the moment.

It's important to remember that you're not taking something away from your querent when you set these boundaries—you're giving them something more valuable—**agency**. You're showing them that tarot is not about being told what to do, but about seeing more clearly so they can choose. And in love, that is the greatest gift you can offer.

Sometimes the cards don't say what the querent wants to hear. The Lovers reversed might show disharmony. The Tower might show a collapse. The Devil might reveal unhealthy attachment.

In those moments, your task is to balance honesty with hope. A blunt "No, he's not coming back" may be true, but it can leave your querent in despair. Instead, you might say: *"The cards suggest this connection isn't moving closer right now. But what I do see is a new chapter of healing opening for you, one where love can meet you more fully."*

This isn't sugarcoating—it's honoring the truth while showing the path forward. You're not denying their longing, but you're also not leaving them stranded in it.

PRACTICE PROMPT

Imagine a client asks: *"Will he come back to me?"*

Pull three cards.

> Version One (Prediction-Focused): Give a direct yes/no answer based on the cards.

> Version Two (Empowerment-Focused): Reframe the question. For example: "What do I need to know about this connection?" or "What is my next step in love, whether he returns or not?"
>
> Then write a response that gives growth, empowerment, and possibility.

Read both aloud. Which one feels more responsible? Which one feels more like the kind of reader you want to be?

Romance readings aren't about handing over certainties—they're about guiding people through the most tender terrain of their hearts. When you set boundaries, reframe loaded questions, and balance honesty with compassion, you give your querent not just an answer, but a path. And that's the true gift of tarot in love.

CHAPTER 5
karma in love readings

When tarot enters the realm of romance, it often brushes against deeper spiritual threads—karma, past-life connections, and soul contracts. These ideas are powerful, but also easily misunderstood. So let's take the time to define them, explore how they show up in love readings, and, most importantly, talk about how to read them responsibly.

What Karma *Is* (and What It Isn't)

Karma is one of the most misunderstood spiritual concepts. Too often, people reduce it to punishment: *"Bad things happen because you did something wrong."* This view makes karma sound like cosmic retribution, a tally system of rewards and punishments doled out by the universe. But karma is not punishment—it is cause and effect.

Every action carries energy. Every word spoken, every decision made, every way we show up in love—these are seeds we plant in the soil of our lives. Karma is simply the unfolding of those seeds over time. Some bloom into joy and connection, others into struggle or lessons. But none of it is arbitrary. Karma is not about judgment; it's about momentum.

In the context of love, karma is often felt as intensity. These are the relationships that spark immediately, where the pull is magnetic, irresistible, sometimes even destabilizing. Karmic connections can feel like *destiny*, but they are not always meant to last forever. Instead, they act like mirrors, drawing us back into old wounds we need to face or lessons our soul is finally ready to learn.

A karmic partner might awaken patterns of abandonment so we can heal our fear of being left. Another might stir up jealousy so we can learn self-worth. Someone else may show us unconditional love so we finally recognize what we truly deserve. These connections are not punishments—they are classrooms of the soul. And in those classrooms, both partners are teachers.

What karma is *not* is a guarantee of suffering. If a relationship is painful, it doesn't mean you're being "punished" for something in this life or another. It means the connection is carrying lessons. Once those lessons are integrated, the karma can shift. The cycle doesn't have to repeat.

It's also important to know that karmic relationships aren't always difficult. Sometimes karma brings gifts—meeting someone who restores our faith in love after heartbreak, or finding a partner who embodies the kindness we ourselves once gave. Karma is not just about wounds; it is also about balance.

So when karma shows up in a love reading, it's not a sentence—it's an invitation. An invitation to ask: *What is this person teaching me about myself? How is this relationship helping me grow? What seeds am I planting now that will shape the love I experience later?*

When we say karma is a "classroom," what do we actually mean? At its core, karmic relationships highlight something our soul needs to understand about love—whether that's how we give it, how we receive it, or how we mistake it.

These lessons often show up in patterns: the same kind of partner appearing again and again, or the same conflict resurfacing in different relationships. The universe isn't "punishing" us—it's that the soul keeps returning to the lesson until we've integrated it. Once learned, the cycle doesn't need to repeat.

Common Karmic Lessons in Love

ABANDONMENT

- *The experience:* A partner leaves suddenly, withdraws emotionally, or is unavailable.
- *The lesson:* To learn that your worth isn't determined by whether someone stays. To anchor in self-trust and stability even when others waver.
- *When learned:* You stop chasing unavailable partners and begin choosing those who are present and consistent.

TRUST & BETRAYAL

- *The experience:* Cheating, lies, secrecy, or repeated disappointments.

- *The lesson:* To recognize red flags, honor intuition, and create boundaries that protect your heart.
- *When learned:* You no longer silence your inner knowing—you act on it.

BOUNDARIES

- *The experience:* Giving more than you receive, feeling drained, or being taken advantage of.
- *The lesson:* To understand that love is mutual, not martyrdom. To know that saying "no" is also an act of love—for yourself.
- *When learned:* You no longer settle for one-sided relationships, but seek reciprocity.

SELF-WORTH

- *The experience:* Settling for less, chasing validation, or clinging to partners who don't meet your needs.
- *The lesson:* To realize that you are already worthy of love, exactly as you are.
- *When learned:* You stop begging for crumbs of affection and begin receiving whole-hearted love.

ATTACHMENT & DETACHMENT

- *The experience:* Obsession, dependency, relationships that feel addictive.
- *The lesson:* To balance passion with freedom, connection with individuality.
- *When learned:* You can love deeply without losing yourself.

FORGIVENESS & RELEASE

- *The experience:* Old wounds resurfacing, cycles of resentment, difficulty moving on.
- *The lesson:* To release bitterness and free yourself from the past. Forgiveness doesn't excuse—it liberates.
- *When learned:* You can close doors without carrying the weight of them into new love.

The beautiful—and sometimes frustrating—truth is that karmic lessons repeat until we integrate them. That's why clients often say, *"Why do I keep attracting the same type of partner?"*

It's not that they're cursed—it's that the soul is still learning. When the lesson is finally absorbed, the cycle shifts. They stop attracting unavailable partners. They stop confusing obsession for love. They stop repeating patterns of abandonment or betrayal.

In readings, this is where tarot shines. The cards help the querent see the pattern clearly, name the lesson, and step into empowerment. For example, pulling the *Eight of Cups* after a cycle of heartbreak might signal: *"This time, you're ready to walk away. The lesson is integrated—you're not chasing what doesn't serve you anymore."*

Karmic love isn't a punishment, and it isn't forever binding. It is a soul-level classroom, sometimes tender, sometimes brutal, always transformative. When you help a querent see their karmic lessons not as fate but as *freedom,* you're giving them one of the greatest gifts tarot has to offer: the ability to write a new story of love.

CHAPTER 6

soul contracts in love readings

A soul contract is the belief that, before we arrive in this lifetime, our souls make agreements with other souls about how we'll meet, what we'll learn together, and how we'll grow through the connection.

These contracts can be profoundly romantic, yes—but not always in the fairy-tale sense. Some contracts are sweet and supportive, designed to help us remember our worth. Others are more difficult, stirring up shadow work and transformation.

Soul contracts are not about punishment or reward. They're about growth. They ensure that no matter what, we encounter the experiences we need most to evolve.

Sometimes that looks like meeting the great love of our lives. Sometimes it looks like heartbreak that cracks us open. Sometimes it looks like friendships that teach us loyalty, or mentors who guide us toward wisdom.

Think of soul contracts as agreements for learning—not life sentences. A contract may last a lifetime, or it may last only a season. Once the growth is integrated, the contract can dissolve.

That's why some relationships that feel "fated" don't last forever: their purpose was never permanence, but awakening.

Types of Soul Contracts in Love

THE SUPPORTIVE CONTRACT

This is the partner who shows up to love you gently, to remind you that tenderness is possible. They may not challenge you fiercely, but they restore your faith in connection.

THE TRANSFORMATIONAL CONTRACT

This is the lover who changes everything—sometimes through passion, sometimes through pain. They ignite deep lessons about self-worth, boundaries, or identity.

THE ANCESTRAL CONTRACT

These are connections that help heal family wounds or generational patterns. For example, someone may break a lineage of unhealthy relationships by choosing differently with their partner.

THE SEASONAL CONTRACT

Some soul contracts are not meant to last forever. They show up for a few months or years, deliver their lesson, and then fade. Their brevity doesn't make them less important—it makes them timely.

THE LIFETIME CONTRACT

And yes, sometimes we meet someone who walks beside us until the end. These contracts hold the energy of stability, growth, and shared purpose. They feel like home because they are meant to stay.

WHAT SOUL CONTRACTS ARE *NOT*

- They are not chains. Just because someone is in your contract doesn't mean you must endure endless suffering for the sake of growth.
- They are not guarantees of "forever." Not every soulmate is meant to be your lifelong partner.
- They are not excuses for harm. A toxic relationship is not "meant to be endured" because of a contract. You always have the power to release.

In tarot, soul contracts often show up through themes of recognition, choice, and transformation. Cards like *The Lovers*, *Judgement*, *The World*, and *The Wheel of Fortune* can signal these agreements, especially when paired with karmic or healing cards like *The Devil* (lesson of attachment) or *The Star* (lesson of healing).

Clients often *feel* soul contracts before they name them: that eerie sense of knowing someone instantly, the magnetic pull that can't be explained, or the sense that the relationship has deeper meaning than its length or circumstances suggest.

Soul contracts remind us that love is never random. Every connection—whether lasting a lifetime or a fleeting season—carries wisdom. When you help a querent see their relationship as part of a contract, you're not binding them to fate—you're freeing them to ask: *What am I meant to learn here? What will I carry forward, even if this ends?*

Because ultimately, the truest soul contract is always with ourselves: to keep growing, to keep loving, and to keep showing up for the lessons that make us whole.

CHAPTER 7

Signs of karmic or soul-contract love in readings

Certain cards in tarot often point to these dynamics, especially when combined:

- **The Lovers** → soul recognition, profound choice, union that feels bigger than the self.
- **The Devil** → karmic ties, unhealthy patterns, attachment that feels binding.
- **Death** → contracts closing, endings that create space for growth.
- **Judgement** → past-life echoes, reunion energy, soul awakenings.
- **The World** → completion of a cycle, fulfillment of a contract.

In Minor Arcana, patterns of repetition (e.g., *Eight of Swords, Five of Pentacles*) can signal lessons the querent is cycling through.

Karma and contracts are not excuses for staying in toxic or abusive relationships. *"We're karmic"* should never mean *"I have to endure suffering forever."*

They don't mean love is doomed. A karmic relationship can evolve into a healthy one if both partners grow—or it can end once the lesson is learned.

They aren't proof of a soulmate being "the one." A soulmate may be here for a season, not a lifetime.

When these themes appear in love readings, your role is not to label relationships as "good" or "bad," but to help the querent see what's being mirrored.

✘ Instead of: *"This is your karmic punishment."*

- ✅ Try: *"This connection may be showing you an old pattern—an invitation to step into healing."*

❌ Instead of: *"This contract ties you together forever."*

- ✅ Try: *"This feels like a soul-level connection. It's here to teach you something profound. The choice is whether you want to keep learning with this person, or carry the lesson forward on your own."*

REFLECTION & PRACTICE

Journal:

> Think of a past relationship that felt magnetic, transformative, or difficult to let go. Which tarot card best represents that connection? What lesson did it leave you with?

Practice:

> Pull three cards on the question: "What is the soul lesson this relationship is here to teach?"
>
> Bonus: Write the answer in Love Letter style, as if the soul itself is speaking.

Karma and soul contracts don't exist to trap us. They exist to free us. When we understand the lesson, we no longer need the cycle. In love readings, naming these patterns isn't about binding people to fate—it's about helping them recognize growth, healing, and choice. Because ultimately, the soul's deepest contract is always with itself.

KARMIC & SOUL CONTRACT SPREAD

This spread is designed to illuminate the deeper lessons of a relationship that feels "fated," "karmic," or soul-level. It doesn't tell someone they're *stuck*—it shows them what they're learning, how to release cycles, and how to carry the gift forward.

The Layout

1. **The Soul Contract** – What brought our souls together in this lifetime?
2. **The Lesson** – What am I being asked to learn through this connection?
3. **The Mirror** – What are they showing me about myself?
4. **The Release** – What is ready to be let go so the cycle can heal?

5. **The Gift** – What wisdom or strength will I carry forward, no matter what happens?

(Optional: Pull a 6th card, **The Future Choice**, to show how the querent can consciously shape what comes next.)

EXAMPLE READING

Cards Drawn: Lovers, Devil, Eight of Swords, Death, Star

- **The Soul Contract (Lovers):** This connection came to awaken choice —between fear and freedom, between illusion and authentic love.
- **The Lesson (Devil):** It teaches the querent about breaking free from unhealthy attachments. The lesson is learning love without bondage.
- **The Mirror (Eight of Swords):** The partner mirrors back self-limiting beliefs—the feeling of being trapped or powerless.
- **The Release (Death):** It is time to release the cycle of repeating old wounds, to let this particular form of the relationship transform.
- **The Gift (Star):** Hope, healing, and the ability to believe in love again. This relationship left behind not just pain, but a deeper capacity for renewal.

"These cards show me that this connection was never random—it arrived to teach you something profound about freedom and healing. The intensity you feel isn't wrong, but it's here to awaken you. The choice is always yours: to keep cycling through this lesson, or to carry it forward and let love transform into something healthier."

This gives clarity without trapping the querent in fate.

CHAPTER 8

tarot cards that often signal karma & soul contracts in love

MAJOR ARCANA

- **The Lovers** → Soul recognition, choices of the heart, contracts that test free will.
- **The Devil** → Karmic bonds, obsession, toxic patterns, relationships that feel binding.
- **The Tower** → Karmic upheaval, sudden events meant to break false structures.
- **Death** → Contracts closing, transformation, endings that clear space for new lessons.
- **Judgement** → Past-life echoes, soul awakening, reunion energy.
- **The World** → Completion of a cycle, fulfillment of a karmic contract.
- **The Wheel of Fortune** → Fate, cycles repeating until learned, divine timing.
- **Justice** → Karmic balance, cause-and-effect in relationships, "what you sow, you reap."
- **The High Priestess** → Hidden soul ties, mystery, intuition recognizing something deeper.
- **The Hanged Man** → Lessons of surrender, waiting, sacrifice in soul agreements.

Minor Arcana – Cups (Emotions & Bonds)

- **Six of Cups** → Past-life connections, nostalgia, karmic reunions.

- **Eight of Cups** → Walking away from karmic cycles, leaving behind unfinished lessons.
- **Ten of Cups** → Soul family, chosen family contracts.

Minor Arcana – Wands (Desire & Destiny)

- **Two of Wands** → Soul contracts that involve long-term choices or destiny paths.
- **Eight of Wands** → Fast-moving karmic encounters (the "swept off your feet" soulmate).
- **Nine of Wands** → Repeating karmic lessons that test resilience.

Minor Arcana – Swords (Karmic Challenges & Lessons)

- **Eight of Swords** → Feeling trapped in a cycle, karmic entanglement.
- **Nine of Swords** → Anxiety tied to unresolved soul contracts.
- **Ten of Swords** → Final karmic endings, lessons that cannot be repeated.
- **Five of Swords** → Power struggles that mirror karmic imbalances.

Minor Arcana – Pentacles (Long-Term Lessons & Contracts)

- **Five of Pentacles** → Abandonment wounds, karmic contracts around loss & support.
- **Seven of Pentacles** → Soul contracts that unfold slowly, testing patience.
- **Ten of Pentacles** → Legacy contracts, ancestral karma, family patterns in love.

When these cards appear together (like *Devil + Lovers* or *Six of Cups + Judgement*), the reading often points to karmic or soul-level lessons. These aren't always "bad"—sometimes they bring profound healing and transformation—but they *always* call for deeper reflection.

JOURNALING PROMPT

Think of a love connection in your past that felt fated, overwhelming, or transformative. Which of these cards best reflects that story? What lesson did the relationship leave behind?

CHAPTER 9

love reading foundations: reader's checklist

Use this as a centering guide before giving any romance reading—whether for yourself or someone else.

Before the Reading

- I pause and breathe, remembering that love readings carry heightened vulnerability.
- I set the intention: *to read with compassion, clarity, and empowerment.*
- I remind myself: *My role is not to predict fate, but to illuminate choices, patterns, and lessons.*

During the Reading

- I choose my tone with care:
    - Am I delivering honesty with compassion?
    - Am I framing truth in a way that empowers, not crushes?
- I watch for loaded questions (like "Are they cheating?" or "Will they come back?").
    - Instead of saying "yes" or "no," I reframe toward the querent's growth:
        - "What do you need to know about this connection?"
        - "How can you best move forward in love?"
- I notice if karmic or soul-contract themes are surfacing.
    - If they are, I ask: *What is the lesson? What is the gift? What is ready to be released?*

After the Reading

- I check in: Did I give clarity instead of confusion?
- Did I leave the querent feeling empowered rather than dependent?
- Did I honor their heart with compassion?

Quick Reminders

- Love readings are sacred ground. Go slow.
- Tone is remembered longer than predictions.
- Karma = classrooms. Soul contracts = invitations. Neither is punishment.
- Your words carry weight. Choose them like love letters.

Pro tip: Keep this checklist near your deck or in your tarot journal. Glance at it before sessions until these practices feel second nature.

CHAPTER 10

client bill of rights in love readings

When you sit down for a love reading, you are entering a sacred space. Your heart, your story, and your questions deserve respect. As a querent, you have rights—guidelines that protect you and ensure your reading serves your growth, not your fear.

Your Rights as a Querent

The Right to Safety:

You deserve to feel held, not judged. Your vulnerabilities will be met with compassion.

The Right to Honesty:

You will receive truth from the cards, spoken with care. No sugarcoating to mislead, and no harshness meant to wound.

The Right to Boundaries:

Your reader will not pry into another person's private thoughts or actions. Tarot is for *your* growth, not surveillance of others.

The Right to Empowerment:

A love reading should give your power back, not take it away. You will never be told you are doomed or fated without choice.

The Right to Clarity:

Confusing or vague messages will be explained. If something feels unclear, you have the right to ask questions until you understand.

The Right to Respect for Timing:

You will not be promised exact dates or guarantees. Instead, you will be shown seasons, cycles, and signs of readiness—so you can meet love with awareness, not waiting.

The Right to Closure & Hope:

Even if the message is difficult, your reading will offer guidance for healing and moving forward. Love readings honor endings as much as beginnings.

Final Promise

Tarot does not dictate fate—it illuminates the heart's path. A love reading is not about prediction alone, but about reflection, empowerment, and support. You are always free to choose your own story.

CHAPTER 11
Foundations of love readings: recap & practice

By now, you've journeyed through the foundations of reading tarot for love. You've explored how love readings differ from general ones, how the tone of your delivery matters, how to hold clients with compassion and boundaries, and how to recognize the deeper soul patterns that show up in romance readings.

This module was not about memorizing a checklist—it was about teaching you to step into the sacred space of love readings with confidence, awareness, and integrity. Let's weave it all together.

Unlike general spreads about career or daily guidance, love readings touch the most vulnerable places of the heart. They arrive charged with hope, fear, and longing. "Is this my soulmate?" carries a weight that "Should I take this new job?" never will. That's why love readings require more than skill—they require tenderness.

The way you speak is often remembered longer than the prediction itself. A blunt answer can crush a querent, while a compassionate one can help them face even the hardest truths with courage.

Compare:

- ❌ *Blunt Three of Swords:* "They don't love you anymore."
- ✅ *Compassionate Three of Swords:* "This card reflects heartbreak, yes—but it also shows healing and new beginnings on the horizon. Your heart will open again."

Same truth. Different tone. Worlds apart in impact.

Clients come with big questions: *"Are they cheating?" "Will they come back?" "When will I meet the One?"* These aren't just questions—they're raw hopes and fears. Your role is to honor their vulnerability while setting clear boundaries. Tarot illuminates patterns, energies, and lessons. It cannot ethically guarantee absolutes like exact timing, another person's thoughts, or fate carved in stone.

When clients are disappointed by what the cards reveal, remember: honesty and hope must walk hand in hand. Always tell the truth, but frame it in a way that empowers them to move forward.

Karma & Soul Contracts

Some love stories carry deeper threads—karmic lessons and soul contracts. These connections often feel magnetic, overwhelming, or fated. But remember:

Karma is not punishment—it's cause and effect. These relationships act as classrooms, teaching lessons about self-worth, trust, boundaries, and healing.

Soul contracts are agreements souls make before this lifetime to help each other grow. Some last a season, others a lifetime. They are invitations, not chains.

Recognizing these patterns in readings helps clients understand the "why" behind the intensity of certain connections—without trapping them in despair or false destiny.

Some cards often carry karmic or soul-contract weight in romance spreads:

Majors: Lovers, Devil, Tower, Death, Judgement, World, Wheel of Fortune, Justice, High Priestess, Hanged Man.

Minors: Six of Cups, Eight of Swords, Five of Pentacles, Ten of Swords, Seven of Pentacles.

When these appear, pause. Ask: *What lesson is being reflected? What does this soul connection teach? What is the gift, even if painful?*

PRACTICE & INTEGRATION

Now that you've built a foundation, it's time to practice with intention. This is where skill becomes confidence.

Practice Prompt 1: Compare the Energy

Lay two spreads side by side:

- Spread A: *"What do I need to know right now?"*
- Spread B: *"What do I need to know about my relationship?"*

Journal the differences. How does your tone shift? How does your body feel different in each?

Practice Prompt 2: Blunt vs. Compassionate

Pull a "difficult" card (Tower, Devil, Three of Swords). Write one blunt interpretation and one compassionate, empowering version. Which feels more aligned with the kind of reader you want to be?

Practice Prompt 3: Reframing Client Questions

Imagine someone asks: *"Will he come back?"* Do a three-card spread. Write two versions of your answer:

1. Prediction-focused.
2. Empowerment-focused (shifting toward the querent's growth).

Which version builds trust? Which one you'd want to receive if it were your own heart on the table?

Practice Prompt 4: Karmic Reflection

Think of a relationship in your own life that felt "fated." Pull three cards and ask: *"What was the lesson of this connection?"* Journal what the cards reveal.

SELF-CHECK QUIZ 🌹

This is not about "passing" or "failing"—it's about checking in with yourself. Answer in your journal:

1. How are love readings different from general spreads?
2. Why does tone matter more than prediction in romance readings?
3. Name two questions clients often ask that need reframing. How would you reframe them?
4. What is karma, in your own words?
5. What is a soul contract, and how is it different from karma?
6. Which tarot cards might point to karmic or soul-contract dynamics?
7. How would you explain the difference between a blunt and a compassionate reading to a beginner?

The foundations of love readings are about trust, compassion, and depth. You're not just flipping cards—you're holding someone's heart story. Every word you speak has the power to wound or to heal. Every spread is an opportunity to reflect not only on the querent's love life, but also on the lessons of the soul.

Now that you've built these foundations, your next step is practice. The more readings you give—whether to yourself, to friends, or to clients—the more fluent you'll become in the language of love. Keep journaling, keep reflecting, keep softening your words into clarity and hope.

Because in the end, love readings aren't about predicting fate. They're about guiding someone back to their own strength, their own choice, and their own heart. And that is the greatest gift you can offer.

PART TWO
types of romance

CHAPTER 12

introduction

When you read tarot for romance, spreads become the scaffolding of your story. They give shape to the question, structure to the energy, and flow to the interpretation. For many readers, spreads feel like maps—they show where to begin, what to explore, and how to tie it all together.

But here's the secret: spreads are guides, not rules. They can focus your reading beautifully, but you don't *have* to use them every time. Some of the most powerful love readings happen when you simply pull cards intuitively, letting the conversation unfold. Spreads are tools, not cages.

Why Use Spreads?

The Pros

- They provide a framework, so the querent knows what each card represents.
- They help you, as the reader, stay focused on the heart of the question.
- They can uncover hidden layers by asking specific sub-questions.

The Cons

- They can feel restrictive if followed too rigidly.
- They may encourage querents to expect cookie-cutter answers.
- They can distract from intuition if you're worried more about placement than meaning.

Think of spreads as conversation starters. They give you a script to begin with —but once the cards are on the table, you can let intuition guide the dialogue.

You'll notice in spreads that cards are often numbered. The numbering is about *order of interpretation*, not a sacred geometry of placement. Whether you lay them in a straight line, a circle, or a cluster on the table, the important thing is that *you know which card is which.*

Some readers like symmetrical patterns. Others prefer organic shapes. Some even design their spreads like constellations or hearts. Do what feels comfortable. The layout is visual—its true power is in the story it unlocks.

Love readings come in many flavors because love questions do, too. A single person may want to know how to attract connection. Someone in a complicated relationship may want clarity on where things are heading. A couple may ask how to deepen their bond. Spreads adapt to these different needs.

Over time, you'll develop your own go-to layouts—the ones that flow easily from your hands. You may even create signature spreads that clients come to you for. That's the beauty of tarot: spreads are endlessly flexible, evolving alongside your practice.

CHAPTER 13

single & searching — attracting love with tarot

"WHAT DO I NEED TO KNOW ABOUT ATTRACTING LOVE?"

Being single carries its own magic. It is a season of possibility, growth, and discovery—but it can also feel frustrating, lonely, or uncertain, especially in a world that often equates love with worth.

As a reader, it's important to honor the tenderness behind these questions while gently reframing them. Rather than reducing love to a timeline, we want to help singles see this moment as fertile ground: a chance to align, heal, and call in the kind of love that truly serves them.

THE TIMING TRAP IN SINGLES READINGS

If you read for singles, you'll hear it again and again: *"When will I meet someone?"* It's the most natural question in the world. People who have been waiting for love often feel impatient, tired of the unknown, and longing for certainty. They want a date on the calendar, a countdown to their soulmate.

But here's the truth: tarot doesn't work like a stopwatch. Love isn't just about a date in time—it's about readiness, alignment, and mutual timing. If you give an exact answer ("In three months you'll meet them"), you risk creating false hope or disappointment if the querent hasn't yet released their old patterns, opened their heart, or stepped into the places where love can actually find them.

This doesn't mean you dismiss their question—it means you translate it into something more meaningful.

Your role as a reader is to shift the focus from *waiting for love to arrive* toward becoming ready to receive love. Instead of seeing timing as a clock, see it as a season, a cycle, an energy state.

❌ **Instead of:** *"You'll meet someone in three months."*

✅ **Try:** *"The cards show the energy of spring—new beginnings, lightness, and openness. Love is aligned with that season, once you've cleared this old story. When you step into renewal, that's when love flows toward you."*

This way, the querent still gets a sense of timing, but it's rooted in energy and growth—not an external promise.

Timing Through Tarot

Seasons: Cards like *The Sun* (summer), *The Hermit* (winter), or suit associations (Cups = spring, Wands = summer, Pentacles = fall, Swords = winter) can gently point to natural cycles of change.

Energy Readiness: The Ace of Cups might suggest new love is near—but only if the querent is emotionally open. The Two of Swords may show a pause until they make a clear choice.

Cycles: Major cards like *The Wheel of Fortune* or *The World* often suggest that love aligns when a chapter closes and a new one begins.

By focusing on these symbols, you can give your querent a sense of movement and rhythm—without creating rigid predictions.

When you reframe timing questions this way, you empower the querent to step into love as a co-creator, not just a passive receiver. You teach them that *time doesn't deliver love—alignment does*. And that is far more hopeful and practical than any calendar date could be.

LONELINESS VS. READINESS IN SINGLES READINGS

Sometimes a querent comes to you not because they're truly ready for love, but because they feel the ache of loneliness. This is tender ground. Loneliness is valid, and it deserves to be named—but loneliness and readiness are not the same thing.

Loneliness says: *"I don't want to feel alone anymore."*

Readiness says: *"I'm open, willing, and capable of sharing life with someone in a healthy way."*

Both states are human, but only one creates fertile soil for lasting love.

The cards often reveal whether someone is seeking love to fill a void, or whether they're genuinely ready to give and receive.

Signs of Loneliness / Inner Work Needed:

- *Five of Pentacles* → feelings of lack, unworthiness, or being left out in the cold.
- *Nine of Swords* → anxiety, fear, or sleepless longing.
- *Devil* → seeking connection out of obsession, addiction, or dependency.

Signs of Readiness / Openness to Love:

- *Ace of Cups* → emotional overflow, willingness to begin again.
- *Three of Cups* → openness to community, joy, and connection.
- *Two of Wands* → visioning the future with space for another.

When these cards appear, you can gently reflect the difference: *"This spread shows me your heart is craving connection, but also that there are places of healing still calling for your attention. Loneliness is a very real feeling—but love flourishes best when you are grounded in self-worth. Let's see what steps can help prepare you for that readiness."*

Holding Hope Without False Promises

Singles don't want to be dismissed with, *"You're not ready, come back later."* That can feel harsh and invalidating. But they also don't want false hope—being told, *"Your soulmate is coming tomorrow!"* when the cards suggest otherwise.

Your role is to balance honesty with hope:

- Remind them that love begins now. It starts with self-love, self-expression, and saying yes to opportunities—not with waiting for someone else to appear.
- Frame the present as part of the love journey. Healing, building confidence, or stepping into community are not "delays"—they are love in motion.
- Show them how tarot offers practical steps — boundaries to strengthen, patterns to release, joy to invite in.

Practical Example

If a querent pulls *Five of Pentacles* (loneliness), *Nine of Swords* (anxiety), and *Ace of Cups* (potential for love), you might say:

"These cards show me your heart is aching with loneliness, and that's a valid and human experience. But they also tell me there's an opening—a fresh start waiting in your emotional world. Before love can find its way in, the cards invite you to nurture

your own worth and bring compassion to yourself. As you do, you create the space for that Ace of Cups—new, nourishing love—to pour in."

This way, you acknowledge their loneliness, honor their hope, and still keep the reading realistic and empowering.

CHAPTER 14

action steps for singles

One of the most important things to remember when reading for singles is that clarity without action rarely leads to change. A reading can reveal all the possibilities in the world, but unless the querent takes a step forward, those possibilities remain in the realm of potential.

It's easy to want love without changing the patterns that keep it out of reach. If a querent says they long for connection but never leaves their comfort zone—avoiding social spaces, refusing dating apps, or closing themselves off emotionally—their chances of meeting someone remain slim. Tarot, when read well, can gently highlight where action is needed and inspire them to move toward it.

The beauty of tarot is that it doesn't just describe what's coming—it shows how to align with it. Cards can offer specific, practical invitations:

- The **Three of Cups** might suggest saying yes to gatherings, joining a class, or connecting with community.
- The **Queen of Wands** could be a call to grow confidence, embrace playfulness, or step into visibility.
- The **Four of Pentacles** may encourage creating stability—whether financial, emotional, or energetic—so the querent feels secure enough to welcome love in.

When you present these insights as steps rather than predictions, the reading becomes not just informative but empowering. You give your querent agency: instead of waiting passively for love to appear, they leave knowing how to embody the qualities and take the actions that draw love closer.

⚑ RED FLAG WATCH FOR SINGLES

One of the tender realities of reading for singles is that sometimes the reason love hasn't arrived yet is because the querent is still tethered to an old cycle. Maybe they're stuck on an ex. Maybe they're giving energy to someone who's emotionally unavailable. Maybe they're repeating a pattern of heartbreak they haven't yet released.

Tarot doesn't call this out to shame them—it calls it out so they can be free.

Cards That Often Signal Stuck Cycles

The Devil → unhealthy attachments, obsession, a cycle of craving what isn't good for them.

Seven of Swords → sneaky or dishonest energy, chasing unavailable partners, or situationships where truth is avoided.

Death reversed → resisting an ending, struggling to let go, staying tied to something that has already run its course.

Eight of Swords → trapped in old stories or self-limiting beliefs.

Five of Cups → focusing on the loss rather than the love still available.

When these appear in singles spreads, it may not be about *when* love is coming—it may be about *what's blocking it from arriving.*

How to Deliver This With Compassion

The key is to avoid blame. Your querent may already feel shame about their patterns. Instead, frame it as loving awareness:

✘ Instead of: *"You're stuck on your ex and that's why you can't find love."*

- ☑ Try: *"These cards suggest your heart is still holding onto someone or something from the past. That's natural—it means your love is deep. But they also show that releasing this will create space for the love that's truly aligned with you."*

✘ Instead of: *"You're chasing unavailable people—it's your fault."*

- ☑ Try: *"The cards are showing a pattern of reaching for love that doesn't give back equally. That doesn't mean you're broken—it means your soul is teaching you what you deserve. Let's look at how you can shift toward relationships that meet you fully."*

These moments are not dead ends—they're invitations. If a spread reveals a red flag, guide the querent toward a path of healing:

- **Release Rituals:** Suggest journaling a goodbye letter, pulling a release spread, or doing a cord-cutting meditation.
- **Action Steps:** Encourage self-love practices, new communities, or even just taking a break from dating to heal.
- **Empowerment:** Remind them that recognizing the cycle is the first step to breaking it. Awareness is freedom.

Red flag cards don't mean love is doomed—they mean love is waiting on the other side of release. Your role as a reader is to guide singles not just toward new beginnings, but also through the endings that make space for them. When you frame red flags with compassion, you help your querent feel hopeful, even in the process of letting go.

SINGLE IS SACRED

For many people, singlehood feels like an in-between state—a waiting room where life is paused until love arrives. They see being single as a gap to be filled, a problem to be solved, or proof that they're "behind."

But singlehood is not waiting. It is living. It is a sacred season of self-discovery, healing, and empowerment. A good love reading has the power to reframe singlehood from lack into opportunity.

Being single is the time when we:

Deepen self-knowledge. Who am I without another person reflecting me back? What do I desire? What lights me up?

Heal old wounds. Past heartbreaks or family patterns often rise when we're alone, giving us the space to tend to them.

Strengthen identity. This is when we build our independence, discover passions, and root in self-worth.

When love eventually enters, it doesn't rescue us from emptiness—it joins a life already rich and full.

As a tarot reader, your task is to reflect this truth with compassion. Singles often come to readings feeling that something is missing. Your words can remind them: *"You are already whole. Love is not here to complete you—it is here to complement you."*

This isn't dismissive—it's empowering. It validates their longing while also affirming their worth in the present moment.

Tarot in Singlehood

Cards that honor the sacredness of being single include:

- **The Hermit** → turning inward, finding wisdom within.
- **Nine of Pentacles** → thriving in independence, building self-sufficiency and joy.
- **Strength** → courage in self-love, power rooted in gentleness.
- **The Star** → healing, renewal, hope that radiates from within.

When these appear in a singles reading, emphasize their beauty: they aren't about "waiting"—they're about becoming.

✘ Instead of: *"You're single because it's not your time yet."*

- ☑ Try: *"This season is about you. The cards show you're building a life that love will be honored to step into."*

✘ Instead of: *"Love isn't coming right now."*

- ☑ Try: *"Love is already here in the way you nurture yourself, your friendships, your passions. Romantic love will arrive as an addition, not a rescue."*

Singlehood is not empty space. It is fertile ground. Remind your querents that love is not a lifeline thrown to save them, but a hand extended to walk beside them. When they see singlehood as sacred, they stop waiting for life to begin and start living the fullness of it—making them even more magnetic to love when it arrives.

THE SINGLE & SEARCHING SPREAD (4 CARDS)

Card 1 What energy am I carrying now?

This card reveals how the querent is currently moving through the world. Are they open-hearted, guarded, hopeful, weary? Love begins with self-awareness.

Card 2 What patterns do I need to release?

Here we see what old stories, wounds, or habits might be blocking love. It could be clinging to past heartbreak, chasing unavailable partners, or doubting self-worth. This card brings clarity on what to let go of.

Card 3 What qualities will attract love?

This card points to the radiant qualities the querent can embody that will naturally draw love in. Confidence? Vulnerability? Playfulness? Steadiness? It's about magnetism, not chasing.

Card 4 What next step brings me closer to connection?

The action card. A practical invitation: say yes to invitations, update your dating profile, focus on self-love, or practice boundaries. Whatever the card reveals, it grounds the reading in something tangible.

Tips for Reading Singles with This Spread

Affirm their worth as they are. The message should never be: *"You're single because you're broken."* Instead, frame it as: *"This time is a preparation space. The more you know and love yourself, the more aligned love will be when it arrives."*

Notice balance in the suits. Cups may highlight emotional openness, Wands point to confidence and attraction, Pentacles to grounding and self-worth, and Swords to clarity in communication and boundaries. For singles, this balance can show where they shine and where they might be unconsciously holding back.

Reframe the idea of "The One." Remind them that love isn't a lottery ticket they're waiting to win—it's a connection they co-create. Tarot helps them see what role they play in that creation.

Be mindful not to promise timelines or destiny. Instead of saying, *"You'll meet someone in six months,"* you might say: *"This card shows the season of opening—it feels like summer energy, vibrant and alive. When you embody this openness, love flows toward you more naturally."* Focus on readiness and alignment, not waiting.

Practice Prompt for Singles

Pull this spread for yourself or a single friend with the question: *"What do I need to know about attracting love?"*

Journal your reflections:

- What did the first card reveal about the energy you're currently carrying into dating or connection?
- Did the second card highlight a pattern you already suspected—or one that surprised you?
- What qualities in the third card feel most alive in you now? Which ones do you want to grow?
- What practical invitation did the final card offer—and how can you embody it today, not "someday"?

After journaling, write a short affirmation inspired by the spread. For example, if your "qualities to attract love" card was the Queen of Wands, you might write: *"I shine brightly, and the right people are drawn to my warmth."*

CHAPTER 15

dating / complicated

"WHERE IS THIS CONNECTION HEADED?"

The early stages of love are intoxicating and confusing all at once. Whether it's a brand-new spark, a situationship that blurs the lines, or a casual dating connection, querents often come to tarot with the same question: *"Where is this going?"*

These are some of the trickiest readings to navigate. New relationships are fragile, undefined, and full of possibility. A single card can feel like the difference between "This is my forever" and "It's already doomed." Your role as the reader is to offer clarity without crushing possibility, to name patterns without turning them into fixed destinies.

Dating readings carry an edge of uncertainty that makes querents especially tender. Singles want to know *when* love is coming, but people in new or complicated situations want to know *if* love is real. Is this connection mutual? Are we on the same page? Am I wasting my time?

The challenge is that energy in this stage is fluid. What you see in the cards reflects the connection *as it stands right now*—but both people are still free to choose. That means your language matters. A blunt, fated answer can shut down hope. A compassionate, empowering answer can help the querent see both the beauty and the work of the moment.

THE DATING / COMPLICATED SPREAD (5 CARDS)

Card 1 Their energy in this connection

How is the other person showing up emotionally, mentally, spiritually?

Card 2 My energy in this connection

What is the querent bringing into this relationship?

Card 3 What we share (strengths)

The glue or spark that draws them together.

Card 4 What challenges we face

Where friction, imbalance, or uncertainty lies.

Card 5 Likely direction of the relationship

The trajectory based on the current energy—NOT a carved-in-stone outcome.

Look for balance or imbalance. Do one person's cards dominate the reading? Are the suits aligned (both Cups = shared emotions, both Wands = shared passion), or are they clashing (one Pentacle, one Sword = stability vs. coldness)? This reveals a lot about dynamics.

CHAPTER 16
how to speak to querents in "it's complicated" love

Name the tenderness. Acknowledge the vulnerability of asking: *"It's scary not knowing where this is headed. Let's look together at what the cards are showing you right now."*

Avoid rigid predictions. Instead of: *"This won't last,"* try: *"The current energy shows distance or hesitation. That doesn't mean it's doomed—it means clarity is needed."*

Empower through choice. Frame challenges as opportunities: *"This connection is real, but the cards suggest mismatched expectations. The question is: do you want to invest in aligning, or does it feel more loving to yourself to step away?"*

Take Cautions and Tread Carefully

Reading for situationships or complicated dating connections is delicate work. Querents are often in a heightened emotional state—anxious, hopeful, and sometimes desperate for clarity. That means your words carry even more weight than usual. A single phrase can either soothe their heart or shatter it. This is why caution isn't about being vague—it's about being responsible.

Don't Declare Feelings as Fact

It can be tempting, when the cards look cold or detached, to say: *"They don't love you."* But remember: tarot reflects energy, not a person's hidden diary.

A better approach might be:

"The cards suggest they're showing up with guarded or inconsistent energy right now. That doesn't mean there isn't feeling—it means this connection isn't being expressed in a steady way."

This keeps the reading true to the cards while leaving space for nuance and growth.

Don't Present Outcomes as Fixed

When querents ask *"Where is this going?"* they're really asking for reassurance. But the future is fluid, shaped by choices on both sides. If you say, *"This relationship is doomed,"* you strip away their agency.

Instead, frame the outcome as trajectory:

"Right now the energy suggests this connection may move slowly or face challenges. That doesn't mean it can't change—it means this is where the current path is leading. You both have choices that can shift the direction."

This empowers the querent to engage with the reading, not resign to it.

Don't Feed Obsession

Complicated relationships can easily tip into obsession. A querent may come back repeatedly with the same question, hoping the cards will eventually say what they want to hear. As a reader, it's your responsibility not to fuel that cycle.

If you notice this happening, gently redirect:

"Instead of asking again if they'll commit, let's ask what you need to know about your role in this connection. How can you care for yourself here? What choices are truly in your control?"

This helps the querent reclaim their power rather than spiraling into dependency on the cards.

Tarot is not here to dictate fate or confirm fears—it's here to illuminate energy, patterns, and choice. When you tread carefully, you show your querent respect and compassion, while also maintaining your integrity as a reader. The most healing readings often come not from definitive answers, but from helping someone see themselves, their connection, and their options more clearly.

> Practice Prompt: Imagine a querent says, *"Does he even love me?"* Pull three cards. Write one version of an answer that declares their feelings as fact. Then rewrite it in a way that reflects energy, possibility, and empowerment. Notice how the second version feels safer, kinder, and truer to tarot's purpose.

EXAMPLE READING

Question: *"Where is this connection headed?"*

Cards Pulled:

1. Their energy → *Knight of Wands*
2. My energy → *Queen of Cups*
3. What we share → *Two of Cups*
4. What challenges we face → *Seven of Cups*
5. Likely direction → *Temperance*

Their energy — Knight of Wands

The other person is showing up as the Knight of Wands—someone full of spark, attraction, and forward drive. This card often signals excitement and passion, but it can also bring inconsistency. The Knight of Wands rushes in with fire and enthusiasm, but may not have the staying power for steady commitment. In romance readings, this energy suggests they're caught up in the thrill of connection but may be less grounded in long-term vision.

My energy — Queen of Cups

The querent, on the other hand, shows up as the Queen of Cups—tender, intuitive, and emotionally invested. This is someone who feels deeply, loves deeply, and craves emotional reciprocity. The contrast here is important: one person is operating from emotion and depth, the other from passion and immediacy. Neither is wrong, but together they create a tension between speed and sensitivity.

What we share — Two of Cups

Despite these differences, the Two of Cups shows the undeniable bond between them. There is real chemistry here, a sense of mutual attraction, a mirror-like connection that draws them together. This isn't one-sided—the energy of this card confirms that both parties feel the pull, even if they express it differently.

What challenges we face — Seven of Cups

The Seven of Cups represents confusion, illusions, or too many possibilities. In this context, it suggests uncertainty about where the relationship is headed. There may be mixed signals, unclear intentions, or simply different expectations. The Knight of Wands might be chasing the thrill while the Queen of Cups is looking for depth, leaving both wondering if they're truly aligned. This card cautions against fantasy—it invites the querent to get clear about what they want and to see the connection realistically.

Likely direction — Temperance

Temperance shows the potential for blending and balance—but only with patience. This is not a "sweep you off your feet into forever" outcome. Instead, it's an invitation for both to slow down, communicate openly, and find harmony between their different approaches to love. Temperance reassures that there *is* possibility here, but it won't be rushed. It asks: *Can fire and water meet without extinguishing each other? Can passion and tenderness weave together into something sustainable?*

Interpretation

This connection is alive with chemistry. One person brings the heat and excitement of new love (Knight of Wands), while the other brings emotional depth and sensitivity (Queen of Cups). Together, they feel the spark of true attraction (Two of Cups), but the relationship is clouded by uncertainty and mixed expectations (Seven of Cups).

The cards don't promise an easy path forward, but they do suggest potential—if both are willing to slow down and meet in the middle (Temperance). The likely outcome isn't instant resolution, but gradual blending: finding balance between passion and depth, between thrill and tenderness.

This relationship has real potential, but clarity and patience are key. Don't rush to define it before the foundation is strong. Honor your depth, and invite them to bring steadiness to their passion. If both step into balance, this connection can grow into something beautiful.

PRACTICE PROMPT

Pull this spread for a fictional couple you know well—a book, movie, or TV show relationship. Practice reading their dynamics without the emotional pressure of a real querent. Notice how the spread plays out in their story. Then, pull the spread for yourself or a friend and compare: how does the energy feel different when it's personal?

Dating and "it's complicated" readings are about possibility, not permanence. They ask the reader to hold space for both the excitement of new love and the anxiety of uncertainty. When you balance clarity with compassion, you empower querents to see not only where the connection is now, but also what choices they can make to guide its direction.

Because at this stage, the truth isn't about destiny—it's about discovery.

CHAPTER 17

long-term / commitment

"HOW DO WE DEEPEN OUR BOND?"

Tarot isn't just for beginnings—it's also for the middle and the long haul. Couples in long-term or committed relationships often come to tarot not to ask *if* there is love, but to ask *how* to keep it alive. Whether it's a marriage of twenty years, a live-in partnership, or a long-term bond, these querents are looking for guidance on growth, healing, and staying connected through the changes of life.

In new love, the question is often about potential. In complicated love, it's about clarity. But in long-term love, the question is about depth: *"How do we keep choosing each other?"*

These querents aren't usually seeking dramatic predictions. They want practical insights: how to communicate better, how to rekindle intimacy, how to weather challenges together. They already know love is work—they're just asking tarot to shine a light on where to focus that work.

The Long-Term / Commitment Spread (6 cards)

Card 1 The current state of the relationship

How things stand right now—overall energy, shared tone, or current phase.

Card 2 What I bring into the bond

The querent's contributions—strengths, attitudes, and baggage.

Card 3 What my partner brings into the bond

The partner's energy—support, challenges, or gifts they contribute.

Card 4 Where we're strong together

The glue: trust, passion, teamwork, or shared values.

Card 5 Where we need growth

The stress points or blind spots—what still needs tending.

Card 6 How we can move forward in harmony

The next step toward healing, unity, or renewed intimacy.

> Look closely at Majors here—they often indicate turning points or karmic themes. Pentacles may point to financial security, shared stability, or long-term roots. Cups reveal the depth of intimacy and emotional nourishment.

CHAPTER 18
cautions for long-term readings

Reading for long-term partnerships is very different from reading for singles or situationships. When a querent comes in asking about a marriage or a decades-long bond, you are stepping into a story that already has deep history, roots, and shared responsibilities. The stakes feel higher: there may be children, shared homes, or lifetimes of patterns at play. Because of that, it's essential to tread carefully, with ethics and compassion at the forefront.

Avoid Telling Someone to "Stay" or "Leave"

This is the golden rule. Tarot is not here to dictate someone's life choices, especially in relationships as complex as marriages or long-term commitments. Declaring *"You should end this"* or *"This is your forever person"* removes the querent's agency and places a weight on your words that is not yours to carry.

✘ Instead, frame the cards as mirrors:

- ✔ *"Here's what the relationship looks like right now."*
- ✔ *"Here are the challenges and strengths present."*
- ✔ *"Here's the direction the energy seems to be moving."*

From there, remind them: *"You are the one who decides what to do with this insight."* Tarot illuminates possibilities, but the choice belongs to the people in the relationship.

Balance Honesty with Hope

A long-term querent deserves the truth, but they also deserve to leave the reading with a sense of possibility. Even if the cards reveal conflict, stagnation, or old wounds, those messages don't have to be delivered as doom.

✗ Instead of: *"This relationship looks dead—there's no future here."*

- ✓ Try: *"The cards show that the bond is carrying heavy energy right now. But they're also showing where growth and healing are possible if both partners choose it. The question becomes: are you both willing to do that work?"*

This balance allows you to stay honest while still opening a door for hope. Remember: even a card like *The Tower* doesn't mean an ending—it means a restructuring.

Empower Both Partners

Even when only one partner is in the room, speak in a way that honors both. Avoid villainizing one side or over-glorifying the other. Relationships are rarely that simple.

If one partner shows up as *The Devil*, don't immediately say: *"They're toxic."* Instead: *"The energy here suggests control or unhealthy cycles. This doesn't automatically mean they are a bad person—it means there are patterns in the relationship that may need attention and boundaries."*

If the querent pulls strong "positive" cards, avoid making them the sole savior of the bond. Emphasize that both people contribute energy—for better or for worse.

This framing not only protects you ethically but also helps your querent see the relationship as a partnership, not a battle of blame.

Why These Cautions Matter

When querents come to you with long-term questions, they're often carrying both love and fear. They may be on the edge of big decisions, or they may just need reassurance. Either way, your words can ripple through their lives in powerful ways. By honoring these cautions, you:

- Protect their agency and dignity.
- Keep the reading empowering, not disempowering.
- Make tarot a supportive tool for growth, rather than a final judgment.

Practice Prompt: Imagine a married querent asks: *"Are we going to make it?"* Pull three cards. First, write the kind of blunt, predictive answer you might give if you weren't being cautious. Then rewrite your response with these three cautions in mind—framing the cards as mirrors, balancing honesty with hope, and empowering both partners. Compare the two versions and notice how different they feel.

CHAPTER 19

the seasons of long-term love

Long-term love is not one steady line—it ebbs and flows, just like the turning of the seasons. Many querents fear that when a relationship feels cold, distant, or difficult, it means the love has died. But tarot helps us reframe: difficulty doesn't always mean failure. Sometimes, the relationship is simply moving through a different season.

When you introduce this idea in a reading, you help couples see their bond not as broken, but as alive—growing, shifting, and evolving. Just as we don't expect summer to last forever, we can't expect relationships to remain in constant bloom. Each season brings gifts, lessons, and opportunities for growth.

Spring Energy — Renewal & Beginnings

Cards: *Ace of Cups, Fool, Page of Wands*

Spring in love is about fresh energy: rekindled passion, new beginnings, or the start of a deeper chapter. For couples, this might show up after a period of struggle, when forgiveness and healing breathe new life into the bond. It can also represent milestones like moving in together, starting a family, or simply rediscovering why they chose each other in the first place.

If this comes up in a spread, remind the querent: *"This is a season of renewal. Love is waking up again. Tend to it gently, like seedlings breaking through the soil."*

Summer Energy — Joy & Flourishing

Cards: *The Sun, Ten of Cups, Three of Cups*

Summer is the time when love feels effortless—joyful, thriving, and abundant. Couples often experience this season during times of celebration (anniversaries, shared accomplishments, family gatherings). This is when the bond is in full bloom, carrying warmth and light.

If these cards appear, encourage gratitude and presence: *"This is your season to celebrate. Let yourselves enjoy what you've built without worrying about the next challenge."*

Autumn Energy — Reflection & Harvest

Cards: *Pentacles, Justice, Hermit*

Autumn represents maturity and reflection. It's when couples begin to harvest the lessons of their past efforts—sometimes enjoying stability, sometimes confronting the consequences of long-ignored issues. It's about deepening roots, reevaluating priorities, and preparing for the next cycle.

In readings, this season may signal a need to slow down and ask: *"What have we learned? What do we need to release? What values do we want to carry forward together?"* It's not about loss, but about wisdom.

Winter Energy — Rest & Renewal Through Challenge

Cards: *The Tower, Four of Swords, Five of Pentacles*

Winter is the hardest season—but also the most transformative. It represents times when relationships feel cold, distant, or shaken by external pressures. This could be illness, financial strain, betrayal, or simply exhaustion. But just as nature rests in winter, couples may need to pause, recover, or rebuild.

If winter energy dominates a reading, reassure the querent: *"This season feels heavy, but it's not forever. Winter strips away what no longer serves, so that spring can come again. Rest, heal, and know that this cycle prepares the ground for renewal."*

When you frame love through the lens of seasons, you shift the narrative. Suddenly, struggles aren't proof of failure—they're part of the natural rhythm of a living relationship. Couples learn to see their bond as a garden: something to nurture, prune, and protect, knowing that every season brings new life.

Practice Prompt:

Pull six cards with the question: *"What season is our relationship in, and what is it asking of us?"*

Which suit dominates? (Cups = emotional renewal, Pentacles = stability lessons, Swords = communication challenges, Wands = rekindled passion.)

Which Major Arcana appears, and what larger cycle is it signaling?

Journal the answer, then write advice you'd give a client to help them embrace this season instead of resisting it.

CHAPTER 20

intimacy beyond romance

When couples ask about passion, what they're often really seeking is *closeness*. But intimacy isn't just about physical chemistry—it's about the many ways we allow ourselves to be known and connected. Over time, long-term relationships thrive not just on romance, but on the balance of emotional, physical, practical, and intellectual intimacy.

Tarot is uniquely suited to highlight which forms of intimacy are flourishing in a relationship and which may need nurturing. When a couple feels "something is missing," it's often because one of these dimensions has been neglected.

Emotional Intimacy (Cups)

Emotional intimacy is the ability to feel seen, heard, and safe in the relationship. It's the heart-to-heart connection: trust, vulnerability, empathy.

Strong Signs: *Two of Cups, Ten of Cups, Queen of Cups* → shows warmth, affection, and mutual understanding.

Weak Spots: *Five of Cups, Four of Cups, Nine of Swords* → suggest grief, emotional distance, or feeling unheard.

How to frame it: *"The cards show that your emotional closeness is thriving—but to deepen it, lean into open-hearted conversations where you both feel safe to be vulnerable."*

Physical Intimacy (Wands)

Physical intimacy includes passion, attraction, and sexual energy—but also everyday affection: touch, playfulness, the spark that keeps the body language alive.

Strong Signs: *Ace of Wands, Knight of Wands, Strength* → passion, chemistry, vitality.

Weak Spots: *Four of Wands reversed, Ten of Wands, Five of Wands* → show fatigue, misaligned desire, or conflict around physical connection.

How to frame it: *"The fire is here, but it may need to be tended. Try creating intentional space for play, passion, and touch that isn't rushed."*

Practical Intimacy (Pentacles)

Practical intimacy is often overlooked, but it's the foundation of long-term relationships: teamwork, shared responsibilities, and building security together. It's how love shows up in the "real world."

Strong Signs: *Ten of Pentacles, Six of Pentacles, Three of Pentacles* → indicate mutual effort, family support, financial partnership.

Weak Spots: *Five of Pentacles, Four of Pentacles, Two of Pentacles* → reveal strain, imbalance, or fear around resources.

How to frame it: *"Love shows up in daily life too—your teamwork is strong, but the cards invite you to check in around how balanced the effort feels between you."*

Intellectual Intimacy (Swords)

Intellectual intimacy is about stimulation of the mind—being curious together, having meaningful conversations, or challenging each other with new ideas. It keeps the relationship lively and evolving.

Strong Signs: *Ace of Swords, Two of Swords (when upright), King of Swords* → clear communication, shared curiosity, honesty.

Weak Spots: *Seven of Swords, Eight of Swords, Nine of Swords* → dishonesty, avoidance, overthinking that blocks open dialogue.

How to frame it: *"The mental connection is as important as the emotional. The cards suggest nurturing this by exploring new conversations, shared learning, or honesty around what's been unspoken."*

When a couple says, *"We've lost our spark,"* they may not mean passion at all—they may mean they don't feel heard, they don't feel like a team, or they've stopped inspiring each other. By noticing which suits dominate in a spread, you can help couples understand where intimacy is flourishing and where it needs attention.

Instead of reducing love to a single dimension, you show them its fullness. And that reframing can be healing in itself: it teaches couples that they *are* connected, even if one area feels neglected—and that every form of intimacy can be rekindled with intention.

Practice Prompt:

Pull four cards, one from each suit, with the question: *"Which kind of intimacy is strongest in our relationship right now, and which needs nurturing?"*

Journal or roleplay how you'd explain these results to a couple. How would you frame the "weak" area with compassion, while celebrating the areas that shine?

CHAPTER 21

legacy & shared dreams

When couples come for long-term readings, they're often not only asking about their present struggles—they're also asking about their future vision. *"What are we building together? What's our purpose as a couple? What do we leave behind?"*

This is where tarot becomes a tool for visioning, not just problem-solving. Long-term love isn't measured only in years—it's measured in what the bond creates: families, homes, shared projects, businesses, art, communities, or simply the story of two lives well lived side by side.

Legacy doesn't always mean children or material inheritance. It can be:

- The *energy* a couple leaves with their community (warmth, example, wisdom).
- The *traditions* they build together—rituals, values, spiritual practices.
- The *dreams* they pursue—shared goals, adventures, or creative projects.
- The *stability* they create for each other, becoming each other's "safe place."

Helping querents see beyond the daily grind into their shared vision can renew their sense of purpose and remind them why they're walking this path together.

Cards of Legacy & Vision

Ten of Pentacles → Family, stability, generational wealth or wisdom, "the life we've built."

The World → Completion, fulfillment, impact that extends beyond just two people.

The Empress → Nurturing, creativity, abundance, fertility (literal or metaphorical).

Three of Pentacles → Building something together; teamwork, collaboration, shared project.

Star → Legacy of hope and healing; the gift of inspiring others by simply being who you are together.

If these cards appear in a long-term spread, invite the querent to zoom out from the day-to-day frustrations and ask bigger questions:

- *"What are we working toward together?"*
- *"What impact do we want our relationship to leave on our family, community, or the world?"*
- *"What dream is ours to bring to life as partners?"*

This reframes the relationship not as a series of conflicts to fix, but as a story they're writing together.

EXAMPLE READING

Question: *"What are we building together as a couple?"*

Cards Pulled: *Three of Pentacles, Ten of Pentacles, The World*

Interpretation:

The Three of Pentacles suggests that this couple is building their bond like a project—brick by brick, with patience and collaboration. The Ten of Pentacles shows that their work isn't just for themselves; it's creating stability and blessings that ripple outward to family, children, or community. The World as the outcome suggests fulfillment and legacy—together they're writing a story that feels complete, impactful, and lasting.

This reading doesn't just reassure them about the present; it inspires them with the sense that they're part of something much larger than their daily struggles.

When you guide couples to think about legacy, you shift them from *reacting to problems* into *envisioning possibilities*. That shift alone can be healing. Suddenly, disagreements about chores or bills look small compared to the dream they're co-creating. They leave not just with insight, but with renewed purpose: *"We're not just surviving. We're building something."*

Practice Prompt:

Pull three cards with the question: *"What legacy are we creating together?"* Journal how you'd explain the result to a couple in a way that lifts their vision beyond the present moment. Then, write how you might reframe the same cards for a single querent, focusing on the legacy they're preparing for love to join.

CHAPTER 22
healing old wounds together

In long-term partnerships, the question is rarely *"Do we love each other?"* More often, it's *"Can our love carry us through what we've been through?"* Couples who have weathered years together usually know their bond is real, but they may feel weighed down by old wounds—betrayal, resentment, communication breakdowns, or the exhaustion of burnout.

Tarot is a powerful tool for helping couples recognize these wounds, name their lessons, and envision paths toward forgiveness and renewal. The cards don't erase the past, but they illuminate how healing is possible when love is still present.

Why Wounds Arise in Long-Term Love

Conflict Patterns: Arguments that repeat without resolution (Five of Swords, Knight of Swords).

Betrayal or Broken Trust: Infidelity, secrecy, or dishonesty (Seven of Swords, Three of Swords).

Burnout & Disconnection: Life stress, overwork, parenting fatigue, emotional withdrawal (Ten of Wands, Four of Cups).

These wounds don't always mean the relationship is ending—they often signal places that need tenderness, attention, and new agreements.

The Healing Spread (4 Cards)

Card 1 What wound are we still carrying?

The root pain that still lingers—whether it's unspoken resentment, broken trust, or unprocessed grief.

Card 2 What strength can help us heal it?

The shared quality that can bring resilience—loyalty, humor, teamwork, spiritual faith.

Card 3 What lesson is hidden in this wound?

How this pain can grow the couple: boundaries, deeper honesty, appreciation, renewed choice.

Card 4 What step can bring forgiveness or renewal?

A tangible action or mindset shift—apologizing, creating new rituals, choosing compassion, or simply deciding to release the weight of the past.

EXAMPLE READING

Question: *"How can we heal what's been hurting between us?"*

Cards Pulled:

1. Wound → *Three of Swords* (betrayal, heartbreak still lingering)
2. Strength → *Ten of Cups* (family love, shared vision for the future)
3. Lesson → *Justice* (the need for fairness, truth, accountability)
4. Step → *Ace of Pentacles* (planting a new seed, rebuilding trust slowly)

Interpretation: The cards reveal a relationship carrying the weight of old heartbreak (Three of Swords). This wound may stem from betrayal, a painful conflict, or simply words and actions that left lasting scars. It lingers not because the love is gone, but because the hurt was never fully acknowledged or processed. The Three of Swords asks us to name the pain instead of pretending it doesn't exist—because healing can only begin where truth is spoken.

And yet, alongside this wound is the Ten of Cups: a reminder that the foundation of this relationship is genuine love, shared history, and a vision of family or emotional fulfillment. This is the bond that keeps them tethered even in difficulty. It shows that despite the hurt, there is something precious still worth protecting—a home, a dream, a sense of belonging they've built together.

Justice as the third card brings clarity to the path forward. Healing won't happen through avoidance or wishful thinking; it must come through honesty, fairness, and accountability. Justice invites both partners to take responsibility for their roles, to tell the truth even when it's uncomfortable, and to set new agreements that honor both people equally. It's about balance: not one person carrying the blame or the weight, but both stepping into alignment with what is fair, transparent, and right.

Finally, the Ace of Pentacles offers a hopeful way forward. This is not a sweeping promise that everything will be instantly fixed—it's a seed. Healing here requires patience and practical effort. Small, consistent actions will matter more than dramatic gestures. Think of it like planting a garden: the Ace of Pentacles reminds them to water trust slowly, to nurture tenderness daily, and to allow growth to come in its own time. Renewal is possible, but it must be rooted in tangible change—apologies backed by action, promises reinforced by consistency, love expressed not only in words but in real, grounded ways.

Together, these cards tell a powerful story: yes, the wound is real, but so is the love. Healing is possible when truth is honored, responsibility is shared, and both partners commit to planting something new together. The relationship doesn't need to return to what it once was—it has the chance to become something wiser, stronger, and more resilient than before.

How to Frame Healing Readings

Be gentle with blame. Instead of, *"Your partner broke this and it may never be fixed,"* try, *"The cards show a wound that still weighs heavily, but also the strength you share that can help you face it together."*

Emphasize choice. Healing is always possible, but both partners must want it. Tarot can illuminate steps, but it cannot force change.

Normalize cycles. All long-term love carries wounds—it's part of the depth of intimacy. The key is how couples choose to tend to them.

When you offer couples a framework for healing, you're reminding them that wounds aren't proof of failure—they're proof that love has been tested. And in many cases, the act of healing *together* deepens intimacy more than smooth years ever could.

> **Practice Prompt:**
>
> Pull this 4-card Healing Spread for a fictional couple (Romeo & Juliet, Ross & Rachel, Gomez & Morticia). Practice explaining the wound, the strength, the lesson, and the step in a way that feels compassionate and empowering. Then, try it again for yourself—choose a personal relationship (romantic or otherwise) and see what the cards reveal about healing.

EXAMPLE READING

Question: *"How can we deepen our bond?"*

Cards Pulled:

1. Current state → *Four of Pentacles* (stable, but guarded)
2. What I bring → *Knight of Cups* (romance, emotional offering)
3. What my partner brings → *King of Pentacles* (security, steadiness)
4. Where we're strong → *The Lovers* (shared values, alignment, choosing each other)
5. Where we need growth → *Five of Swords* (conflict, defensiveness)
6. How we move forward → *The Star* (healing, renewal, faith)

Interpretation: Right now, the relationship is steady (Four of Pentacles) but maybe too tightly held—there's stability, but also fear of change. The querent brings romance and emotional tenderness (Knight of Cups), while their partner offers grounded stability and support (King of Pentacles). Together, they are strong in their shared values and the choice they've made to be together (The Lovers).

But the challenges lie in conflict patterns (Five of Swords)—perhaps arguments that get competitive, or words that wound more than they heal. The Star as the final card is beautiful—it shows the potential for deep renewal and healing if both are willing to bring vulnerability and forgiveness into the bond.

This reading doesn't tell the querent whether to stay or go—it shows them what's alive in the relationship and where the real work is. With care, this bond can absolutely deepen and continue to flourish.

> **Practice Prompt**
>
> Imagine pulling this spread for a friend's relationship. How would you explain the results in a way that empowers *both* partners, even though only one asked the question? Write two versions:
>
> • One blunt, predictive version.
>
> • One compassionate, growth-centered version.
>
> Notice how the second version creates more space for possibility, and more dignity for both people in the relationship.

Long-term readings are about nourishment, not fortune-telling. They remind us that love isn't just about falling—it's about choosing, every day, to show up with honesty, tenderness, and effort. Tarot becomes the mirror that shows couples where their strengths lie, where they're hurting, and how they can weave their story more tightly together.

When done with compassion, these readings don't just answer questions—they can truly heal relationships.

CHAPTER 23

long-term relationship card guide

Tarot cards take on special nuances in the context of long-term or committed partnerships. These interpretations highlight how the cards often "speak" when the question is: *"How do we deepen our bond?"*

Majors in Long-Term Love

- **The Lovers** → Alignment of values, choosing each other daily. Can also highlight tough choices if paths are diverging.
- **The Hierophant** → Marriage, shared traditions, long-term spiritual or cultural bonds.
- **The Empress** → Nurturing energy, home-building, family or fertility.
- **The Emperor** → Structure, security, stability; sometimes a warning of rigidity.
- **The Devil** → Cycles of control, unhealthy attachment, or codependency that need addressing.
- **The Tower** → Disruption that shakes the foundation—can be painful, but often clears the way for rebuilding truthfully.
- **The Star** → Healing, forgiveness, and renewal after difficulty.
- **Temperance** → Patience, balance, learning to blend differences into harmony.
- **The World** → Completion of a cycle, stepping into a new phase together.

Cups in Long-Term Love

- **Two of Cups** → Intimacy, partnership, mutual respect—still choosing each other.
- **Ten of Cups** → Family harmony, shared happiness, emotional fulfillment.
- **Five of Cups** → Lingering hurts or disappointments that need to be processed.
- **Eight of Cups** → One or both may feel emotionally checked out; a need for honest talk.
- **Ace of Cups** → Renewal of love, opening the heart again, emotional reset.

Wands in Long-Term Love

- **Four of Wands** → Celebrations, milestones (anniversaries, home, weddings).
- **Six of Wands** → Pride in the relationship, mutual recognition.
- **Seven of Wands** → Defensive energy—protecting love, but sometimes too guarded.
- **Ten of Wands** → Burdens of responsibility, one partner feeling overwhelmed.
- **Knight of Wands** → Rekindled passion, but can also signal restlessness or inconsistency.

Pentacles in Long-Term Love

- **Four of Pentacles** → Stability, security, but also emotional guardedness.
- **Six of Pentacles** → Balance of giving and receiving, reciprocity in effort.
- **Ten of Pentacles** → Family, legacy, building something enduring together.
- **Five of Pentacles** → Struggles with finances or health, needing to weather storms together.
- **Ace of Pentacles** → A fresh start in material stability—new home, shared financial goals.

Swords in Long-Term Love

- **Two of Swords** → Avoidance, unspoken truths, decisions left hanging.
- **Five of Swords** → Conflict patterns, arguments where no one "wins."
- **Seven of Swords** → Secrecy, avoidance, or trust issues that need transparency.

- **Nine of Swords** → Anxiety, fear, cycles of worry impacting the bond.
- **Ten of Swords** → Feeling betrayed, or hitting a rock-bottom moment that demands honesty.
- **Ace of Swords** → Breakthrough conversations, clarity, communication reset.

CHAPTER 24

self-love

"HOW DO I LOVE MYSELF THE WAY I DESERVE?"

Every querent comes to tarot carrying questions of the heart, but sometimes the most powerful love reading has nothing to do with another person at all. Self-love is the foundation of every healthy relationship, and yet it's often the one people overlook. Without it, connections become unbalanced, desperate, or dependent. With it, relationships become expansive, joyful, and rooted in worthiness.

Self-love spreads are about shifting focus inward: instead of waiting for someone else to show us love, we learn to show it to ourselves first. This isn't about arrogance or selfishness—it's about tending to our own garden so that when love arrives, it has fertile ground to grow.

Why Self-Love Readings Matter

Many querents will resist these spreads at first. They came to ask about their crush, their ex, their marriage—why should they read about themselves? But the truth is, every relationship is a mirror of the relationship we have with ourselves. If we neglect our own needs, we attract neglect. If we doubt our worth, we attract partners who reflect that doubt. When we root into self-love, we become magnetic to love that honors us.

Self-love as the *most important love reading of all*. Gently redirect querents who are obsessing over external validation to self love. You're not dismissing their desire for romance—you're showing them that the path begins within.

THE SELF-LOVE SPREAD (4 CARDS)

Card 1 How I'm currently treating myself

Reveals the inner dialogue—are they kind and encouraging to themselves, or critical and neglectful?

Card 2 What wounds need my care

Highlights old hurts, limiting beliefs, or unhealed parts of the self that need tenderness.

Card 3 How I can show myself love right now

A practical step or action—rest, boundaries, celebration, compassion.

Card 4 The gift waiting when I do

The outcome of practicing self-love—confidence, renewal, freedom, magnetism.

When working with self-love spreads, it's important to remember that not every card points outward toward romance or another person. Many cards, especially the Courts and the Majors, are mirrors of the self. They show us the roles we inhabit, the archetypes we embody, and the soul-level lessons we are invited to embrace.

The Court Cards: Inner Personas of the Self

Court Cards often represent aspects of personality rather than external figures. In self-love readings, they can be read as the "inner voices" or roles the querent is being called to embody.

Pages → The student within us: curious, vulnerable, learning. A Page in a self-love reading may reveal the part of you that longs to explore, take risks, or start fresh.

Knights → The part of the self in motion: passionate, seeking, sometimes restless. Knights may show where you need to take action or direct energy more consciously.

Queens → The nurturer within: intuitive, wise, deserving of respect. Queens often highlight areas where you must honor yourself, set boundaries, and receive with grace.

Kings → The sovereign self: mastery, authority, leadership. Kings call you to claim your power and make choices from a place of confidence and clarity.

> Example: In a self-love spread, the Queen of Pentacles might not point to an

external person at all—it could be reminding the querent to nurture themselves, honor their body, or invest in their own well-being.

The Major Arcana: Soul Lessons of Self-Love

Where the Court Cards reflect personal roles, the Major Arcana reveal larger archetypal lessons. In self-love readings, Majors often act as milestones on the querent's soul journey, showing the deeper truths they are being asked to integrate.

Strength → Courage through compassion; meeting yourself with gentleness rather than force.

The Star → Hope and healing; believing in your worth and radiance, even after difficulty.

The Hermit → The gift of solitude; recognizing that self-love often blooms in quiet reflection.

The Empress → Nurturing and creative abundance; learning to receive as well as to give.

The World → Wholeness and completion; remembering that you are already enough as you are.

> Example: If Strength appears in the "How can I love myself right now?" position, the cards may be reminding the querent to stop battling their flaws and instead meet themselves with gentleness. If The Star appears as "The gift waiting when I do," it promises the renewal of hope, radiance, and self-trust.

By framing the Courts as facets of the self and the Majors as archetypal lessons, you help querents stop looking outside for validation and instead recognize the depth of wisdom already within. These cards become invitations to inhabit roles, integrate lessons, and walk the path of self-love with more awareness.

Practice Exercise:

Pull one Court and one Major. Journal about:

- What inner persona does the Court reveal in you right now?
- What soul lesson is the Major inviting you to embody?
- How do these two cards "talk" to each other about your self-love journey?

CHAPTER 25

Tips for reading self-love spreads

Self-love spreads are often some of the most transformative readings you can give, because they shift focus from the desire for external validation into the deeper work of building inner strength. The goal isn't to replace romance—it's to create the fertile ground where healthy love can take root. When guiding querents through these readings, keep the following principles in mind:

Self-Love Is Not "Settling"

One of the biggest hurdles for querents is the belief that focusing on self-love means "giving up" on romance. Many come to tarot wanting to hear about a soulmate, a reunion, or a new relationship, and self-love may feel like a consolation prize. As a reader, it's your role to reframe this.

Self-love is not a substitute for partnership—it's the foundation upon which all healthy partnerships are built. Without it, relationships risk becoming unbalanced, dependent, or filled with unmet needs. With it, love can thrive in a way that honors both people.

Example Language:

✗ Instead of: *"This spread is about you because you're not ready for love yet."*

✓ Try: *"This spread is about you because every relationship you step into is shaped by how you love yourself. The stronger that love becomes, the stronger your future connections will be."*

Notice and Track Patterns

Self-love spreads often work best when repeated over time. Encourage querents to revisit these spreads monthly or quarterly and track recurring themes.

When the same card appears again and again, it's not random—it's a lesson the soul is circling back to, asking for deeper integration. For example, if the Four of Swords keeps showing up, the querent may need more consistent rest and reflection. If the Strength card repeats, self-compassion in the face of fear is still a lesson calling for attention.

By highlighting these patterns, you help the querent see their growth over time and understand that self-love is a journey, not a single destination.

Translate the Cards Into Action

The most powerful self-love readings don't stop at description—they inspire practice. Self-love is a lived experience, and the cards can be translated into actionable steps the querent can take in daily life.

For instance:

Ace of Pentacles → A reminder to ground in routine, begin a new healthy habit, or treat oneself to something nurturing.

Knight of Wands → An invitation to embrace joy, spontaneity, or creative expression—say yes to play and passion.

Nine of Pentacles → Encouragement to celebrate independence, indulge in beauty or luxury, and acknowledge personal accomplishments.

The Hermit → Guidance to take space for reflection, journaling, or solo time that reconnects them with inner wisdom.

By giving practical steps, you ensure the reading doesn't remain abstract. The querent leaves not only with insight but also with a path forward—something they can *do* to embody the message of the cards.

Self-love spreads can be the most resisted by querents—yet they are often the most transformative. By reframing self-love as foundational, tracking repeating themes as soul-level lessons, and translating each card into a practical invitation, you show that tarot isn't just about predicting when love will arrive. It's about preparing the heart, strengthening the self, and making space for love to flourish when it does.

Practice Exercise

> Pull one card with the question: "What is one way I can show myself love today?"

> Write down a practical action step inspired by that card.
>
> Repeat this daily for a week. At the end of the week, journal about how these actions shifted your self-perception and mood.

There is a natural desire to skip this spread because you might be craving answers about someone else. That's normal. But it's important to remember, no external relationship can give what we refuse to give ourselves. Skipping self-love doesn't make romance come faster—it makes it harder to sustain when it does arrive.

Instead of framing this as a detour, frame it as preparation: *"Every card you pull here strengthens the love you're able to offer and receive later."*

EXAMPLE READING

Question: *"How do I love myself the way I deserve?"*

Cards Pulled:

1. How I'm treating myself → *Five of Pentacles* (self-neglect, feeling unworthy)
2. What wounds need my care → *Nine of Swords* (anxiety, self-criticism)
3. How I can show myself love → *Strength* (gentle compassion, courage rooted in softness)
4. The gift waiting when I do → *The Star* (renewal, hope, radiant healing)

Interpretation: The spread begins with the Five of Pentacles, showing that the querent has been moving through life with a sense of lack—whether that's financial, emotional, or spiritual. In the context of self-love, this card often reflects feelings of unworthiness or neglect, like standing outside in the cold while warmth glows just beyond reach. It suggests that the querent may be shutting themselves out of their own compassion, focusing only on what they lack instead of what they already carry inside. This is the starting point: recognition of the neglect they've been placing on their own heart.

The Nine of Swords deepens this picture by pointing to the inner wounds that need care. This card highlights anxiety, sleepless nights, or the sharp edges of self-criticism that play on repeat in the querent's mind. It reveals that much of the pain is not coming from the outside, but from the harsh stories they tell themselves. Together, the Five of Pentacles and Nine of Swords speak of a person who has been both abandoned *and* their own abandoner—longing for kindness but withholding it from themselves.

And then, Strength arrives as the turning point. This card reminds us that love of the self is not about force or perfection—it is about courage wrapped in gentleness. Strength whispers that the querent does not need to conquer their flaws but instead meet them with patience, kindness, and soft resilience. Where the Nine of Swords lashes with criticism, Strength offers the lion's heart: calm, steady, and compassionate even in the face of fear. Self-love, here, is about becoming the nurturing presence they've always needed—reassuring themselves instead of punishing, soothing instead of scolding.

Finally, The Star shines as the gift waiting on the other side of this journey. The Star is a card of renewal, hope, and radiant healing. It promises that when the querent begins to treat themselves with compassion and care, their light will return—not just quietly, but in a way that radiates outward. The Star suggests that this healing will restore their sense of worth and inspire others around them. It's the promise that by learning to love themselves, they'll not only heal their own wounds but also become a beacon of gentle hope to others.

Taken together, the spread tells a story of someone who has been caught in a cycle of neglect and self-criticism, but who carries within them the courage and tenderness to step into deep healing. The message is clear: *you are not broken—you are waiting to be reclaimed.* By practicing compassion and meeting themselves where they are, the querent will move from scarcity to abundance, from self-criticism to self-acceptance, and from despair into radiant renewal.

How to Deliver This in a Reading (Example Phrasing):

"You've been so hard on yourself—almost like standing outside your own heart, not letting yourself in. The cards show that the biggest wound here isn't that you're unworthy—it's that you've convinced yourself of that story. But Strength is reminding you that true self-love doesn't come from fixing yourself, it comes from treating yourself with compassion, even in your messy, fearful moments. And when you do, The Star shows up—the promise of hope, renewal, and a light that shines from within you. You'll not only feel better—you'll become magnetic to love and connection in ways you haven't before, because you'll finally see the beauty that's been in you all along."

Practice Prompt

Do this spread for yourself once a month. Record the results in your tarot journal and track the patterns. Which wounds keep asking for your attention? Which gifts keep showing up? Over time, you'll see your relationship with yourself evolve, just like you would in any long-term partnership.

CHAPTER 26

self-love affirmation builder

Tarot is a mirror, but affirmations are the echo. When you pull a card for self-love, you're being shown an image, an archetype, an energy to embody. Turning that into an affirmation anchors the lesson into daily life. It takes the wisdom of the spread out of the reading and into the querent's language—words they can repeat, write, or carry with them.

How It Works

> Pull a single card with the question: "What truth do I need to affirm about myself today?"
>
> Translate the card's energy into an "I" statement. This can be simple or poetic, but it should be empowering.
>
> Repeat it daily. Say it aloud, write it in a journal, or place it on a post-it where it will be seen.

Examples

The Sun → *"I radiate joy and warmth. My light is worthy of being seen."*

Strength → *"I am stronger than my fear. I meet myself with courage and compassion."*

The Star → *"I am a vessel of healing and hope. My presence is enough."*

Nine of Pentacles → *"I thrive in my independence. I am abundant, capable, and whole."*

Five of Cups → *"I honor my grief, but I also honor the love still present in my life."*

Ace of Cups → *"I am open to love—beginning with my own heart."*

Tips for Building Affirmations

Keep them present tense. ("I am," "I have," "I choose")—this brings the energy into the now.

Balance softness and strength. Affirmations should be tender but empowering.

Make them personal. Encourage querents to adapt them—let the words feel natural in their own voice.

Practice Prompt

Pull three cards and write one affirmation for each. Then, choose your favorite and make it your mantra for the week. At the end of the week, journal: *How did living with this affirmation shift how I treated myself?*

CHAPTER 27

the court cards as self-love voices

Page of Cups — The Inner Dreamer

This voice invites playfulness, creativity, and openness to emotional expression. It reminds you to imagine freely, to listen to your heart, and to reconnect with wonder.

Page of Pentacles — The Inner Student

This aspect of self is grounded, curious, and practical. It encourages you to take small, steady steps toward growth—like starting a new habit, skill, or routine that nurtures you.

Page of Swords — The Inner Curiosity

This voice wants to know the truth, even if it's uncomfortable. It asks you to question your own stories, seek clarity, and explore your inner world with honesty.

Page of Wands — The Inner Adventurer

This is the spark of excitement within, urging you to take risks, try new things, and step into joy. It reminds you that self-love thrives on fun, exploration, and a willingness to say yes.

Knight of Cups — The Inner Romantic

This aspect of you loves beauty and poetry. It encourages you to court yourself —write love notes, indulge in things that delight your senses, and treat yourself with tenderness.

Knight of Pentacles — The Inner Steward

This voice values consistency and loyalty. It reminds you that self-love isn't just about indulgence—it's about steady, practical care. Build routines that protect your well-being long-term.

Knight of Swords — The Inner Clarifier

This is the part of you that cuts through confusion with honesty. It invites you to speak truth to yourself, to stop hiding behind excuses, and to embrace clarity over avoidance.

Knight of Wands — The Inner Fire

This self-love voice is passionate, bold, and energetic. It urges you to follow your excitement, embrace spontaneity, and pursue joy with enthusiasm.

Queen of Cups — The Inner Nurturer

This voice teaches compassion, tenderness, and emotional safety. It invites you to treat yourself the way a loving mother would—gentle, kind, and validating.

Queen of Pentacles — The Inner Provider

This aspect of you values comfort, grounding, and care. It reminds you to tend to your body, your home, and your physical needs with reverence and love.

Queen of Swords — The Inner Truth-Teller

This voice is wise, discerning, and boundary-driven. It invites you to honor your truth, speak with clarity, and practice the kind of self-love that comes from saying no when necessary.

Queen of Wands — The Inner Confidence

This is your radiant, magnetic self. It encourages you to celebrate yourself, shine brightly, and step unapologetically into visibility.

King of Cups — The Inner Healer

This aspect of self is emotionally balanced, compassionate, and mature. It teaches you to navigate emotions with grace, honoring both strength and vulnerability.

King of Pentacles — The Inner Protector

This voice values stability and security. It calls you to provide for yourself—financially, emotionally, and physically—so that you always feel supported and safe.

King of Swords — The Inner Judge

This is the voice of wisdom, integrity, and discernment. It encourages you to lead yourself with clarity and fairness, cutting through illusions with truth.

King of Wands — The Inner Leader

This is your bold, empowered self. It asks you to step into your own authority, take action in service of your joy, and lead your life with vision and passion.

PART THREE

timing in love

CHAPTER 28

why "when will i meet them?" is tricky

Why "When Will I Meet Them?" Is Tricky

In love readings, few questions appear as often as: *"When will I meet my soulmate?" "When will we get married?" "When will they text me back?"* At first glance, these questions seem natural. When the heart longs for love, waiting can feel unbearable. People want a calendar date, a countdown, a promise that their story will soon begin or return.

But here lies one of the greatest challenges in tarot: timing.

Tarot reflects energy, cycles, and readiness—not fixed dates etched in stone. The cards illuminate patterns, highlight lessons, and reveal the direction of movement. They show the season, not the clock. A card may suggest that a relationship is aligned with the energy of spring, or that love will appear once old wounds are healed—but it cannot guarantee an exact day or hour.

This is because people change. Choices shift. Free will is always at play. What feels true in this moment may change tomorrow if someone makes a new decision, takes a different path, or chooses a new way of loving. Tarot captures the living, breathing flow of possibility, not a predetermined destiny.

Relying on exact predictions in timing questions can create more harm than help. If someone is told, *"You'll meet your soulmate in three months,"* they may place all their hope on that promise. And if life unfolds differently, the result is disappointment, doubt, or even dependency—returning to the cards again and again, desperate for a new countdown.

The truth is that love does not follow a stopwatch. It follows the rhythm of readiness: the readiness of the self to give and receive, the readiness of another to arrive, the readiness of both to meet in alignment.

When it comes to love, tarot is not meant to be a calendar—it is a compass. It points to where the energy is flowing, where growth is possible, and where the heart is being called. Instead of predicting exact dates, the cards guide toward seasons of transformation, cycles of renewal, and the steps needed to prepare for connection.

Tarot isn't a stopwatch—it's a compass. It does not count down to love's arrival but shows the direction in which the heart must walk to meet it.

THE DEEPER TRUTH OF TIMING

Cycles vs. Clocks

Tarot often speaks in cycles rather than numbers. The Wheel of Fortune, The Moon, or The World remind us that love arrives when a cycle turns, when one chapter ends and another begins. Unlike a clock that ticks predictably, cycles flow according to energy, healing, and readiness. This is why "when" questions rarely find satisfying answers—the cards point to a turning tide, not a date on the wall.

Seasons as Timing Symbols

The imagery of the cards themselves often hints at *seasons of energy*. The Sun glows with summer warmth, The Hermit whispers of winter introspection, Cups often suggest spring, while Pentacles align with autumn. These aren't deadlines—they are metaphors for what energy needs to be embodied before love can flow in.

Why Exact Predictions Can Harm

Giving a specific date risks doing more harm than good. Imagine telling someone, "You'll meet your person in three months." If nothing happens, despair sets in—*"The cards lied."* If something *does* happen, dependency grows—*"Tell me what happens next, on what date, in what way."* The querent becomes less empowered and more reliant on tarot as an external authority rather than on their own choices.

Reframing the Question

The most empowering way to approach timing is to shift the question from

"When?" to *"What needs to be in place?"* or *"What season of my life will align with love?"* Instead of a deadline, the cards offer preparation.

✗ Instead of: *"When will I meet them?"*

✓ Try: *"What energy will I be in when I'm ready to meet them?"*

✗ Instead of: *"When will they call me?"*

✓ Try: *"What needs to happen before this connection can move forward?"*

Hope vs. Fixation

It's natural for people to want hope when they ask about timing, but fixation on dates often fuels obsession. The role of tarot is to bring hope through direction, not countdowns. Remind that querent: *"Love isn't late. Love is aligning."*

CHAPTER 29

how to phrase timing questions with care

Timing is one of the trickiest areas in love readings because it sits at the crossroads of desire and uncertainty. Querents want guarantees—dates, deadlines, and certainty about "when" love will arrive. But tarot works in cycles, energy, and readiness, not in clocks. That means the way a question is phrased can make all the difference in the clarity and compassion of the answer.

THE PROBLEM WITH "WHEN WILL I MEET THE ONE?"

Questions like *"When will I meet the One?"* assume that:

1. There is only one destined partner.
2. Love arrives at a fixed time regardless of choices.
3. Tarot should act as a stopwatch rather than a mirror.

This framing makes love sound like a lottery ticket someone is waiting to win, instead of a living relationship shaped by free will, self-growth, and timing on both sides. A reading given from this place often leads to false hope, disappointment, or passivity—querents sitting back and waiting rather than stepping into their role as co-creators of love.

Shifting the Question

The true gift of tarot is not to act as fortune-teller, but as compass. When a querent asks "when," the reader can gently redirect toward "how" and "what" —questions that explore readiness, cycles, and preparation.

✘ Instead of: *"When will I meet the One?"*

☑ Try: *"What energy needs to shift in me before I'm ready to meet love?"*

✗ Instead of: *"When will they come back?"*

☑ Try: *"What cycle or season does this relationship need to move through before clarity returns?"*

✗ Instead of: *"When will I get married?"*

☑ Try: *"What steps can I take now that bring me closer to lasting commitment?"*

Why Reframing Matters

Reframing timing questions is not just a matter of wording—it changes the *entire energy* of the reading. The way a question is asked shapes the kind of answer that tarot can give. A poorly framed question—"When will I meet the One?"—narrows the scope of the reading into an unrealistic demand for a deadline. A reframed question—"What energy do I need to cultivate to welcome love?"—opens the space for tarot to speak about growth, readiness, and possibility.

This subtle shift keeps the reading empowering. Instead of leaving someone waiting passively for fate to deliver love, reframing points them toward the actions, insights, and healing that prepare them for the love they desire. It transforms a reading from prediction into participation, from passivity into co-creation.

Compassion: Reframing honors the querent's longing without shutting it down. If someone asks, *"When will they text me back?"* simply saying *"Tarot can't give you that"* can feel cold or dismissive. But shifting it to, *"Let's see what you need to know about this connection and where the energy stands right now,"* validates their vulnerability and still offers them meaningful guidance.

Empowerment: Instead of leaving with a date circled on the calendar, the querent leaves with practical steps they can take today. Tarot shows them how to align themselves with the love they seek: what patterns to release, what qualities to embody, what environments or communities to step into. This gives them agency. They become an active participant in their own love story rather than a passive observer.

Clarity: When questions are framed around energy and readiness, the answers go deeper than surface predictions. They reveal patterns, emotional cycles, and spiritual lessons. For example, a spread may show that love is aligned with "spring energy" or that new romance arrives once the querent steps into the openness of the Ace of Cups. This kind of clarity gives direction rooted in growth rather than a false promise of dates and deadlines.

Reframing is the bridge between longing and empowerment. It acknowledges the ache of "when?" while guiding it into the wisdom of "how?" and "what now?" In doing so, tarot readings become not only more accurate but also more healing. They leave the querent with a sense of hope and agency—two of the greatest gifts a love reading can offer.

CHAPTER 30

a reader's role in redirection

One of the most important skills in love readings is learning how to redirect questions. Querents often arrive with very specific, emotionally charged questions — *"When will they text me back?" "When will I meet the One?" "When will we get married?"* These questions come from longing, uncertainty, or fear. The role of the reader is not to dismiss that longing, but to gently guide it toward a framing that tarot can meaningfully answer.

Redirecting questions isn't about correcting someone or scolding them for asking the "wrong" thing. It's about honoring the vulnerability underneath the question while offering a way to approach it that's more fruitful, compassionate, and empowering. Tarot cannot control another person's free will or stamp a date on the calendar—but it *can* reveal the energy of the moment, the lessons being learned, and the path that will bring the querent closest to love.

Meeting the Heart Behind the Words

When someone asks, *"When will they text me back?"* the literal question is about timing—but the heart behind the words is about reassurance. What they really want to know is: *"Do they still care? Will this silence end? Am I forgotten?"* Redirecting honors this deeper need without locking the reading into a false countdown.

For example, instead of saying:

✘ *"Tarot can't answer that,"*

you might say:

☑ *"That's such an understandable question. Rather than looking at exact timing, let's ask the cards what you need to know about this pause in communication, and how you can best respond when the connection does open again."*

This way, the emotional need for clarity is acknowledged, and the reading stays ethical, useful, and compassionate.

The Tone of Redirection

How you redirect matters as much as what you say. A querent is already vulnerable; being too blunt can feel dismissive or shaming. Gentle phrasing works best—empathizing with the ache while guiding it toward a more empowering angle.

- ✗ *"Tarot doesn't work like that, you're asking the wrong thing."*
- ☑ *"That's a really common and understandable question. Here's a way we can look at it that might give you more clarity and power."*

When questions are reframed around energy, cycles, and readiness, the answers become more accurate and more helpful. Instead of a dead-end ("wait three months"), the querent walks away with insight they can use right now. They learn what energy they're carrying, what needs healing, and what steps can bring them closer to the love they desire.

Tarot is not a stopwatch—it's a compass. It doesn't tick down the minutes until love arrives; it points to where the querent is headed, and what might be needed to align with love's arrival. The way a question is phrased sets the tone for the entire reading. By redirecting timing questions with care, a reader ensures that the querent leaves not with false deadlines, but with direction, reassurance, and empowerment.

Redirection is an act of compassion. It honors the vulnerability in the question while transforming it into something tarot can answer truthfully. Done well, it gives the querent not only clarity but also dignity—they feel seen, supported, and empowered rather than shut down.

CHAPTER 31
redirect script library for common love questions

1. "When will I meet the One?"

✗ Literal Question: "Give me a date."

✓ Redirect: *"That's such a natural question—we all want to know when love is coming. Rather than looking at an exact date, let's see what energy is building around you and what needs to shift before love enters. The cards can show when you're most aligned, which is often more helpful than a calendar prediction."*

2. "When will they text/call me back?"

✗ Literal Question: "Predict their actions."

✓ Redirect: *"I hear the longing behind that—waiting can be so hard. Instead of focusing on their exact timing, let's ask what this silence is teaching you right now, and how you can best navigate the connection when communication does open again."*

3. "Will they come back to me?"

✗ Literal Question: "Guarantee reconciliation."

✓ Redirect: *"That's a very tender question. Let's reframe it a little—rather than just yes or no, we can ask what energies are still alive in this connection, and what's possible moving forward. That way, you'll see not only where they stand, but also what choices are open for you."*

. . .

4. *"Are they cheating on me?"*

✗ Literal Question: "Spy on someone's private actions."

✓ Redirect: *"I can hear how much pain and uncertainty this is causing you. Tarot can't ethically look into another person's private actions, but it can show what energy surrounds this relationship and whether it feels honest, balanced, or aligned. That way you'll know what truths are asking to be seen."*

5. *"Are they the One?"*

✗ Literal Question: "Confirm soulmates/destiny."

✓ Redirect: *"That's a beautiful question—and it comes from such a hopeful place. Instead of trying to label them as 'the One,' let's ask what role this relationship is meant to play in your life right now, and what lessons or gifts it's bringing. That can tell you if it's a soulmate, a teacher, or something else important to your path."*

6. *"Will I ever get married/have a family?"*

✗ Literal Question: "Absolute prediction of life outcome."

✓ Redirect: *"This is such a heartfelt question. Tarot may not guarantee a yes or no on something so life-spanning, but it can show what energies support long-term partnership for you, and what steps you can take now that move you closer to the kind of future you're dreaming of."*

7. *"What is he/she/they thinking about me right now?"*

✗ Literal Question: "Read their private thoughts."

✓ Redirect: *"That's so understandable—we all want to know what's going on in the other person's head. Tarot can't ethically read their private thoughts, but it can show the energy of the connection, how they're showing up in it, and what you most need to know about their role in your story."*

8. *"Am I destined to be alone?"*

✗ Literal Question: "Fatalistic self-judgment."

✓ Redirect: *"That's such a raw and honest question, and I want to honor the vulnerability in it. Instead of fate deciding, let's look at what's shaping your path toward love and what you can do to open the way. Tarot can highlight what might be blocking connection and how to step into relationships more aligned with you."*

Pro Tip: Always start with empathy. Acknowledge that their question makes sense, then gently pivot to the reframing. This way, they feel validated and not scolded, but still leave with a healthier, more useful answer.

CHAPTER 32

tarot tools for timing

Even though tarot isn't a stopwatch, it does carry symbolic ways of hinting at timing. These symbols are rarely about exact dates on a calendar—instead, they reveal the *seasonal energy, numerical rhythm,* or *transformational stage* that must unfold before love enters in its next phase. Timing through tarot is more about *recognizing cycles* than predicting deadlines.

Seasons in the Suits

One of the most traditional ways to glimpse timing is through the four suits of the Minor Arcana, each of which can correspond to a season.

Wands → Summer

Wands are fiery, hot, and full of movement, aligning with the energy of summer. They can suggest love appearing in a time of adventure, heat, and risk-taking—or when the querent themselves steps into bold, visible action.

Cups → Spring

Cups hold water, emotion, and new life. Like spring, they speak of renewal, fresh beginnings, and the opening of the heart. When Cups dominate, love may align with seasons of emotional openness, creativity, and growth.

Swords → Autumn

Swords align with air, cutting clarity, and the harvesting of truth. Autumn is a time of change, reflection, and letting go. Timing through Swords often points to a season of decision-making, honesty, or releasing what no longer serves before love can deepen.

Pentacles → Winter

Pentacles are grounded and slow-moving, like the stillness of winter. They suggest timing rooted in patience, foundation, and preparation. Love here unfolds when stability is created, when the querent has built security within themselves or their life.

Example: If someone asks about new love and pulls the Two of Cups alongside several Pentacles, you might say: *"This feels like a connection that blossoms slowly, in a winter season of grounding and preparation."*

Numbers on the Cards

The numbers on the Minor Arcana can also serve as markers of time. These aren't rigid promises of "weeks" or "months," but they can give rhythm to the unfolding.

Ones/Aces → Immediate openings, beginnings, fresh sparks.

Twos → A short cycle, perhaps two weeks or two months, or a stage of choice and alignment before action.

Threes → Expansion, often connected to community or external connections —three months, or after three meaningful interactions.

Higher Numbers (7–10) → Longer cycles, suggesting more work or time is needed before the energy resolves.

Example: The **Three of Cups** could point to "three months" until love enters, but it may also mean *"after three important social connections"* or *"in the next joyful gathering season."* Timing here is flexible, always tied to energy rather than a stopwatch.

Major Arcana as Stages

The Major Arcana reveal timing not through dates but through archetypal stages of the soul's journey. Each card acts like a milestone, showing what inner or outer event must occur before love moves forward.

Death → After an ending or transformation. Love cannot enter until an old story closes, whether that's a breakup, a shift in identity, or the shedding of outdated patterns.

The Star → During healing or after hope is restored. Timing here suggests that love arrives in the wake of vulnerability, faith, and renewal. It often shows up when the heart has softened and begun to shine again.

The World → When a major cycle completes. This is the card of arrival, integration, and wholeness. It may signal that love appears once a long journey is resolved, a lesson is learned, or a life chapter has come full circle.

Other Majors can also carry timing clues:

The Fool → The very beginning of a journey, a leap of faith.

The Hermit → A winter-like pause for solitude and reflection.

Wheel of Fortune → When the cycle naturally turns; an event or shift that changes the landscape.

Example: If someone asks about marriage and Temperance appears, you might say: *"The timing of this commitment depends on balance. The cards suggest not rushing—marriage comes when both of you have found your rhythm together."*

The real magic of timing in tarot happens when you weave these symbols together. A spread full of Pentacles with the number "Four" and the appearance of the Hermit might suggest: *"This love unfolds slowly—think four months or in the season of winter, after a time of reflection and inner work."*

Notice how this isn't a rigid promise—it's a symbolic roadmap. It tells the querent that patience, grounding, and solitude are part of the timing, which empowers them to engage with the process instead of just waiting.

While tarot does not give exact dates—it gives symbolic timing through seasons, numbers, and stages. These hints are not about "waiting for the clock to strike" but about understanding what energy must shift, what cycles must complete, and what readiness must emerge before love can truly arrive.

CHAPTER 33

timing quick reference in tarot

SEASONS IN THE SUITS

Wands → **Summer** (heat, passion, action)

Cups → **Spring** (renewal, openness, fresh emotions)

Swords → **Autumn** (clarity, harvest, letting go)

Pentacles → **Winter** (patience, grounding, stability)

NUMBERS ON THE CARDS

(Weeks, months, or cycles — use context + intuition)

Aces (1) → Immediate beginnings, fresh sparks.

Twos (2) → Choices, partnerships; short cycles.

Threes (3) → Expansion, community; often "three months" or "after three key encounters."

Fours (4) → Stability, pauses; slower unfolding.

Fives (5) → Challenge, change; timing requires adjustment first.

Sixes (6) → Flow, harmony; timing comes after resolution.

Sevens (7) → Delays, inner work; longer cycles.

Eights (8) → Movement, progress; energy shifts quickly once momentum builds.

Nines (9) → Near completion; timing soon but not final.

Tens (10) → Culmination, closure; timing aligns at the end of a cycle.

MAJOR ARCANA AS TIMING ANCHORS

The Fool → At the very beginning, when a leap is taken.

The Hermit → Winter; solitude before movement.

Death → After an ending or transformation.

Temperance → When balance is restored; patience required.

The Star → During healing; after hope returns.

The Wheel of Fortune → When the cycle naturally turns; a shift outside your control.

The World → When a chapter completes; arrival at wholeness.

> **Pro Tip:** Timing is never absolute in tarot. Use these symbols as *clues* rather than deadlines. They show not just *when* love may arrive, but *what needs to happen first*—a season of healing, a lesson learned, a cycle completed.

CHAPTER 34

right timing vs. exact dates

When it comes to love, timing is always the question that hovers at the edges of the reading. *"When will I meet them?" "When will this relationship deepen?" "When will the pain end?"* The ache for certainty is human. Yet the truth is that tarot is not at its best when treated like a stopwatch—it doesn't hand us a date, a time, or a countdown. Instead, tarot shines brightest when revealing right timing: the conditions, lessons, and states of readiness that make love possible.

Right timing is about alignment, not schedules. It's when your energy and someone else's meet in resonance, when the lessons have been learned, when the heart is open enough to receive what it has been asking for. Tarot reflects this not in days on a calendar, but in cycles and symbols.

Consider this example: if **The Lovers** and **The Star** appear together in a timing spread, the message is not, *"You'll meet someone in May."*

Instead, the story they tell is: *"Love will blossom once you've moved through healing and opened your heart again."* The Star shows the restoration of hope; The Lovers speaks of choosing love consciously. Together, they point to a season of readiness rather than a specific date.

This way of reading timing does more than give information—it gives power back to the querent. Instead of passively waiting for fate to deliver, they see the role they play in creating the conditions for love. They can focus on their healing, their growth, and their choices, knowing that when they are aligned, love flows naturally.

PRACTICE PROMPTS

Pull a card with the question: *"What energy needs to shift before love comes in?"*

> Journal about the readiness this card suggests. For example, The Chariot may point to focus and direction, while The Empress could suggest nurturing self-worth.

Try a second reading with: *"What season feels most aligned for love to enter my life?"*

Pay attention to imagery, suit associations, or seasonal cards like The Sun (summer) or The Hermit (winter).

> Reflect afterward: Did the answers feel more like cycles, lessons, or conditions rather than calendar dates?
>
> How does that shift your perspective on timing?

Timing questions reveal something profound: when people ask *"When?"* they are rarely seeking numbers on a page. What they are truly asking for is hope, reassurance, and guidance. They want to know if love is possible, if their longing is valid, if their story still holds a promise of connection.

As a reader, your role is not to act like a clock. Your role is to reveal the rhythm of love—the cycles of endings and beginnings, the readiness of the heart, and the seasons that make growth possible.

Tarot cannot circle a date on a calendar, but it can tell us when the soul is ready to bloom. And in matters of the heart, that readiness is worth far more than a number.

CHAPTER 35

reading right timing

CASE STUDY

Question: *"When will love come into my life?"*

Cards Pulled:

Five of Pentacles → Feelings of lack, loneliness, or unworthiness.

Death → A major ending, transformation, or letting go.

Ace of Cups → Emotional renewal, a fresh start, new love blossoming.

Reading the Spread Literally

At first glance, a querent—especially one asking about timing—might jump to a straightforward prediction:

- **Five of Pentacles** → *"Five weeks."*
- **Death** → *"After a breakup."*
- **Ace of Cups** → *"Then you'll meet someone new."*

This kind of linear, countdown-style reading can be tempting because it offers the illusion of certainty. It sounds simple, clean, and reassuring: *"In five weeks, after you let go of something, a new relationship will begin."*

But this approach risks oversimplification. Life is not always that neat, and love especially does not follow a rigid schedule. Timing is fluid. Free will shifts things. Healing cannot be rushed just to fit a calendar. A literal interpretation may give momentary comfort, but if life doesn't unfold exactly as predicted, it can leave the querent discouraged, disappointed, or questioning the validity of tarot altogether.

Shifting Into "Right Timing"

Instead of locking into dates and numbers, the more fruitful way to read this spread is through the conditions the cards describe. The focus becomes: *what needs to happen for love to flow in naturally?*

Five of Pentacles: This card shows the querent in a season of loneliness or self-doubt, where love feels scarce or out of reach. Importantly, this is not a punishment. It's a reflection of how they are currently relating to themselves and their worth. The "timing" here is not about waiting five weeks—it's about moving through a state of lack and recognizing the need for warmth, self-care, and reconnection with others.

Death: Transformation is the threshold. Love won't arrive until the querent has shed what no longer serves them. This may mean letting go of an ex, releasing grief, or dismantling limiting beliefs about what they "deserve." Death teaches that love comes when space has been cleared, when the old story is allowed to fall away. The timing is linked to courage in endings, not dates on a calendar.

Ace of Cups: This is the gift waiting on the other side of release. Once the querent moves through transformation, their heart opens like a vessel ready to overflow. The Ace suggests that new love is indeed close, but its arrival depends on the completion of the Death stage. The message is: *"As soon as you've made space and softened into renewal, love blossoms."*

Here, the timing is symbolic. It is a sequence: **Loneliness → Release → Renewal.** Love's arrival is not set by weeks or months but by the querent's readiness to move through these stages.

✘ A literal reading says, *"Love in five weeks."*

✓ A right timing reading says, *"Love arrives when loneliness is tended, endings are honored, and the heart is open to renewal."* One gives a countdown; the other gives a roadmap.

✘ The message isn't: *"In five weeks you'll meet someone."*

The message is:

✓ *"Love will arrive when you release the pain and patterns of the past (Five of Pentacles + Death). The Ace of Cups shows that new love is waiting, but it can only pour in once the ending is honored and completed. Timing here is less about a date and more about your readiness. When you feel transformed and emotionally open again, that's when love finds you."*

How to Deliver This to a Querent

"You've been carrying loneliness and old heartbreak, and the cards are asking you to release that before new love can enter. The ending is important—it's the clearing. Once you allow yourself to let go, love comes quickly. The Ace of Cups shows new romance is close, but the timing depends on your healing. In other words, love doesn't wait on the calendar—it waits on your readiness. The good news? The Ace is here. New love *is* possible—it's not a question of if, but of when your heart feels free enough to receive it."

The cards didn't predict a number—they revealed a sequence of readiness. Loneliness → Release → Renewal. That's the "true timing" of love.

CHAPTER 36

redirecting timing questions in practice

Timing questions are really love's way of asking, "When will my heart be met?"

Behind every *"When will I meet them?"* or *"When will they call?"* is a longing for reassurance, for hope, for a promise that love is not out of reach. Tarot isn't a clock that ticks toward a deadline—it's a mirror that shows us cycles, readiness, and the energy of the heart. The art of the reader is to honor the vulnerability behind the question while gently guiding it into a form the cards can truly answer. In doing so, timing becomes less about counting days and more about recognizing when the soul is ready to open.

Querent: *"When will I meet someone?"*

Literal Request: They want a number, a date, a countdown.

Validate the Longing

Before redirecting, acknowledge the feeling behind the question.

> *"That's such a natural thing to wonder. Waiting for love can feel so uncertain and tender."*

Reframe the Focus

Gently shift the question away from clocks and toward conditions, cycles, or readiness.

"Tarot usually shows timing not as exact dates, but as energy and stages. Instead of asking 'when,' let's look at what needs to shift for love to flow in."

Phrase with Empowerment

Offer the querent a new way to think about their timing.

"The cards can show what season, lesson, or transformation aligns with your next love. That gives you a sense of movement and direction without locking you into a false deadline."

EXAMPLE IN ACTION

Querent: *"So... when will I meet them?"*

Reader:

"That's a really understandable question. The cards don't usually give exact dates, but they do show when the energy is right. For example, they might say 'in the springtime, when you're opening to joy again' or 'after you've released an old heartbreak.' Would you like me to phrase it that way for you—so you know what needs to be in place for love to find you?"

Key Reminder: Redirecting isn't about denying or scolding—it's about transforming a yes/no countdown into a roadmap. Done with compassion, it makes the querent feel both validated and empowered.

PART FOUR

red flag & green flag cards

CHAPTER 37

what red & green flags mean in tarot

In the language of love and relationships, people often talk about "red flags" and "green flags." These are the signals we pick up on—sometimes consciously, sometimes intuitively—that tell us whether a relationship feels healthy or whether it carries potential risks. A red flag might be a partner who refuses to communicate, a pattern of dishonesty, or a dynamic that drains self-worth. A green flag might be mutual respect, emotional openness, or a steady foundation that feels safe to grow within.

Tarot mirrors these signals beautifully. Each card is a snapshot of energy, and that energy can sometimes align with patterns that feel supportive and nourishing—or with patterns that raise caution. In romance readings, certain cards naturally show up as red flag indicators: the Devil, the Tower, the Seven of Swords. Others light up as green flags: the Two of Cups, the Ten of Pentacles, the Star.

But here's the most important truth: **no tarot card is inherently good or bad.** Just like in life, a red flag is not always a deal-breaker, and a green flag is not a guarantee of "happily ever after." Instead, they are signals—clues that help us understand what energy is present and what choices need to be made.

Think of tarot as a lantern shining light on a path. If it shows a red flag, it isn't condemning the relationship—it's saying, *"Here's a place where caution and awareness are needed."* If it shows a green flag, it isn't promising perfection—it's saying, *"Here's a strength you can lean into and build upon."*

This perspective is critical for ethical readings. If we treat red flag cards as doomsday omens, we risk frightening the querent or stripping away their agency. If we treat green flag cards as guarantees, we risk giving false hope. The real art of the reader is to interpret these signals with nuance, compassion, and clarity.

FOR EXAMPLE:

The Devil as a red flag may suggest unhealthy attachment, but it can also invite awareness of where desire or dependency is shaping the connection.

The Two of Cups as a green flag suggests mutual attraction and emotional reciprocity, but it still asks the question: *Are both partners choosing to show up fully here?*

The key is to read the signals as part of a larger story. One card never tells the whole tale—it's the patterns, the combinations, and the context that matter most.

> **The Reader's Role:** Your job is not to declare a verdict of "stay" or "leave." Your role is to help the querent see the signals clearly, understand what they might mean, and make empowered choices. Red flags call for awareness and boundaries. Green flags call for trust and celebration. And always, the querent retains the power to decide how to respond.

CHAPTER 38

common red flag cards

Every relationship has challenges, but in tarot some cards consistently highlight dynamics that require extra caution. These are the cards that raise eyebrows in a love spread—the ones that whisper of imbalance, instability, or dishonesty. In modern language, we call these *red flags*.

It's important to remember: **a red flag card doesn't mean a relationship is doomed.** It doesn't mean you should automatically advise someone to leave. What it does mean is that the querent is being asked to pause, look closely, and bring awareness to what may be off-balance. These cards are not verdicts—they are invitations for reflection.

⚑ **The Devil**

Core Meaning in Love: Unhealthy attachments, obsession, control, codependency.

How It Shows Up: A relationship that feels magnetic but toxic; cycles of passion followed by pain; difficulty letting go even when it hurts.

Gentle Framing: Instead of, *"You're trapped in a toxic relationship,"* try:

"This card suggests a bond that feels powerful but may not be balanced. Ask yourself: does this connection nourish you, or does it drain you? Where do you feel free, and where do you feel controlled?"

⚑ **The Tower**

Core Meaning in Love: Sudden collapse, shocking revelations, instability in the foundation.

How It Shows Up: A breakup no one saw coming, betrayal, or a truth that shakes the relationship to its core.

Gentle Framing: Instead of, *"Everything is about to fall apart,"* try:

"This card shows disruption—something breaking open so the truth can be seen. While painful, it can also clear the way for greater honesty and alignment."

⚐ Five of Swords

Core Meaning in Love: Toxic conflict, winning at all costs, no one truly wins.

How It Shows Up: Constant arguments, manipulation, or a dynamic where one person always "takes" while the other loses.

Gentle Framing: Instead of, *"This person is abusive,"* try:

"This card suggests conflict where both sides may end up feeling hurt. Notice whether arguments here bring growth—or if they leave only resentment."

⚐ Seven of Swords

Core Meaning in Love: Deception, secrecy, dishonesty, sneaking around.

How It Shows Up: Lying, cheating, hidden agendas, or avoiding necessary conversations.

Gentle Framing: Instead of, *"They're lying to you,"* try:

"This card suggests something is hidden or not fully honest. Do you feel safe and respected here? Trust your intuition about what may not be spoken."

⚐ Lovers (Reversed)

Core Meaning in Love: Disharmony, misalignment of values, love as illusion or temptation.

How It Shows Up: A relationship built on attraction but not true compatibility; choices made for lust rather than alignment; two people not walking the same path.

Gentle Framing: Instead of, *"This isn't real love,"* try:

"This card suggests a disconnect—are your values and goals aligned, or are you moving in different directions?"

⚐ Three of Swords

Core Meaning in Love: Heartbreak, betrayal, painful truths, love triangles.

How It Shows Up: Discovering a partner's infidelity, feeling abandoned, or old heartbreak resurfacing in the current relationship.

Gentle Framing: Instead of, *"This person will break your heart,"* try:

"This card suggests pain or disappointment connected to this bond. It may be pointing to betrayal, or simply to wounds that still feel raw. Healing and clarity are needed here."

⚐ Eight of Swords

Core Meaning in Love: Feeling trapped, powerless, or stuck in limiting beliefs.

How It Shows Up: A dynamic where someone feels unable to leave or speak their truth; relationships that breed fear instead of freedom.

Gentle Framing: Instead of, *"You're stuck in this and can't get out,"* try:

"This card shows where you may feel bound or silenced in the connection. The truth is, you hold more power than it feels right now. What small steps could begin to set you free?"

⚐ Nine of Swords

Core Meaning in Love: Anxiety, sleepless nights, emotional torment.

How It Shows Up: Constant worry about the relationship, suspicion, or unresolved guilt haunting one or both partners.

Gentle Framing: Instead of, *"This relationship is only causing suffering,"* try:

"This card reflects deep anxiety around the connection. The question isn't just about the relationship, but about what's keeping you awake at night. What reassurance or clarity do you most need right now?"

⚐ Ten of Swords

Core Meaning in Love: Painful endings, betrayal, collapse.

How It Shows Up: Breakups that feel final, betrayal that can't be ignored, or the complete exhaustion of a relationship dynamic.

Gentle Framing: Instead of, *"It's over and hopeless,"* try:

"This card shows a cycle that has reached its breaking point. While painful, it also suggests that no more harm can be done—there's only healing and rebuilding ahead."

⚐ Five of Cups

Core Meaning in Love: Dwelling on loss, grief, regret.

How It Shows Up: Being unable to move on from an ex, replaying old heartbreak, or focusing on what's missing instead of what's still alive in the connection.

Gentle Framing: Instead of, *"You'll never get over them,"* try:

"This card shows sorrow that's taking center stage. It acknowledges your grief, but also reminds you that not all love is lost—there's still something worth turning toward."

⚐ The Moon (Reversed)

Core Meaning in Love: Confusion, illusion, manipulation, gaslighting.

How It Shows Up: A relationship clouded by mixed signals, dishonesty, or emotional distortion that makes it hard to tell what's real.

Gentle Framing: Instead of, *"They're manipulating you,"* try:

"This card suggests uncertainty and blurred truths in the connection. It may feel like not everything is being revealed clearly. What would help you feel more grounded and certain here?"

⚐ The Hierophant (Reversed)

Core Meaning in Love: Rejection of commitment, secrecy, resistance to tradition or shared values.

How It Shows Up: One partner avoids formalizing the bond, hides the relationship, or refuses to align on foundational beliefs.

Gentle Framing: Instead of, *"They'll never commit to you,"* try:

"This card suggests resistance to commitment or a mismatch in values. The question is: do their choices align with what you truly want and deserve in love?"

⚐ How to Frame Red Flags with Kindness

The power of a red flag reading isn't in pointing fingers—it's in illuminating the imbalance so the querent can choose how to respond.

✘ Instead of: *"This person is lying to you."*

☑ Try: *"The cards suggest secrecy or a lack of full honesty. It may be important to ask yourself if you feel fully safe and respected here."*

✘ Instead of: *"This relationship is over."*

☑ Try: *"The cards show instability in the foundation. This doesn't have to mean an ending, but it does suggest something important is being revealed. The question is whether this truth can be worked with, or whether it shows a need to rebuild on stronger ground."*

Red flag cards are not a judgment—they are signals. The most empowering way to read them is to ask: *"Where is the imbalance, and what choices do you have to shift it?"*

CHAPTER 39

the red flag spread

Red flag cards can feel heavy when they appear in a reading. This spread is designed to bring clarity, compassion, and empowerment—so the querent doesn't leave feeling hopeless, but instead with insight and choices.

The Spread (5 Cards)

1. **The Red Flag** → What energy or pattern in this relationship needs attention?
2. **The Hidden Truth** → What isn't being seen or acknowledged clearly?
3. **The Impact** → How this energy is affecting the relationship dynamic right now.
4. **The Choice** → What action, boundary, or decision the querent has power over.
5. **The Healing Path** → What energy will guide growth, clarity, or release.

This spread moves the focus from *doom and gloom* into *awareness and choice*. It acknowledges what's hard without leaving the querent stuck in it. The "Healing Path" card especially ensures that the reading ends with light and direction, not despair.

EXAMPLE READING

Question: *"Why does this connection feel so unstable?"*

Cards Pulled:

1. The Red Flag → **Seven of Swords** (dishonesty, secrecy)
2. The Hidden Truth → **Moon reversed** (confusion, illusion, something unclear)
3. The Impact → **Nine of Swords** (anxiety, sleepless worry)
4. The Choice → **Justice** (seeking truth, demanding fairness, accountability)
5. The Healing Path → **Ace of Swords** (clarity, honest conversation, truth revealed)

Interpretation:

The spread shows dishonesty at the center of this connection (Seven of Swords), and the Moon reversed confirms that not all is being revealed. The impact is clear: the querent is in a constant state of anxiety and doubt (Nine of Swords). Justice as "The Choice" shows they do have agency—they can ask for honesty, set boundaries, and decide what fairness looks like for them. The Ace of Swords as "The Healing Path" suggests that clarity is both the medicine and the outcome here. Whether the relationship continues or not, truth is what frees the querent from fear.

How to Deliver It With Kindness

✘ Instead of: *"This person is lying and this relationship is doomed."*

✔ Try: *"The cards suggest there are secrets here that are causing you real distress. It's taking a toll on your peace of mind. Justice shows you have the right to clarity and fairness. The Ace of Swords encourages an honest conversation—the truth, even if hard, is what will heal you and guide your next step. This isn't about making you powerless—it's about reminding you that your voice and your boundaries matter."*

Practice Prompt

Pull this spread for yourself with the question:

"What red flag pattern have I repeated in love, and how can I break it?"

> Journal your reflections, especially on The Choice and The Healing Path.
>
> Notice how even in the toughest cards, the spread always brings the focus back to agency, empowerment, and healing.

CHAPTER 40

common green flag cards

Green flag cards are the encouragers of love readings. They highlight moments of reciprocity, healing, and joy—signs that a connection has fertile ground to grow upon. They don't promise perfection or "soulmate status," but they do shine a light on strengths, harmony, and potential.

Just like with red flags, it's important to remember: **no card is a guarantee.** A green flag doesn't mean a relationship will automatically last forever—it means the energy present is supportive, nourishing, and worth noticing. Your role as a reader is to affirm these positive qualities while keeping the querent grounded in reality.

⚑ Two of Cups

Core Meaning in Love: Mutual attraction, emotional reciprocity, heartfelt connection.

How It Shows Up: Two people meeting eye-to-eye, sharing vulnerability, and creating a sense of equality. It often appears in new relationships where both parties are genuinely interested and emotionally present.

Gentle Framing: Instead of, *"This is your soulmate,"* try:

"This card suggests mutual feelings and a real sense of connection. The energy here is open, equal, and respectful—this bond is worth exploring further."

⚑ Ten of Pentacles

Core Meaning in Love: Long-term security, family, shared goals, legacy.

How It Shows Up: Couples who are thinking about building a home together, blending families, or investing in shared stability. It signals not just romance, but practical commitment and lasting partnership.

Gentle Framing: Instead of, *"This means you'll marry and live happily ever after,"* try:

"This card shows a relationship with the potential for longevity and shared vision. It's about building a life together—partnership as something rooted, secure, and future-focused."

⚑ The Star

Core Meaning in Love: Hope, renewal, healing, intimacy born of vulnerability.

How It Shows Up: After heartbreak, this card often arrives as reassurance that love can heal. It may signal a partner who creates space for openness, honesty, and emotional authenticity.

Gentle Framing: Instead of, *"This is perfect, everything will be healed instantly,"* try:

"This card suggests a relationship rooted in hope and honesty. There's a sense of renewal here—an invitation to be your authentic self and to be loved in that truth."

⚑ The Sun

Core Meaning in Love: Joy, authenticity, clarity, playful openness.

How It Shows Up: A relationship where people feel safe to be themselves, where joy is shared openly, and where truth is celebrated instead of hidden. It can also mark a time when the querent feels emotionally lit up by love.

Gentle Framing: Instead of, *"This is definitely the happiest you'll ever be,"* try:

"This card shows warmth, openness, and joy at the heart of this connection. It's a reminder that love thrives when it feels safe to be authentic and playful."

⚑ Ace of Cups

Core Meaning in Love: Emotional renewal, pure affection, the overflowing beginning of love.

How It Shows Up: A fresh start in romance, a deepening of existing feelings, or the tender first stirrings of emotional openness. The Ace of Cups is pure possibility—love at its most innocent and true.

Gentle Framing: Instead of, *"This guarantees a new relationship,"* try:

"This card suggests new emotional beginnings. It shows your heart opening to love, and with that openness comes the possibility of deep connection."

⚑ Four of Wands

Core Meaning in Love: Celebration, stability, joyful milestones, creating a shared foundation.

How It Shows Up: A relationship moving toward stability—living together, celebrating commitment, or simply finding that sense of "home" in each other. It reflects harmony, joy, and a foundation worth building on.

Gentle Framing: Instead of, *"You'll definitely get married,"* try:

"This card shows stability and joy being celebrated. It suggests this connection has the energy of creating a home together—whether literal or emotional—and that's something to cherish."

⚑ Six of Pentacles

Core Meaning in Love: Balance, generosity, mutual support.

How It Shows Up: A relationship where both partners give and receive equally, where effort is shared, and kindness flows naturally. It can also highlight one partner's generosity lifting the other up in healthy ways.

Gentle Framing: Instead of, *"They'll always take care of you,"* try:

"This card suggests reciprocity and generosity at play. It shows a connection where giving and receiving feel balanced—a reminder that healthy love thrives on mutual care."

⚑ Ten of Cups

Core Meaning in Love: Emotional fulfillment, harmony, deep joy.

How It Shows Up: A family vision, whether literal (marriage, children, blending homes) or symbolic (deep emotional joy shared with others). It's the emotional "happily-ever-after" card, but in practice it points to connection that feels whole and deeply satisfying.

Gentle Framing: Instead of, *"You've found your forever love,"* try:

"This card shows harmony, joy, and emotional fulfillment. It points to a bond that carries the energy of family, belonging, and shared happiness."

⚑ The Empress

Core Meaning in Love: Nurturing, abundance, sensuality, growth.

How It Shows Up: A relationship that feels life-giving and creative, often overflowing with affection and care. Can also point to fertility (literal or symbolic), flourishing love, or partners who deeply nurture each other's well-being.

Gentle Framing: Instead of, *"This means you'll have children,"* try:

"This card suggests a love that feels nourishing and abundant. It's about care, creativity, and growth—a reminder that love should help you flourish, not wither."

⚑ The World

Core Meaning in Love: Wholeness, fulfillment, integration, completion.

How It Shows Up: A relationship where both partners feel whole on their own but come together in harmony. Can mark a bond that feels fated, aligned, or like the completion of a cycle leading to greater maturity.

Gentle Framing: Instead of, *"This is the end-all-be-all of your love story,"* try:

"This card suggests a sense of wholeness and fulfillment in the connection. It reflects balance, maturity, and the feeling of having come full circle together."

⚑ Strength

Core Meaning in Love: Compassion, patience, courage rooted in gentleness.

How It Shows Up: A relationship where patience and kindness outweigh harshness, where challenges are met with empathy instead of anger. Strength often signals emotional maturity and respect in how love is expressed.

Gentle Framing: Instead of, *"This guarantees a strong bond forever,"* try:

"This card suggests love expressed through compassion and gentleness. It reflects courage in vulnerability and patience in growth—the kind of strength that sustains intimacy."

⚑ King & Queen of Cups

Core Meaning in Love: Emotional maturity, empathy, depth, and sensitivity.

How It Shows Up: These court cards often reflect a partner—or the querent themselves—who shows up with emotional steadiness, compassion, and the ability to hold space for deep connection. When they appear together, they signal a partnership rooted in mutual care and emotional intelligence.

Gentle Framing: Instead of, *"You've found your perfect match,"* try:

"This card suggests emotional depth and maturity within the relationship. It shows a capacity for deep compassion and empathy—qualities that create a safe and nourishing bond."

How to Frame Green Flags with Kindness

Green flag cards are invitations to celebrate, but they should never be handed out as guarantees. Instead of presenting them as proof of a destined love story, frame them as strengths to nurture:

"This looks promising, and here's how you can encourage it."

"This card highlights trust, joy, and reciprocity—qualities that make a bond strong."

Green flag cards encourage hope and show what's worth building upon, while keeping the querent grounded in the truth that love always requires effort, presence, and choice.

CHAPTER 41
the green flag spread

This spread is designed to celebrate what's healthy in a connection and show how those strengths can be deepened. It works beautifully for both new and long-term relationships, and it can even be used for self-love (seeing what qualities make you magnetic).

THE SPREAD (5 CARDS)

1. **The Green Flag** → What strength or gift is shining in this connection?
2. **The Shared Spark** → What brings joy, attraction, or harmony between you?
3. **The Support System** → What stability or mutual care is present here?
4. **The Growth Edge** → What part of this bond is worth investing more energy in?
5. **The Blessing** → What this connection offers at its best.

Where red flag readings focus on awareness and protection, the green flag spread celebrates what's working. It affirms the querent's intuition when they feel good about a relationship, and it gives them practical insight into how to cultivate even more love and joy.

EXAMPLE READING

Question: *"What strengths define this relationship, and how can we grow them?"*
Cards Pulled:

1. The Green Flag → **Two of Cups** (mutual connection and reciprocity)
2. The Shared Spark → **The Sun** (joy, openness, authenticity)
3. The Support System → **Six of Pentacles** (balance, generosity, shared effort)
4. The Growth Edge → **Strength** (compassion, patience through challenges)
5. The Blessing → **Ten of Cups** (emotional fulfillment, shared happiness)

Interpretation:

This spread glows with green flags. At the core is genuine reciprocity (Two of Cups)—a bond where both give and receive equally. The Sun shows that joy and authenticity are central: this is a connection where both people feel free to be themselves. The Six of Pentacles reminds us that balance and generosity support the relationship; it's a give-and-take that keeps the love steady. Strength as the growth edge suggests that patience and compassion will be the keys to sustaining this bond through challenges. The Ten of Cups as the blessing shows the potential for true happiness and shared fulfillment—a partnership that feels like family, joy, and belonging.

How to Deliver It With Kindness

✗ Instead of: *"This is perfect, you've found your forever person."*

✓ Try: *"The cards show strong green flags here—mutual care, joy, generosity, and the potential for deep happiness. No relationship is without challenges, but these strengths give you an incredible foundation to build upon. This connection has real promise, and the cards encourage you to nurture these qualities."*

Practice Prompt

Pull this spread for yourself with the question: *"What green flags am I bringing into love right now?"*

- Journal your reflections, especially on The Growth Edge.
- What qualities in yourself are already magnetic?
- What strengths can you nurture further to create even healthier connections?

CHAPTER 42

the red + green flag spread

This spread is designed to reveal both the cautions (red flags) and the strengths (green flags) of a relationship. It gives a balanced perspective so the querent isn't lost in idealization *or* fear—they see where the love shines, and where it asks for awareness or boundaries.

THE SPREAD (7 CARDS)

1. **The Heart of the Connection** → What energy defines this relationship right now.
2. **The Green Flag** → What's healthy, supportive, or worth celebrating.
3. **The Red Flag** → What challenge, risk, or imbalance needs attention.
4. **The Shared Joy** → What keeps the bond magnetic and meaningful.
5. **The Hidden Strain** → What may be unspoken, avoided, or draining.
6. **The Choice** → What the querent has agency over—where their power lies.
7. **The Potential Path** → Where this connection could go if both parties grow in awareness.

Love has a way of amplifying everything—it can feel like the highest high or the lowest low. When querents come to tarot about a complicated relationship, they're often caught in extremes. On one side, they may be over-romanticizing the bond, clinging to the hope that it's "meant to be" no matter what. On the other, they may catastrophize, assuming that one red flag means everything is doomed. Both extremes cloud judgment.

The Red + Green Flag Spread works because it brings the full picture into view. By laying out both the strengths and the challenges side by side, the querent can see the complexity of the connection with clarity. The spread validates the good—the moments of joy, reciprocity, and genuine love—while also acknowledging the struggles that cannot be ignored. This balance gives the reading both honesty and hope.

Another strength of this spread is that it doesn't end with the relationship itself—it ends with *agency*. By including a position for "The Choice," the cards remind the querent that they are not powerless, no matter what dynamic they are in. The cards may reveal imbalance or instability, but they also highlight the querent's ability to set boundaries, to choose truth, to honor their own needs.

Finally, the spread ends with "The Potential Path," a card that reframes the future as possibility rather than fate. It says: "Here's what this connection could grow into if both people are willing to meet the challenges honestly." This ensures that the querent leaves not with fear or false promises, but with insight, perspective, and choice.

In short, this spread works because it grounds the querent. It offers the full truth—both the cautions and the blessings—while holding space for free will. It helps them leave the reading not confused or dependent, but empowered to navigate their love life with awareness and strength.

EXAMPLE READING

Question: *"What do I need to understand about this complicated relationship?"*

Cards Pulled:

1. Heart of the Connection → **The Lovers** (a powerful attraction, but also a choice point)
2. Green Flag → **Two of Cups** (mutual attraction, shared vulnerability)
3. Red Flag → **Devil** (unhealthy attachment, control)
4. Shared Joy → **The Sun** (playfulness, honesty, shared laughter)
5. Hidden Strain → **Seven of Swords** (secrecy, things left unsaid)
6. The Choice → **Justice** (truth, accountability, alignment with values)
7. Potential Path → **Temperance** (healing, balance, the slow blending of energies)

Interpretation:

This connection is defined by powerful attraction (The Lovers), but it's at a crossroads where choices matter. On the green flag side, the Two of Cups shows genuine mutual affection—there is real connection and reciprocity here. On the red flag side, the Devil warns of unhealthy patterns: obsession, control, or dynamics that could slip into codependency. The Sun as shared joy reminds us that this relationship brings warmth and laughter, while the Seven of Swords as hidden strain suggests secrets or avoidance that undermine that light.

Justice in the choice position shows that the querent has power here: to ask for truth, to clarify values, and to ensure fairness in the bond. Temperance as the potential path shows that balance is possible—but only if both partners are willing to be honest and to bring patience and healing into the connection.

How to Deliver It With Kindness

✘ Instead of: *"This is toxic, you should leave."*

or

✘ *"This is perfect, you've found your soulmate."*

✅ Try: *"This relationship carries both green and red flags. There's real connection here, but also patterns that could become heavy if left unchecked. The cards encourage you to celebrate the joy you share while also being clear about your needs for honesty and balance. The potential for growth exists—but it requires both of you showing up with truth and patience."*

> **Practice Prompt**
>
> Pull this spread for a fictional couple (like Elizabeth & Darcy, Romeo & Juliet, or even your favorite TV duo). Notice how the red and green flags weave together into a realistic picture of love that is never just one thing. Then try it for yourself —or a past relationship—and see what the cards reveal about both the beauty and the challenges.

CHAPTER 43

reader's script for the red + green flag spread

If you're struggling with how to introduce a tarot spread, try saying this out loud. Make it your own by journaling it and practicing with a friend.

> This spread is designed to give us a balanced look at your connection. Every relationship has both green flags—things that feel healthy, joyful, and worth celebrating—and red flags—areas that may need extra attention, honesty, or healing.
>
> The cards won't tell us to stay or leave. That choice is always yours. Instead, they'll help us see what strengths are present, what challenges may be influencing the connection, and where your own power lies in navigating it.
>
> We'll begin with the heart of the connection—the overall energy that defines where things are right now. Then we'll look at both the green flag (what's working well) and the red flag (what needs care or caution).
>
> From there, we'll explore the shared joy—the light that makes this bond feel meaningful—and the hidden strain—what might be unspoken or weighing on the relationship.
>
> Finally, we'll close with two powerful cards: the choice, which shows what agency you personally have in this situation, and the potential path, which reveals where this connection might go if both people are willing to grow in awareness.
>
> This spread is not about judgment—it's about clarity. By seeing both the beauty and the challenges together, you'll have a fuller picture of what's really happening, and the tools to decide what feels right for you.

PART FIVE

sensitive topics in love readings

CHAPTER 44

why sensitive topics matter

When people come to tarot with questions about love, it's rarely just for entertainment. More often, they approach the cards at the most vulnerable crossroads of their lives. The questions they bring are born from longing, grief, fear, or uncertainty. They ask about the lover who betrayed them, the relationship they desperately want back, the person they cannot let go of, or the affection that is not being returned. These aren't casual curiosities—they are heart-level aches, and they deserve to be treated with care.

Sensitive topics in love readings—infidelity, breakups, unrequited love, and the classic "will they come back?"—carry enormous emotional weight. For many querents, these questions are less about facts and more about survival. They're not only wondering *what will happen*; they're quietly asking, *Am I lovable? Am I safe? Am I going to be okay?*

This is why sensitive topics matter so much. A careless word in these readings can deepen the wound. If a reader is blunt without compassion, or careless with interpretation, the querent may leave the reading feeling worse—more hopeless, more confused, more dependent. On the other hand, when handled with clarity and empathy, these same readings can be life-changing. They can affirm dignity, restore hope, and empower someone to navigate heartbreak or uncertainty with strength instead of despair.

Tarot doesn't exist in isolation—it exists in human hearts. When the cards reveal painful truths, the responsibility falls on the reader to deliver them in a way that honors the querent's humanity. Compassion does not mean sugar-coating or false hope. It means naming the reality with gentleness, offering perspective, and reminding the querent of their own resilience and agency.

A sensitive reading should never take power away. Instead, it should return power to the querent. It should say, *"Yes, this hurts. Yes, this is complicated. And here's how you can move forward with strength."*

That's why sensitive topics matter: they reveal not only what the cards say, but also who we are as readers. Will we use our words to wound, or to heal? Will we feed obsession, or foster clarity? Will we leave someone dependent on us, or remind them that the power has always been in their hands?

Handled well, these readings don't just answer questions about love. They hold space for heartbreak, illuminate the path through it, and remind us that even in loss, love still teaches, heals, and transforms.

CHAPTER 45

infidelity

THE BIG FOUR SENSITIVE TOPICS

Tarot for love is tender ground. These four themes—infidelity, breakups, reconciliation ("will they come back?"), and unrequited love—are the most common, the most emotionally charged, and often the hardest to read. Each one carries a mix of fear, hope, grief, and vulnerability. Below, we'll take them one at a time, breaking down how to recognize them in the cards, how to approach them ethically, and how to frame your insights with compassion.

Few questions cut as deeply as *"Are they cheating on me?"* It's one of the most painful inquiries a querent can bring to the cards, because beneath it is often more than suspicion—it's fear, grief, or the memory of past betrayals. When someone asks this, they're already in a heightened state of anxiety. Their body is braced, their heart is pounding, and often they're torn between two painful possibilities: confirmation of their worst fear, or dismissal of their intuition. That makes your role as the reader especially delicate.

What to Look For in the Cards

Certain archetypes often appear in spreads when themes of secrecy, broken trust, or hidden dynamics are present.

SEVEN OF SWORDS → SECRECY, SNEAKING, DISHONESTY.

This card is the classic "something happening behind closed doors" energy. It can suggest avoidance, half-truths, or dishonesty. But it can also mean secrecy in other forms—hiding feelings, keeping plans private, or withholding communication. It points to something not being shared openly, rather than offering absolute proof of betrayal.

DEVIL → UNHEALTHY ATTACHMENT, CONTROL, TEMPTATION.

The Devil can reveal patterns of obsession, power struggles, or codependency. In the context of infidelity, it may suggest someone feels trapped in unhealthy dynamics or drawn to temptation. But it can also show a querent's own feeling of being chained to fear or suspicion. It's about cycles of control, secrecy, or addiction—not always literal cheating.

THREE OF CUPS (REVERSED) → THIRD-PARTY ENERGY, IMBALANCE.

Upright, this card often means joyful connection, friendship, or celebration. Reversed, it can point to too many people being involved—jealousy, gossip, or a third party creating tension. It doesn't automatically mean an affair, but it does highlight that something in the bond feels crowded or unbalanced.

FIVE OF SWORDS → BETRAYAL, CONFLICT, SELFISHNESS.

This is the energy of "winning at any cost." It can reflect betrayal, sharp words, or someone acting in ways that serve themselves rather than the relationship. It doesn't prove infidelity, but it can show harm being done through dishonesty, disrespect, or cruelty.

No Card Alone Proves Infidelity

It's critical to remember: **tarot is not a surveillance system.** No card can definitively prove that someone is cheating. The Seven of Swords might show a surprise party just as easily as an affair. The Devil could point to workaholism or toxic family ties, not a secret lover. The cards don't hand us courtroom evidence—they illuminate patterns, dynamics, and emotional truths.

What these cards point toward is *dishonesty, secrecy, or imbalance.* That might mean infidelity—but it could also mean a partner hiding financial stress, struggling with addiction, or closing off emotionally. The ethical reader avoids absolute claims about another person's behavior. Instead, the focus should always return to the querent's lived experience:

- Do you feel safe in this relationship?
- Do you feel your boundaries are honored?
- Are your needs for honesty, openness, and respect being met?

If the answer is no, then the issue is already alive—whether or not physical cheating has taken place.

The Approach

Avoid blunt accusations. Tarot is not a surveillance camera. It cannot (and should not) confirm exactly what someone is doing behind closed doors. What it can show is whether trust has been eroded, secrecy is present, or boundaries are being crossed.

✗ Instead of: *"Yes, they're cheating."*

✓ Try: *"The cards suggest that something isn't being shared openly here, and that lack of honesty is taking a toll on your peace of mind. What boundaries or conversations would help you feel secure?"*

This reframes the issue: instead of spying on another person's actions, you're helping the querent clarify what they need in order to feel safe in love.

Additional Layers to Infidelity Readings

The Emotional Landscape

Infidelity questions are rarely just about *cheating*. They're about trust. They're about safety. They're about the querent's sense of worth. Even if the suspicion turns out to be unfounded, the fact that they're asking the question shows there's already a crack in the foundation of trust. The reading, then, isn't just about what the other person may or may not be doing—it's also about how the querent is experiencing the relationship, and what they need in order to feel secure.

Neutral vs. Loaded Cards

Not all cards in an infidelity spread will scream "red flag." Neutral or supportive cards—like Temperance, Justice, or the Hierophant—might appear to highlight the importance of truth, balance, or agreements. These can be just as revealing: sometimes the cards are less about exposing secrets and more about encouraging communication and clarity.

Energetic Patterns vs. Events

Infidelity spreads are best understood as showing patterns rather than events. For example:

- The Devil might not mean a physical affair, but could show someone hiding an addiction that erodes intimacy.
- Seven of Swords might not mean sneaking out to see someone else, but could suggest emotional withdrawal or secrecy about feelings.

- Three of Cups reversed could just as easily mean outside influences (friends, gossip, meddling family) rather than a third lover.

The nuance matters, because misinterpreting a card could cause unnecessary harm.

Reader Responsibility

These are the moments where the weight of being a reader is heaviest. Tarot should *never* be used to accuse someone's partner outright. Even if a spread shows repeated secrecy, dishonesty, or betrayal energy, the way forward is to reflect what the querent needs to know for themselves—not to hand down a verdict. Your role is to help them understand:

- What energy is alive in the connection?
- Where are the blind spots?
- What conversations or boundaries might be needed?
- What does the querent need in order to feel safe and respected?

Redirection When Needed

Sometimes, the most compassionate thing is to redirect the question. If a querent demands a yes/no about cheating, you might shift toward:

- *"What truth is missing in this connection?"*
- *"What would bring me peace, regardless of what they're doing?"*
- *"What steps can I take to feel safe and respected in this relationship?"*

This way, even if their partner isn't cheating, you've still given them clarity about what they need in order to trust again.

Self-Compassion for the Querent

Remind them: their suspicions don't make them paranoid or broken. They're responding to something in the dynamic that feels off. Tarot can affirm that what they're sensing is valid, even if the cards don't confirm an affair. It's about honoring their intuition, not amplifying fear.

CHAPTER 46

how to frame infidelity readings with compassion

Infidelity readings carry enormous weight. The wrong words can deepen wounds, while compassionate language can bring clarity, healing, and empowerment. The goal is not to accuse, prove, or deny, but to hold space for the truth of the querent's experience and guide them toward agency.

Avoid Absolutes

When it comes to infidelity, querents are often bracing for a yes-or-no answer. They want certainty—confirmation of their worst fears or reassurance that nothing's wrong. But the truth is, tarot cannot and should not be used as a lie detector.

Framing a reading as an absolute verdict—

✘ "Yes, they're cheating."

✘ "No, you're imagining things."

—doesn't just risk inaccuracy. It risks harm. A blunt "yes" can devastate someone based on a symbolic spread, while a careless "no" might leave them staying in a harmful situation. Both extremes disempower the querent, either by crushing them with fear or by invalidating their intuition.

Tarot is not a spyglass. It does not give *courtroom-level evidence*. What it *does* reveal are the energies and patterns at play: secrecy, avoidance, dishonesty, imbalance, broken trust, or conversely, openness, clarity, and honesty. These are the signals, not verdicts.

A more compassionate approach reflects those patterns without declaring absolutes. For example:

✅ *"The cards suggest secrecy or something unspoken in this relationship. That doesn't automatically mean infidelity, but it does highlight that honesty and openness may be missing."*

This framing acknowledges the querent's concern while shifting the focus from accusation to empowerment. It says: *"Your feelings are valid. The cards are showing you there's a lack of clarity here. Now let's explore what you need in order to feel secure, respected, and safe in this relationship."*

By avoiding absolutes, you:

- Protect the querent from unnecessary devastation or false reassurance.
- Keep the focus on trust, communication, and boundaries rather than spying on another person's private life.
- Honor the limits of tarot while still providing insight that is compassionate, truthful, and useful.

In other words, avoiding absolutes doesn't weaken the reading—it strengthens it. It transforms the role of tarot from detective to guide, from judge to mirror, and from punisher to healer.

Validate the Querent's Feelings

When someone asks, *"Are they cheating on me?"* it's not a casual curiosity—it's a cry from a place of tension, fear, or mistrust. Even if the partner is faithful, the fact that the question is being asked means something already feels "off." Doubt itself is painful. A sense of distance, secrecy, or broken trust can wound just as deeply as the act of cheating.

That's why validation is so important. Before even touching the cards, take a moment to acknowledge the vulnerability the querent has brought to the table. Their feelings are not paranoia, drama, or weakness. They are real signals from the body and heart that safety may be missing. By naming this aloud, you affirm their experience and give them the dignity of being heard.

Example:

✅ *"It's clear that you're feeling uneasy in this connection. That feeling is important —it deserves to be honored. Let's look at what the cards reveal about what might be hidden, and how you can navigate this with clarity and self-respect."*

This simple validation does several things at once:

- **It diffuses shame.** Many querents worry they're "crazy" for doubting, especially if they've been gaslit or dismissed before. Hearing their unease named as valid can be healing in itself.
- **It shifts focus inward.** By centering the querent's experience first, you remind them that the reading is about their clarity, not their partner's secrets.
- **It creates safety.** Once a querent feels seen, they're more open to hearing what the cards have to say, even if the message is difficult.

Validation is not about feeding fear. It's about meeting the querent where they are and acknowledging the reality of their emotional state. From that place, the reading can move into reflection, clarity, and empowerment.

Focus on Safety and Boundaries

Infidelity readings are never really just about the partner's actions—they're about whether the querent feels safe, respected, and valued in their relationship. Trust is the bedrock of love, and when it cracks, even slightly, the entire connection feels uncertain. That's why the most powerful role of tarot in these readings isn't to expose another person's secrets—it's to bring the querent back to themselves, their boundaries, and their needs.

A spread may show secrecy, avoidance, or dishonesty—but instead of stopping at *"something is hidden,"* ask: *"What does this mean for the querent's safety and trust?"* This keeps the focus on empowerment, not accusation.

For example:

The **Seven of Swords** doesn't just point to sneaking around—it asks, *"Do you feel honesty and transparency here? If not, what boundaries would restore it?"*

The **Devil** isn't only temptation—it's a mirror for unhealthy patterns. It says, *"Where are you feeling trapped? What chains do you need to break?"*

The **Five of Swords** doesn't simply mean betrayal—it points to conflict where nobody wins. It asks, *"Are you being respected, or does this feel like a battle you can't win?"*

By framing cards this way, you shift the reading from surveillance of the partner's behavior into empowerment of the querent's choices.

Guiding Questions for Safety and Boundaries

When infidelity themes appear, here are gentle questions you can weave into the interpretation:

- *What would help you feel safe in this connection?*

- *Are your needs for honesty and openness being met?*
- *What boundaries would bring you peace, regardless of what your partner chooses?*
- *If nothing changed tomorrow, how would you feel staying in this relationship as it is today?*

These questions move the querent away from obsessing about the partner's actions and toward clarity about their own.

EXAMPLE FRAMING

✖ Instead of: *"They're hiding something, and you can't trust them."*

✅ Try: *"The cards suggest that there's a lack of openness here, and that's leaving you feeling unsafe. Whether or not that means cheating, the impact on you is real. The guidance here is to ask yourself: what boundaries or conversations would help you feel secure and respected?"*

This approach doesn't minimize their fear—it honors it. But it also reminds them that the solution lies in their agency, not in the surveillance of their partner.

Redirect Toward Empowerment

Infidelity questions can trap a querent in obsession: they want to know what their partner is doing every second, hoping tarot will act as an all-seeing eye. But obsession doesn't bring peace—it drains it. The more someone spirals into *"Are they? Aren't they?"* the further they drift from their own power.

As a reader, one of the greatest gifts you can give in these moments is redirection. Redirection doesn't mean dodging the question or sugarcoating the pain. It means guiding the querent toward what tarot can truly reveal: their own strength, their choices, and their path forward.

Instead of fixating on what the partner might be doing, redirect the spread to what the querent can do to feel clear, safe, and whole.

How to Reframe the Question

When asked: *"Are they cheating on me?"* try shifting toward:

- *"What truth is missing in this connection?"*
- *"What do I need in order to feel safe and respected here?"*
- *"How can I best navigate the uncertainty I'm feeling?"*
- *"What steps can I take to either rebuild trust or choose peace?"*

These reframes still honor the emotional urgency of the question—but instead of leaving the querent powerless, they point to steps that bring healing and clarity.

EXAMPLE IN PRACTICE

Suppose the spread includes **Seven of Swords, Devil, and Strength.**

✗ A blunt response might be: *"They're lying and controlling you. You can't trust them."*

☑ A redirected, empowering response might be: *"These cards show secrecy and unhealthy patterns—whether that's literal cheating or another form of dishonesty, something important is missing. Strength reminds you that you have the courage to face this truth. The real question is: what do you need in order to feel safe here? And if that safety isn't available, what choice will honor your heart the most?"*

Here, the reading doesn't deny the possibility of betrayal, but it makes the querent the agent of change—not a passive victim of their partner's actions.

Empowerment is the antidote to obsession. Tarot can reveal dishonesty, secrecy, or imbalance, but the most important message is always this: *"You are not powerless. You have a choice. You deserve trust and love that honors you."*

Blunt vs. Compassionate Framing

Sometimes the cards show painful dynamics: secrecy, betrayal, or dishonesty. The temptation is to deliver that message bluntly—quick, direct, almost clinical. But blunt words can cut too deeply, leaving the querent raw, ashamed, or hopeless.

Compassionate framing delivers the same truth, but in a way that honors the querent's humanity. It validates their feelings, reflects the message, and empowers them to make choices.

Here are several common scenarios with side-by-side examples:

EXAMPLE 1: SECRECY OR DISHONESTY (SEVEN OF SWORDS)

✗ **Blunt:** *"They're sneaking around. You can't trust them."*

☑ **Compassionate:** *"The cards suggest secrecy or something being withheld. That doesn't automatically mean cheating, but it does highlight that honesty is missing. What would help you feel safe and respected in this relationship?"*

EXAMPLE 2: TOXIC PATTERNS (DEVIL)

❌ **Blunt:** *"This relationship is toxic. They're controlling you."*

✅ **Compassionate:** *"The Devil here points to unhealthy dynamics—patterns of control, fear, or temptation. Whether or not infidelity is involved, it's leaving you feeling chained. The question the cards raise is: how can you free yourself from what doesn't serve you?"*

EXAMPLE 3: THIRD-PARTY ENERGY (THREE OF CUPS REVERSED)

❌ **Blunt:** *"There's a third person. They're cheating."*

✅ **Compassionate:** *"This card suggests imbalance—too many people or distractions in the connection. It might be another person, or it might be outside influences like friends or gossip. Either way, the energy shows that your bond needs clearer boundaries in order to thrive."*

EXAMPLE 4: CONFLICT AND BETRAYAL (FIVE OF SWORDS)

Blunt:

❌ *"They betrayed you. They don't care who gets hurt as long as they win."*

✅ **Compassionate:** *"This card shows conflict where no one truly wins. It suggests you may be feeling betrayed or defeated in this connection. The guidance here is to ask: what choices would protect your peace, rather than pulling you into battles that only leave you hurt?"*

EXAMPLE 5: QUERENT'S OWN INTUITION (HIGH PRIESTESS)

❌ **Blunt:** *"You're paranoid—you're making this up."*

✅ **Compassionate:** *"The High Priestess shows that your intuition is strong. Even if cheating isn't happening, your body is telling you something feels off. Trust that feeling—it's calling for attention and clarity, whether from your partner or from your own boundaries."*

Blunt framing names the pain but risks shattering trust. Compassionate framing names the same truth *and* offers a path forward. The goal is never to water down reality—it's to speak truth with gentleness, so the querent leaves with dignity intact and steps they can take.

When the Cards Show Hope

Not every infidelity spread points to betrayal beyond repair. Sometimes the cards reveal that while trust has been fractured, the relationship still carries the potential for healing. These moments are tender: the querent is looking not just for confirmation of pain, but also for signs of whether it's worth trying again.

- **Temperance** → The path of moderation, balance, and slow rebuilding. This card suggests that healing is possible, but it requires patience, honesty, and effort from both sides.
- **The Star** → Hope, renewal, and the light that guides after darkness. It speaks to emotional healing, forgiveness, and the belief that connection can be restored.
- **Six of Cups** → Reconnection through shared history, nostalgia, or the sweetness of remembering why love mattered in the first place.
- **Justice** → A need for fairness, truth-telling, and accountability. When handled well, it can clear the air and rebuild trust.
- **Ace of Cups** → A fresh emotional beginning, the possibility of starting again with open hearts.

Hope must always be balanced with honesty. If the cards suggest repair, frame it in a way that highlights **choice** and **mutual responsibility**—not a guarantee that things will magically "go back to normal."

✗ Instead of: *"Yes, you'll get back together and everything will be fine."*

✓ Try: *"The energy here suggests broken trust, but also the possibility of healing if both partners are willing to be honest and rebuild together. The cards encourage clear conversations and a slow return to balance. This isn't instant forgiveness—it's a path of patient repair."*

Hope Matters. It acknowledges possibility without creating false promises. It honors the querent's longing to know if the relationship can survive. It creates space for free will—the partner must choose honesty and growth for repair to work. It models that tarot is not about doom, but about clarity: "This is what could unfold if both people commit to healing."

EXAMPLE INTERPRETATION

Spread: **Three of Swords, Temperance, The Star**

- **Three of Swords** shows the heartbreak and fracture in trust.
- **Temperance** reminds that healing is possible—but it will be a slow blending, not an overnight fix.
- **The Star** offers hope: a renewed sense of openness, vulnerability, and light after pain.

Framing:

"This reading acknowledges that heartbreak has already occurred. But it also shows a path forward. Healing is possible here, if both people are willing to commit to honesty, patience, and rebuilding step by step. The Star promises renewal—but only through Temperance's slow, steady work."

Closing with Care

Infidelity readings are some of the most emotionally charged sessions a tarot reader can hold. Whether the cards suggest secrecy, conflict, or even hope for healing, the way you close the reading matters as much as the interpretation itself. The querent came to you carrying fear, pain, or doubt. They need to leave feeling steadier, not more broken.

A good closing helps the querent digest the reading, rather than leaving them overwhelmed. It shifts the focus from the partner's choices back to the querent's agency. It affirms their worth regardless of what their partner may be doing.

Core Principles for Closing an Infidelity Reading

Center the Querent's Value

Remind them they deserve honesty, respect, and safety in love. This affirmation helps lift them out of self-blame or fear.

EXAMPLE:

"Whatever happens in this relationship, remember this: you are worthy of love that is honest and safe. The cards are showing where trust feels fragile, but your worth has never been in question."

Point Toward Choice

Leave them with the understanding that they have agency. The cards reveal dynamics, but they do not make the choice for them.

EXAMPLE:

"These cards show that there's work to be done around honesty and openness. The decision of whether to stay or step away belongs to you, and the cards are offering guidance for what you need in order to feel whole in either path."

Offer Gentle Next Steps

Give them something practical to hold onto, even if small: a conversation to start, a boundary to consider, or a self-care practice to soothe the heart.

EXAMPLE:

"The energy here suggests that a heartfelt conversation is needed. Before you approach it, consider journaling what you most need to feel safe and respected. This clarity will help guide that dialogue."

EXAMPLE CLOSINGS

If the cards suggest secrecy:

"There's an energy of something unspoken here. The most important step now is to decide what honesty and safety mean for you, and how to communicate those needs clearly."

If the cards suggest toxicity:

"The Devil here shows unhealthy patterns weighing on the bond. Remember: you are not powerless. You have the strength to name your needs and choose the relationships that honor you."

If the cards suggest hope:

"The Star promises healing, but it comes through patience and truth. This isn't just about waiting—it's about building slowly, with honesty and compassion at the center."

Closing with care means the querent doesn't leave with doom hanging over their head, nor with false hope. Instead, they leave with a mirror of their worth and the reminder that they have power, choice, and clarity—even in the most uncertain circumstances.

Tarot in these moments is not about predicting betrayal—it's about restoring dignity.

CHAPTER 47

infidelity check-in spread

Cards Pulled:

1. What I Know in My Gut → **High Priestess**
2. What's Hidden or Unspoken → **Seven of Swords**
3. What I Need for Safety & Clarity → **Strength**

Card 1 Honor Intuition (High Priestess)

The High Priestess as the first card is powerful—it reflects the querent's inner knowing. Even before the reading, they sensed something was wrong. This doesn't necessarily mean infidelity is confirmed, but it validates the fact that their *feelings* are real and deserve attention. Their nervous system is telling them something is off. This card affirms: *"You are not imagining this. Your inner wisdom is speaking, and it deserves to be trusted."*

This sets the tone for the entire reading: the querent's intuition is not paranoia, it is guidance.

Card 2 Acknowledge What's Hidden (Seven of Swords)

The Seven of Swords appearing in the "What's Hidden" position signals secrecy, avoidance, or dishonesty. This is the card of sneaking around—not always in the literal sense of cheating, but in the emotional sense of withholding truth. It may mean their partner is hiding something, avoiding vulnerability, or not being fully honest.

This is where readers must tread gently:

Instead of saying, *"They're lying to you,"* frame it as: *"This card suggests that something isn't being shared openly. Whether that's another person, an unspoken truth, or simply avoidance, the effect on you is the same—you're left feeling uncertain and unsafe."*

Notice how this keeps the focus on the **impact** rather than the accusation.

Card 3 Return to Empowerment (Strength)

The final card, Strength, shifts the tone from suspicion to empowerment. Strength says: *"You have the courage and inner calm to handle this with dignity."* It calls for setting boundaries gently but firmly, and having the bravery to ask the hard questions.

Instead of spiraling in doubt, Strength invites the querent to step into their power:

- Speak their truth clearly.
- Ask for openness directly.
- Decide what they need in order to feel respected—and stand by it.

Strength reminds them that their worth is not defined by their partner's honesty, but by their own self-respect.

Pulling It Together

This spread tells a story:

- The querent already *knows* something is wrong (High Priestess).
- The relationship is carrying secrecy or avoidance (Seven of Swords).
- Their path forward is to reclaim their power with courage, compassion, and boundaries (Strength).

This isn't a verdict on whether cheating has or hasn't occurred. Instead, it's a mirror: *"Your intuition is valid, the secrecy is real, and your strength will carry you to clarity and safety."*

Closing Example Script

Here's how you might actually phrase this in a reading:

"The High Priestess shows that deep down, you already know something is off. Your body and intuition are alert, and that matters. The Seven of Swords suggests secrecy or avoidance—something is being withheld, even if it's not outright cheating. What's important here is how it leaves you feeling: unsafe, uncertain, and in need of clarity. The Strength card is your answer. It shows that you have the courage to face this honestly and to name what you need. Whether that means asking hard questions,

setting firmer boundaries, or choosing a new direction, the power is in your hands. These cards are reminding you that you don't have to sit in fear—you can take steps that bring you clarity and peace."

This way, the reader delivers truth without doom, and the querent walks away with dignity, courage, and a clear next step.

CHAPTER 48

breakups

THE BIG FOUR SENSITIVE TOPICS

One of the most tender, painful moments in love is its ending. Querents may arrive in the middle of heartbreak asking, *"Why did this end?"* or, *"How do I move on?"* These are not casual questions. They are the raw cries of someone whose world has shifted, who is grieving the loss of love, safety, or a future they thought was certain.

Tarot cannot erase heartbreak—but it can hold space for it. It can reflect the depth of grief while also pointing toward renewal. A good breakup reading acknowledges the ache of endings without rushing the querent toward premature healing.

What to Look For in Breakup Readings

Certain cards appear frequently in breakup spreads. They don't just signal endings—they highlight what the querent is being asked to face, release, or integrate:

- **Death** → the natural end of a cycle, transformation, and release. This card can feel final, but it also opens the door to new beginnings.
- **Three of Swords** → heartbreak, sorrow, betrayal, or separation. It names the pain clearly, validating what the querent is feeling.
- **Five of Cups** → grief, mourning, dwelling on what was lost. Yet it also carries the promise of healing—two cups still stand behind the figure, unnoticed in sorrow.
- **The Tower** → sudden collapse, shattered illusions, foundations that could not hold. It hurts, but it clears space for truth and authenticity.

Other cards may also show the *aftermath* of a breakup:

- **Nine of Swords** → sleepless nights, obsessive thinking.
- **Ten of Swords** → painful finality, rock bottom, but also the promise of dawn.
- **Eight of Cups** → walking away to seek deeper emotional fulfillment.

The Approach

The heart of a breakup reading is validation. When love ends, the pain is real and often profound. Even if the relationship wasn't healthy, even if the querent *knows* it was the right decision, the loss still hurts. Tarot has the power to sit with that ache and say, *"Yes, I see you. This matters. Your grief is real."*

Many querents arrive with guilt or pressure—friends may tell them to *"just move on"* or dismiss their heartbreak as weakness. But tarot readings are sacred pauses. They allow the querent to stop rushing, to sit with the truth of their feelings, and to know they are not alone in carrying them.

When a card like the Three of Swords appears, the goal is not to sugarcoat it— it's to name the heartbreak clearly: betrayal, sorrow, grief. Yet naming is not the same as condemning. Naming validates. It says: *"You are not broken for hurting. This is part of love's story."*

By holding the space where pain is spoken aloud, tarot gives permission to mourn. And mourning is not weakness—it is a form of strength.

While grief needs recognition, tarot does more than reflect pain—it shines a light on what the pain teaches. Every ending is also a threshold. Every wound carries a hidden lesson.

- **Death** teaches that endings are natural, and they clear space for transformation. What once was has served its purpose; something new is waiting to be born.
- **The Tower** shakes illusions to the ground so that only truth remains. Painful collapses make way for stronger foundations in the future.
- **The Three of Swords** cuts sharply, but the presence of pain also reveals the depth of love once felt. With time, that depth becomes a source of compassion, empathy, and resilience.
- **Temperance** comes after the pain, reminding us that healing is gradual, a blending of sorrow and renewal, where balance is restored drop by drop.
- **The Star** brings hope: the promise that after destruction, after heartbreak, the heart can shine again—more authentic, more open, more radiant.

Tarot doesn't erase the pain, but it shows the larger arc of meaning within it. Where the human heart sees only loss, tarot whispers of cycles, of renewal, of the way endings seed beginnings.

The Middle Path: Neither Despair nor False Cheer

A breakup reading should never linger so long in despair that the querent feels doomed, nor skip so quickly to positivity that the grief feels dismissed. The art of the reader is to walk that **middle path**—to witness the pain honestly, while also pointing toward the light ahead.

- Too much focus on despair leaves the querent trapped in sorrow.
- Too much focus on cheer risks sounding hollow, as if the heartbreak didn't matter.

Instead, tarot provides balance: *"Yes, this hurts deeply. Yes, you are allowed to grieve. And yes, healing is already in motion. The cards show that your heart, though broken now, will find its way to wholeness again."*

A breakup reading is not just fortune-telling—it is soul-tending. It validates the grief of endings, illuminates the wisdom inside the wound, and gently guides the querent toward healing.

CHAPTER 49

breakup spread

Breakups are tender terrain. A spread that balances grief, insight, and hope gives structure to what can otherwise feel overwhelming. This four-card spread is designed to validate the pain while also opening a door toward renewal.

THE BREAKUP SPREAD (4 CARDS)

Card 1: Why Did This End?

This position shines a light on the lesson, dynamic, or pattern that led to the breakup. It doesn't assign blame—it clarifies what wasn't aligned.

Example cards:

- **Death** → the relationship had reached its natural conclusion; its season ended.
- **Five of Wands** → constant conflict, competition, or misaligned goals.
- **Justice** → the truth came out, and balance had to be restored.

> *Interpretive note:* This card can help the querent understand the deeper reason, beyond surface events. It reframes the ending not as meaningless loss but as part of their soul's growth.

Card 2: What Pain Am I Carrying Now?

This position validates the current wound. It shows what's still heavy in the heart, so the querent feels seen in their grief.

Example cards:

- **Three of Swords** → heartbreak, betrayal, emotional pain.
- **Nine of Swords** → anxiety, sleepless nights, looping thoughts.
- **Five of Cups** → mourning, focusing on loss, feeling left behind.

Interpretive note: Don't rush past this. Sometimes the querent just needs to hear, "Yes, this hurts. Your pain is real, and it matters."

Card 3: What Am I Being Asked to Release?

Here the spread shifts toward healing. This card shows what story, attachment, or wound must be let go for the heart to find peace.

Example cards:

- **Eight of Swords** → releasing self-limiting beliefs or cycles of entrapment.
- **Devil** → letting go of unhealthy attachment, obsession, or codependency.
- **Ten of Swords** → releasing the cycle of betrayal, recognizing rock bottom as a turning point.

Interpretive note: Frame this as liberation, not judgment. The card isn't saying "you're broken"—it's pointing to what freedom is waiting when they let go.

Card 4: What Hope Is Waiting for Me?

The final card always points toward renewal, reminding the querent that love and life are not over.

Example cards:

- **The Star** → healing, hope, emotional renewal, the heart shining again.
- **Ace of Cups** → fresh emotional beginnings, openness to love.
- **Six of Swords** → moving into calmer waters, leaving pain behind.
- **Ten of Pentacles** → long-term stability and future happiness.

Interpretive note: This card doesn't predict *exactly when* love will return—it promises that love, healing, and joy are part of the querent's future.

CHAPTER 50

"will they come back?"

THE BIG FOUR SENSITIVE TOPICS

Few questions carry the same mix of hope and heartbreak as *"Will they come back?"*

It's one of the most common—and one of the trickiest—questions in love readings.

At its core, this question is rarely just about the person. It's about longing, grief, unfinished feelings, and the ache of uncertainty. Querents ask because they're still holding onto a thread: maybe of love, maybe of regret, maybe of hope.

And this is where the challenge comes in: tarot cannot guarantee another person's free will. People change, choices shift, circumstances evolve. What feels true in the cards today may be different tomorrow if that person makes a new decision. This is why a "yes" or "no" answer is not only unreliable—it can be harmful.

THE APPROACH

When someone asks, *"Will they come back?"* the temptation as a reader is to reach for a clear yes or no. But tarot doesn't work like a coin toss—it's not meant to stamp a verdict on another person's choices. Instead, the strength of tarot lies in reframing the question into something more revealing, more compassionate, and ultimately more healing.

A good reframe does three things: it acknowledges the querent's longing, it keeps the focus on what tarot can actually illuminate, and it returns power to the querent.

FLUENT TAROT: MATTERS OF THE HEART

Moving from Yes/No to Energy & Insight

✗ Instead of locking into prediction, you can redirect toward questions like:

- ✓ *"What is the energy between us right now?"*

This allows you to read honestly about how the connection feels in its current state—whether it's warm, cold, distant, hopeful, or complicated. The querent gets a snapshot of truth, not a fantasy of certainty.

- ✓ *"What do I need to understand about this connection in its current form?"*

Here the reading becomes about clarity. Sometimes the querent is clinging to illusions or mixed signals. This phrasing helps reveal what's *actually* present, not just what they wish were true.

- ✓ *"How can I move forward in wholeness, whether they return or not?"*

This question shifts the focus back to the querent's empowerment. Instead of waiting by the phone or door, they leave with guidance for how to heal, grow, and step into their own strength—independent of another person's actions.

Tarot reflects energy, patterns, and possibilities—not fixed promises. The energy of a connection can change with a single choice, a single conversation, a single act of will. To treat the cards as a guarantee of another's return risks creating disappointment, obsession, or even dependency.

By reframing, you're not denying the querent's desire—you're honoring it while offering a healthier, more useful perspective.

The Gentle Language of Redirection

When reframing, tone is everything. You don't want the querent to feel scolded for asking the question. Instead, meet their vulnerability with warmth:

✗ Instead of: *"Tarot can't tell you that, don't ask those kinds of questions."*

✓ Try: *"That's such a natural question—you miss them, and you want to know what's possible. Rather than focusing on a yes or no, let's ask the cards what the energy looks like right now, and what will help you feel grounded and clear whether or not they return."*

This honors the longing while guiding them toward insight that actually serves them. The way you deliver the message matters as much as the cards themselves.

✗ Instead of: *"No, they're gone forever."* OR *"Yes, they'll definitely return."*

✓ Try: *"The cards suggest their energy feels distant right now. That may or may not shift—but what stands out is what you can focus on to feel whole and empowered, regardless of their choices."*

This reframing gently shifts the spotlight back onto the querent's own healing and agency. It acknowledges the reality of their longing, but it doesn't feed obsession or dependency.

CHAPTER 51

Example spread

THE RETURN QUESTION

3-Card Spread Positions:

1. The energy of the other person right now.
2. The energy of the connection between us.
3. What I need to know about moving forward.

Example Draw:

- **Eight of Cups** → they are walking away, focused on personal searching.
- **Five of Cups** → the connection feels rooted in grief and loss.
- **Ace of Cups** → the querent's path forward is emotional renewal and self-love.

Interpretation:

The Eight of Cups shows that the other person is in a place of distance—they're walking their own path for now. The Five of Cups validates the sorrow and grief of this connection, acknowledging that the loss is felt on both sides. But the Ace of Cups shifts the message toward renewal: a new chapter of love, whether with someone else or with oneself, is waiting once the healing is embraced.

Instead of leaving the querent with despair, this reading affirms: *"Yes, the grief is real. But so is the hope. Love is not gone—it is taking a new form that begins with you."*

These questions about return are tender because they reveal how deeply someone has given their heart. Even if the answer is that the person won't come back, the querent should never leave the reading feeling empty or powerless.

Handled with compassion, this type of reading can do two powerful things at once:

- Validate the depth of the querent's love and longing.
- Empower them to find healing, clarity, and wholeness in the present moment.

CHAPTER 52

what to look for

WILL THEY COME BACK

Certain cards can offer clues about the *energy* of the connection:

Distant / Unlikely Return:

- **Eight of Cups** → walking away for good, soul searching elsewhere.
- **Five of Pentacles** → abandonment, separation, feeling shut out.
- **World** → a cycle has completed, closure is here.

Possible Return / Lingering Energy:

- **Six of Cups** → nostalgia, someone looking back, a reunion vibe.
- **Judgement** → second chances, resurrection of what was thought lost.
- **Wheel of Fortune** → cycles repeating, doors reopening.

Focus on Querent's Growth:

- **Strength** → learning courage and boundaries.
- **Hermit** → healing in solitude.
- **Ace of Cups** → new love, self-love, emotional renewal.

Remember: these aren't guarantees—they're signals of the present energy, and the surrounding cards always tell the fuller story.

CHAPTER 53
the return or release spread (6 cards)

To shift the question from *"Will they?"* to *"What serves me?"* This spread explores the other person's current energy, the state of the connection, and—most importantly—whether holding on or letting go leads to the healthiest path.

Card Positions

Card 1 Their Energy Right Now

How the other person is showing up emotionally, mentally, or spiritually at this moment.

Examples:

- **Eight of Cups** → walking away, seeking elsewhere.
- **Six of Cups** → nostalgia, remembering the past.
- **Knight of Wands** → passionate but inconsistent energy.

Card 2 The Energy of the Connection

What exists between the querent and this person in the present—ties, distance, unresolved threads.

Examples:

- **Two of Cups** → a strong emotional bond remains.
- **Five of Cups** → grief, loss, focusing on what's gone.
- **Devil** → attachment, obsession, unhealthy pull.

Card 3 What Holds Me Back from Letting Go

The belief, fear, or wound that makes it hard to release this connection.

Examples:

- **Four of Pentacles** → fear of losing stability.
- **Nine of Swords** → anxiety, overthinking, replaying scenarios.
- **Five of Pentacles** → fear of abandonment or being unworthy of love.

Card 4 What I Gain by Holding On

What (if anything) is still serving the querent by keeping hope alive.

Examples:

- **Strength** → patience, resilience.
- **Hanged Man** → perspective gained in the waiting.
- **Seven of Cups** → fantasy or illusion (which can also signal it's *not* truly serving).

Card 5 What I Gain by Releasing

The gift, freedom, or healing available when the cord is loosened.

Examples:

- **The Star** → renewal, self-love, hope in a new form.
- **Ace of Cups** → fresh emotional beginnings.
- **Six of Swords** → calmer waters, peace, forward movement.

Card 6 The Guidance for My Heart

The most important message the cards want the querent to carry forward. This card acts as a compass—whether that's about patience, closure, or a new path.

Examples:

- **Temperance** → healing will take time, balance is key.
- **Wheel of Fortune** → cycles are shifting, release control.
- **Ten of Pentacles** → love that lasts is still ahead.

EXAMPLE READING

Question: *"Will they come back, or is it time to move on?"*

Cards Pulled:

1. Their Energy → **Knight of Wands** (in and out, not consistent)
2. Connection → **Five of Cups** (grief and loss dominate)
3. What Holds Me Back → **Nine of Swords** (anxious replaying, sleepless nights)
4. What I Gain by Holding On → **Seven of Cups** (illusions, daydreams, but little clarity)
5. What I Gain by Releasing → **Ace of Cups** (new emotional beginnings, self-love, fresh start)
6. Guidance → **The Star** (healing, hope, renewal after heartbreak)

Interpretation:

This spread shows the other person as passionate but unreliable (Knight of Wands), with the current energy of the bond rooted in grief and loss (Five of Cups). The querent's struggle is their mind's constant replay of the connection (Nine of Swords), which keeps them awake at night. Holding on may only offer fantasy without solid ground (Seven of Cups). In contrast, release offers the gift of renewal (Ace of Cups) and opens the heart to new beginnings. The Star closes the reading with reassurance: healing is already in motion, and the querent's heart will shine brightly again.

Message to the Querent:

"This connection has meaning, but the cards suggest it's kept alive more by memory than by reality. The love you long for hasn't disappeared—it is waiting as a fresh beginning, one that opens once you release the grip of the past. Trust the healing that is already underway."

Why This Spread Works

- It acknowledges the longing instead of dismissing it.
- It shows both sides: what holding on does, and what letting go could open.
- It returns agency to the querent. Instead of waiting helplessly, they leave knowing what choice serves their heart best.

CHAPTER 54

unrequited love

THE BIG FOUR SENSITIVE TOPICS

The Tender Ache of Unrequited Love

Perhaps the most delicate and vulnerable of all love questions is the ache of unrequited love: when someone longs for another who doesn't return their feelings. Querents in this place often come to the cards with heavy hearts, their questions full of both hope and despair. They may ask:

- *"Why don't they love me back?"*
- *"How can I make them notice me?"*
- *"Is there still a chance for us?"*

The pain of one-sided love cuts deeply because it holds a paradox. It mixes hope with rejection, longing with silence, dreams with disappointment. When someone pours so much energy into a love that isn't reflected back, it can feel like standing in the spotlight of your own desire while the other person never turns their head.

This kind of experience often feels intensely personal, as though it were a judgment on one's value or worthiness. The inner dialogue can quickly become cruel: *"If I were enough, they'd choose me. If I were lovable, they'd stay."* That sense of being unseen or unwanted presses on old wounds of inadequacy, abandonment, or shame.

But this is precisely where tarot's wisdom becomes medicine. The cards don't come to confirm the story of *"I am not enough."* Instead, they gently reframe the truth — *"This love is not aligned."*

When feelings are not mutual, it doesn't mean the querent is broken or unworthy. It simply means that this particular connection does not hold the reciprocity that true love requires. Love is not meant to be begged for, chased, or forced into existence. A healthy, mutual bond flows naturally—it is two hearts meeting in the same place at the same time, both willing, both open.

The beauty of tarot is that it can hold the ache of this longing without dismissing it. It validates the sorrow, the yearning, the questions—but it also redirects the focus from *"Why don't they want me?"* toward *"Where will I be met with love that flows freely?"*

In this way, tarot transforms rejection into redirection. It reminds the querent: *"The problem is not that you are unlovable. The truth is that love cannot bloom where the soil is not fertile. You deserve a connection where your presence is not only accepted, but celebrated."*

What to Look For

Certain cards often appear in unrequited love spreads, reflecting imbalance, longing, or disconnection:

- **Four of Cups** → emotional disengagement, disinterest, someone not noticing what's offered.
- **Five of Pentacles** → feelings of being left out, rejected, or unworthy.
- **Lovers reversed** → misalignment, attraction without harmony, unequal connection.
- **Seven of Pentacles** → waiting, investing energy without reciprocity.
- **Page of Cups (reversed)** → immature or unavailable emotions.
- **Knight of Swords (reversed)** → someone chasing elsewhere, not staying present.

Remember: no single card says *"They don't love you."* These cards point to mismatched timing, energy, or capacity for connection.

The most important thing in an unrequited love reading is to **protect the querent from self-blame.** Unreturned love is not evidence that someone is unlovable. It's evidence of misalignment. Two people can be kind, attractive, intelligent, even compatible on paper—but if the emotional energy is not equal, the relationship cannot thrive.

A balanced love is mutual. Anything less is not sustainable, and tarot can help illuminate that truth without crushing the querent's hope or self-esteem.

Instead of reading for ways to "win them over," focus on what the querent *needs* in love, and where their energy is best directed for a reciprocal connection. This reframes rejection as redirection: away from forcing something closed, toward opening to what is truly meant for them.

🌹 Kind Framing

How you deliver the message matters as much as the message itself.

Instead of:

✗ *"They don't love you."*

✗ *"This is hopeless."*

✅ Try: *"The cards suggest this connection isn't balanced in energy, and that's painful. But what they also show is your worthiness of a love that flows freely, without you having to fight for it."*

✅ *"This reading shows me that while this person may not meet you where you are, the cards are pointing toward a bigger truth—you are ready for a love that celebrates you fully."*

This helps the querent see that love is not about convincing someone—it's about finding someone whose heart is already open to theirs.

Unrequited love is not just about *them*—it's about the querent's relationship to longing, to self-worth, and to hope. Tarot's role here is not to "prove" whether the person will ever return feelings, but to gently reveal:

- Where the energy of imbalance lies.
- Why the querent deserves more than breadcrumbs.
- How the heart can heal and re-open to true reciprocity.

This transforms the reading from *painful rejection* into *powerful redirection*.

Unrequited love readings are about shifting the focus from *"Why not them?"* to *"What kind of love is waiting that will meet me fully?"* Tarot does not diminish the ache—but it does transform it into wisdom, dignity, and hope.

CHAPTER 55

example spread: one-sided love

Positions:

1. What I feel in this connection.
2. What they feel (their energy).
3. Why the connection feels blocked.
4. What I most need to hear.
5. Where my love energy is best directed.

Example Draw:

1. **Knight of Cups** → the querent is open, romantic, ready to pursue love.
2. **Four of Cups** → the other person is disengaged, not noticing or not interested.
3. **Lovers reversed** → misalignment, not mutual.
4. **Strength** → the message is to meet oneself with courage and compassion.
5. **Ace of Pentacles** → plant new seeds elsewhere, build love in grounded and nourishing ways.

Interpretation:

The cards clearly show that while the querent is emotionally open and ready (Knight of Cups), the other person is disengaged (Four of Cups), creating an unequal dynamic (Lovers reversed). This isn't a verdict on the querent's value —it's a mismatch of timing and energy. Strength reminds them to honor their own worth with gentleness, and the Ace of Pentacles points toward building a new beginning that can blossom into something mutual.

Gentle framing to querent:

"This connection feels like it isn't being met equally, which I know hurts. But the cards are also showing your strength, your worth, and the new opportunities waiting to grow. Love should not be begged for—it should be shared freely. The love you deserve will not need convincing."

CHAPTER 56

how to hold space in an unrequited love reading

Unrequited love readings are some of the most vulnerable moments you'll face as a reader. The querent is often hurting, longing, or feeling rejected. Your role is not to confirm their worst fears or inflate false hope, but to walk with them through the ache and point them toward dignity, healing, and hope.

Here's a flow you can follow:

Validate the Pain

Start by acknowledging the depth of the querent's feelings. The worst thing you can do is dismiss or minimize their longing—it's real, it matters, and it deserves respect.

> "I can feel how much this connection means to you. It's not easy to carry feelings that aren't returned, and it makes sense that you'd want clarity."

This shows the querent that you see them—not just their question.

Reveal What the Cards Show About the Energy

Instead of declaring "yes" or "no," describe the dynamics present. Are the cards showing distance? Disengagement? Misalignment? Or do they reveal the querent's heart being open while the other person's is closed?

Example: *Four of Cups* might suggest disinterest, while *Lovers reversed* could show misalignment of values or attraction without harmony.

Emphasize that these cards don't say the querent is unworthy—they say the energy between them is not balanced.

Reframe the Story

This is where the healing happens. Gently shift the narrative from *"I am not enough"* to *"This love is not aligned."*

"The cards suggest this connection isn't balanced in energy. That's painful, but it doesn't mean you're unlovable. It means this particular bond doesn't hold the reciprocity you deserve."

This helps the querent separate their self-worth from the outcome of the connection.

Empower the Querent with Choice

Move the focus away from the other person's lack of response and back to the querent's agency. What do they need to nurture in themselves? Where can their love flow that will be fully received?

Look for cards that highlight healing and redirection:

- *Strength* → courage and self-compassion.
- *The Star* → renewal, hope, and new light after loss.
- *Ace of Cups* → a fresh start in love, beginning with the self.

Frame this as an invitation, not homework.

"This reading suggests you deserve to be celebrated, not overlooked. Let's explore what steps can help you open to a love that meets you fully."

Close with Gentle Hope

Even in the face of rejection, leave the querent with a sense of dignity and possibility. Not false promises, but genuine encouragement.

"This chapter may not bring the love you long for, but it is pointing you toward the love that will. You are not unseen—you are simply being redirected to a connection that can honor you the way you deserve."

It honors the pain without letting the reading wallow in it. It clarifies the truth without being cruel. It empowers the querent to see themselves as worthy, not rejected. It leaves hope intact, but re-anchored in self-love and future possibility rather than obsession with someone unavailable.

CHAPTER 57

the unrequited to empowered spread

To help the querent understand the reality of the one-sided connection, release shame or self-blame, and open to love that is mutual, healthy, and aligned.

Card Positions

Card 1 My Feelings

What I am bringing into this connection—my hopes, desires, emotional investment.

Examples: Knight of Cups → longing and romance, Ten of Wands → emotional heaviness.

Card 2 Their Energy

Where the other person truly stands in this dynamic.

Examples: Four of Cups → disinterest, Lovers reversed → misalignment, Page of Cups reversed → emotional immaturity.

Card 3 Why This Connection Feels Powerful

The soul-level reason I am so drawn to them. This often reveals projection, karmic echoes, or unmet needs.

Examples: Devil → karmic tie/attachment, Six of Cups → nostalgia or past-life echoes, Two of Pentacles → indecision.

Card 4 Why It Isn't Balanced

What blocks this bond from becoming mutual.

Examples: Five of Pentacles → unworthiness themes, Seven of Cups → illusion/fantasy, Eight of Swords → self-limiting beliefs.

Card 5 The Lesson This Connection Is Teaching Me

What my soul is meant to learn here, so the ache transforms into wisdom.

Examples: Strength → self-compassion, Temperance → patience and balance, The World → closure and integration.

Card 6 What Opens When I Release or Redirect

The gift, freedom, or love waiting once I stop pouring energy into what isn't flowing back.

Examples: Ace of Cups → new love or self-love, Star → healing and renewal, Ten of Pentacles → aligned long-term bonds.

Crd 7 Message for My Heart

The closing word of encouragement, guidance, or hope—the thread that ties the reading together.

Examples: Sun → joy and clarity, Wheel of Fortune → cycles turning, Empress → you are worthy of abundant love.

EXAMPLE READING

Question: *"Why don't they feel the same way, and how can I move forward?"*

Cards Pulled:

1. My Feelings → Knight of Cups (romantic pursuit, open heart)
2. Their Energy → Four of Cups (disinterest, not noticing what's offered)
3. Why It Feels Powerful → Devil (karmic tie, magnetic but unhealthy pull)
4. Why It Isn't Balanced → Seven of Cups (illusions, fantasy clouding reality)
5. Lesson → Strength (learning self-compassion, taming inner doubt)
6. What Opens → Ace of Cups (fresh start, emotional renewal, new love)
7. Message → The Star (healing, hope, trust in a brighter path ahead)

Interpretation:

This spread reveals the querent's heart as wide open and romantic (Knight of Cups), but the other person is disengaged and not receptive (Four of Cups). The connection feels magnetic because of karmic pull (Devil), but that magnetism is rooted in unhealthy attachment. The lack of balance (Seven of Cups) shows the querent may be caught up in fantasy rather than grounded reality.

The lesson here is Strength—to meet themselves with courage and gentleness rather than self-criticism. By releasing the pull toward someone unavailable, the querent opens the way for Ace of Cups—a fresh start in love, a chance to give and receive in equal measure. The Star closes the reading with hope: this hurt is not the end of their story, but the beginning of healing that will draw in love that truly matches their heart.

It doesn't scold the querent for longing. It validates the pull, explains the imbalance, reframes the lesson, and shows what becomes possible when they redirect their love. The final message ensures they leave the reading not just with understanding, but with hope and empowerment.

CHAPTER 58

reading honestly without crushing hope

One of the hardest tightropes in romance readings is this: how do you speak the truth without taking the air out of someone's heart?

Put yourself in their shoes. Imagine you've just bared your soul to someone—you've told them about the ache of waiting for a message, or the fear that your love isn't being returned. Your heart is already raw, and now you've handed it to a reader, asking them to hold it for a moment. What would you want in return?

Would you want someone to snap, *"No, they're not coming back, get over it"*? Probably not. Even if that were the truth, it would sting in a way that shuts you down instead of opening you up. What you'd want is honesty, yes—but delivered with compassion, with humanity, with the recognition that you're not just asking a question, you're asking for care.

That's what this part of tarot is about: learning to balance truth with tenderness.

Honesty is essential. If the cards show blocks, you name them. If the energy feels distant, you say so. But honesty doesn't mean harshness. It doesn't mean declaring "it's hopeless" or "you're wasting your time." Instead, you can frame it in a way that acknowledges the reality while also leaving room for healing. For example: *"The cards suggest that the energy between you feels blocked right now. That doesn't mean you're unworthy of love—it means this path may not be flowing easily, and your next step may come through release or redirection."*

It's a subtle shift, but it changes everything. Instead of crushing someone with a closed door, you're showing them another doorway: one that leads to clarity, to empowerment, to choice.

Validation matters too. Before you even interpret the cards, take a moment to honor their feelings. You might say, *"It makes sense that you're feeling this way. Of course you'd want answers—it's hard to sit in uncertainty."* That simple act of validation can soften the hardest truths, because the querent knows they've been seen and not dismissed.

And always—always—offer empowerment. The most damaging readings are the ones that leave someone with nothing to do but wait or despair. Tarot is not here to slam doors; it's here to open windows. If you must tell someone that their desired path looks blocked, balance it with a way forward: a step they can take, a reflection they can hold, a piece of self-love they can practice. It may not be the outcome they dreamed of, but it is a path they can walk.

At the end of the day, the goal is not to predict perfectly—it's to help someone walk away from the table stronger than they arrived.

CHAPTER 59

Ethics & Empowerment

When it comes to love readings, ethics aren't an afterthought—they're the heartbeat of the work. Romance is tender ground, and people often come to tarot at their most vulnerable. The way you frame your words can either create empowerment or deepen dependency. That's why ethics matter so much.

First, let's talk about spying.

It's tempting, right? Someone sits down across from you and asks, *"What are they thinking about me right now?"* or *"Are they texting someone else?"* These questions are born from fear, insecurity, and longing—they're completely human. But tarot is not meant to be a surveillance camera into another person's private mind. That crosses a boundary, because it reduces another person's autonomy into a card flip. Instead of playing detective, you can redirect gently: *"Let's ask what you need to know about this connection right now, and how you can navigate it in a way that honors your needs."* Suddenly, the focus shifts from prying into someone else's secrets to empowering the querent with clarity about their own role.

Next: absolutes.

Love is messy, alive, unpredictable. No card—or reader—can promise, *"Yes, he'll marry you"* or *"No, you'll be alone forever."* Those kinds of statements are not only unethical, they're disempowering. They lock the querent into a fate as if nothing they do could change it. Instead, tarot shows possibilities, patterns, and energies. You can frame it as: *"The cards suggest the energy is leaning toward commitment, but the choice will always be between you both. Here's what you can do to nurture that direction."* That way, the message is hopeful and grounded, not a fixed prophecy.

Finally, the most important ethic: encourage agency.

Every love reading should leave the querent with more power in their hands than when they came in. They should walk away not just knowing what *might* happen, but what they *can* do. If a spread shows distance, give them tools to decide, Do they want to reach out? Do they want to set boundaries? Do they want to redirect their love elsewhere? Tarot is not about chaining people to dependency—it's about showing them the keys to their own choices.

Because here's the truth, love readings that focus only on prediction can keep people stuck, waiting for fate to rescue them. But readings that focus on empowerment help people step into their own worth, their own agency, their own love story.

And let me pause to say this, I know these ethics conversations come up a lot. That's because they matter. Love readings aren't light entertainment—they touch the rawest parts of people's hearts. Questions about spying, absolutes, or dependency show up again and again because querents are searching for certainty in the very places they feel most vulnerable. As readers, it's our responsibility not to take that lightly. Every time we sit with someone in their longing, fear, or heartbreak, we're being entrusted with something sacred. The way we handle it—with compassion, clarity, and care—can make the difference between leaving them more broken or more whole.

I am here to empower, not to bind. Tarot is not about dependency—it is about freedom.

CHAPTER 60

practice prompts

The only way to grow comfortable with sensitive topics is to *practice*. These exercises are designed to help you stretch your voice as a reader—balancing truth, tenderness, and empowerment. Try them in your journal, with a practice partner, or even by role-playing aloud. Notice not just *what* you say, but *how it feels* when you say it.

Blunt vs. Compassionate

Prompt: Write out how you would respond to the question:

"Is he cheating?"

- Once bluntly
- Then again with compassionate framing

The blunt version might sound harsh or absolute: *"Yes, the cards say he's lying."* or *"No, you're imagining things."*

The compassionate version might sound like: *"The cards show secrecy or something unspoken in this connection. That doesn't automatically mean infidelity, but it does highlight the importance of trust and open communication."*

When you finish writing both, reflect:

- Which response would you want to hear if you were the querent?
- Which feels more ethical?

> How can you train yourself to choose compassion without losing honesty?

Honoring Grief While Uplifting

Prompt: Pull three cards for *"How can I move on from heartbreak?"*

> First, write down what each card might say in its most direct form.

For example:

- *Five of Cups* → mourning, loss, grief.
- *Strength* → courage, inner resilience.
- *Ace of Pentacles* → a fresh, stable beginning.

Now, turn that into a mini-reading that validates pain *and* points to growth:

"These cards show that your grief is real and heavy right now (Five of Cups), but they also remind you of your strength—you are not broken beyond repair (Strength). The Ace of Pentacles suggests that small new beginnings are waiting, perhaps through grounding yourself in daily routines or fresh opportunities. Healing won't be instant, but step by step, you're rebuilding a foundation for a new chapter."

REFLECTION:

> Did your reading acknowledge the pain without sugarcoating?
>
> Did it also leave space for hope?

Redirection Practice

Prompt: Imagine someone asks: *"Will she come back to me?"*

Instead of answering directly, practice reframing.

For example:

Original question: *"Will she come back?"*

Redirected: *"What is the energy between us right now?"* or *"What do I need to focus on to feel whole whether or not she returns?"*

Then, pull a few cards and write how you would explain this to the querent. Notice how the energy shifts—suddenly, the focus is not just on the other person's choice, but on the querent's healing, clarity, and empowerment.

These practice prompts aren't about getting the "right" answer—they're about finding your *voice* as a reader. Every time you choose compassionate framing, validation, and empowerment, you strengthen your ability to hold space for love in its most vulnerable forms.

Sensitive topics are where tarot proves its deepest worth. It's easy to read when the cards point to joy, attraction, or new beginnings—but the true test of a reader's skill comes when the questions are tender, raw, or painful. Infidelity. Breakups. Longing. Loss. These are the moments when the querent's heart is most exposed, and when the way you hold that heart matters most.

Tarot is not a fortune-telling trick. It is not here to deliver blunt verdicts or pat answers. Tarot is a mirror for the soul, a language that helps people see their inner truth reflected back at them. When someone comes to you with the ache of betrayal or the heaviness of grief, what they often need most is not prediction, but presence. They need to be reminded that their feelings are valid, that they are not alone, and that even in the darkest moments, there is a way forward.

This is where your words carry real weight. A careless phrase can deepen a wound. But a compassionate truth can help someone begin to heal. Tarot is not only about outcomes—it is about perspective, empowerment, and love in all its forms.

When you hold sensitive topics with both clarity and tenderness, you do more than answer a question—you create a safe space. You help someone breathe easier. You remind them that endings are also beginnings, that longing can become self-discovery, that rejection can be redirection. You give them not just a reading, but a moment of healing.

And that is why this work matters.

REFLECTION PROMPT:

Take a moment and journal.

> What does it mean to you to hold someone's heart in your hands through tarot?
>
> How do you want your querents to feel when they walk away from your table?
>
> Write your answer as a personal commitment—a reminder of the kind of reader you aspire to be when faced with life's tenderest questions.

PART SIX

shifting into the love letter voice

CHAPTER 61
what is the love letter voice?

Most tarot writing keeps a certain distance. It observes, analyzes, explains. The familiar phrasing goes something like: *"This card suggests... you may feel... the energy points to..."* And that's useful—it gives clarity, structure, and objectivity. But when it comes to love, distance often isn't what the querent is craving.

The Love Letter Voice changes the axis completely. Instead of analysis, it offers intimacy. Instead of describing love, it becomes love. It speaks in the first person, as if the soul of the connection, the archetype behind the card, or even Love itself were writing directly to the querent.

This shift does something subtle but profound, it bypasses the intellect and speaks straight to the heart. The difference is palpable.

Traditional third-person: *"The Two of Cups suggests harmony and emotional connection."*

Love Letter Voice: *"I see you as my equal, my reflection. When I meet your gaze, I remember what wholeness feels like."*

One is informative. The other is intimate.

Think of this voice as a translation layer. You're still reading the cards with skill, ethics, and clarity—you're not abandoning structure or inventing promises. Instead, you're clothing the truth in tenderness. You're taking the bones of interpretation and wrapping them in skin, breath, and heartbeat.

It's poetry, yes—but it's poetry *anchored in craft*. The imagery, archetypes, and symbolism of the tarot give you the raw material; the Love Letter Voice gives it wings. What might have been a lesson becomes a whisper, a reminder, a vow.

And this matters because love questions are never just about information. They're about longing, vulnerability, and the ache of being human. When you use the Love Letter Voice, you meet the querent not as a teacher pointing to the board, but as a companion sitting beside them, saying, *"I see you. Let me speak to you in the language your heart understands."*

Love questions live in the body. First-person language bypasses distance; it lets the querent feel the message, not just analyze it. This voice softens defenses, invites empathy, and helps the heart metabolize truth—especially when the news is nuanced or bittersweet.

Where the voice comes from (and naming it)

When you write in the Love Letter Voice, you aren't pretending to channel someone's private thoughts word-for-word. That would cross ethical lines and risk planting false hope. Instead, you're giving voice to an energy, archetype, or higher truth that the cards reveal. This distinction is what makes the practice safe, empowering, and deeply moving.

Think of it like tuning a radio. The cards give you the frequency, and you choose how to translate it into words that the heart can hear. Being clear about *where the voice comes from* sets the tone and keeps the reading grounded.

The Connection's Archetypal Voice

This isn't "him" or "her"—it's the **field of energy between them.** You're speaking as the relationship itself: the pull, the rhythm, the bond. This is especially powerful in "Where is this connection headed?" spreads.

Example: "Between us lives both fire and hesitation. When you lean in, I blaze. When you retreat, I flicker."

The Querent's Higher Self

Sometimes what the querent most needs is to hear from their own deepest wisdom. Writing the love letter as if it's their *own soul speaking back* helps them reclaim agency.

Example: "I know you long to be chosen, but I am already choosing you. Love yourself the way you dream of being loved, and watch how others rise to meet you."

The Card's Archetype

The tarot is full of characters who carry strong voices already. The High Priestess can whisper with mystery, The Emperor can promise safety, The Star can shine with hope. Writing directly from the archetype makes the message both vivid and timeless.

Example (The Star): "I am the hope you thought you lost. I am still here, waiting in your bones, humming your name beneath the night sky."

A Compassionate Future Partner Energy

This one requires care and consent, but can be beautiful when done well. Instead of pretending to "see" the literal future spouse, you let the cards give a symbolic voice to the love that is *on its way*. This style is best for spreads about readiness or future love.

Example: "I am walking toward you already, but I need you to walk toward yourself first. Meet me in your joy, and there I will be."

The Importance of Prefacing

Because the Love Letter Voice is intimate, you always want to *name the perspective clearly*. This avoids confusion and makes sure the querent understands they are receiving symbolic, archetypal wisdom—not someone else's diary.

A simple preface works wonders:

"I'll translate the cards as a love letter from the energy of this connection to you."

or

"This is how your higher self might speak to you through these cards."

Framing it this way creates transparency while preserving the intimacy. The querent gets the magic of hearing their reading as a personal letter, but without the ethical risk of thinking you're reading someone else's private mind.

CHAPTER 62

boundaries & ethics

THE GUARDRAILS OF THE LOVE LETTER VOICE

The Love Letter Voice feels tender, direct, and deeply personal. It can make a reading sound like the very words a querent longs to hear whispered in their ear. And that is exactly why it must be handled with extraordinary care. Without strong boundaries, this style of reading risks slipping from healing into harm.

Think of boundaries as the frame around a love letter: they keep the beauty in focus and prevent the message from spilling into illusion.

Never Promise Another Person's Actions

One of the most common—and most dangerous—pitfalls in love readings is slipping from possibility into promise. When you phrase a message in the Love Letter Voice, it feels intimate, immediate, and personal, almost as if you're channeling someone's diary. That intimacy is beautiful—but it also magnifies the risk of false hope.

If you say:

✘ *"I will propose next month."*

✘ *"I'll text you tomorrow."*

The querent will likely take it literally. They may wait by the phone, decline other opportunities, or put their emotional wellbeing on hold. And when reality doesn't unfold as promised, the heartbreak cuts twice as deep: once from the relationship, and once from the tarot itself. Instead of feeling guided, they feel misled.

FLUENT TAROT: MATTERS OF THE HEART

Tarot is not here to lock people into waiting rooms of disappointment. It's here to show *energies, tendencies, and emotional truths*. And when delivered in the Love Letter Voice, those truths can still feel intimate without making claims you cannot guarantee.

How to Shift Ethically

The key is subtle but powerful — speak desire and energy, not calendar events.

Instead of claiming actions, express longings, tendencies, or conditions that are present right now:

✅ *"I want to meet you in honesty."*

✅ *"I feel the urge to reach for you, but I need courage to follow through."*

✅ *"My heart is restless with wanting, but fear still holds me back."*

✅ *"I imagine returning to you, but I don't yet know if I will step forward."*

Notice how each of these speaks from the energy the cards reveal—the pull, the conflict, the desire—without crossing into guarantees. It leaves the querent with insight into the connection's current landscape, while keeping the truth of free will intact.

The difference may feel small, but it changes everything:

❌ **A false promise** creates dependency.

✅ **An honest reflection** creates empowerment.

When you keep the voice anchored in *energy* rather than *certainty,* you give the querent both intimacy and integrity. They walk away not with a date circled on the calendar, but with a map of the heart's landscape—the fire, the hesitations, the desires, and the fears. That map is infinitely more useful than a countdown clock.

Avoid Manipulation

The Love Letter Voice is seductive—literally. It draws people in with beauty and intimacy. That power should never be used to bind someone to waiting, obsessing, or surrendering their agency.

A responsible love letter always brings the querent back to themselves. It affirms their choices, their power, their worth.

Unethical example:

❌ *"Wait for me, no matter how long it takes."*

Ethical reframe:

☑ *"I don't know how long it will take. If you wait, let it be because it feels good in your soul—not because you must. I offer blessings for whatever path you choose."*

This way, the reading liberates rather than entraps.

Clarity Within Poetry

Poetry is a spell. It softens truth so the heart can hold it. But when a reading points to release—or any hard message—ambiguity can wound. If the querent can't tell what you meant, they'll cling to the most hopeful interpretation and stay stuck. Your job is to keep the tenderness—and add a steady hand.

- Ambiguity breeds obsession. Vague metaphors make people parse every line for a secret yes.
- Clarity calms the nervous system. A kind, direct line lets the body exhale, grieve, and move.
- Ethics live in the verbs. Say what is and what isn't, without hedging or hidden promises.

The three-beat clarity recipe

1. **Name the truth.** (Yes/No/Not yet/Conditional.)
2. **Name the why** in *energy* terms, not blame.
3. **Offer a blessing or next step** that returns agency to the querent.

"I cannot stay. The fire that warmed us is fading, and I won't pretend it isn't. Carry what was good and choose the road that chooses you back."

Vague → Clear (across common scenarios)

Ending / Release

✘ **Too vague:** "I'm a wave that drifts beyond your shore."

☑ **Clear but kind:** "I cannot stay. I bless what we shared, but my path is no longer here. Your heart deserves to be met fully, and I cannot give that."

Unrequited love

✘ **Too vague:** "I'm a closed window waiting for summer."

☑ **Clear but kind:** "My feelings can't meet yours right now. That hurts to name, and it's true. I never set out to hurt you. You deserve more than I can offer. Please give your love to someone who can stand in it with you."

On–off / Inconsistent partner

✘ **Too vague:** "I'm a comet—rare, bright, unreliable."

✅ **Clear but kind:** "I know I attract attention, but you should know I'm also inconsistent. I come close and pull away. If you need steady love, I cannot promise to be that person."

Timing / "Not yet"

❌ **Too vague:** "When the orchard ripens, I'll remember the path."

✅ **Clear but kind:** "Fear and healing still stand between us. If the day arrives when I can meet you fully, it will be from honesty—not from delay. Now isn't the time."

5) Reconciliation request

❌ **Too vague:** "Ashes sometimes remember their flame."

✅ **Clear but kind (No):** "I won't return to romance. What we had taught me a great deal, and it is complete. May we both move toward what truly fits."

✅ **Clear but kind (Conditional):** "A return is possible only if we rebuild on truth and new agreements. Without that, it would repeat the past. That wouldn't be healthy for either of us."

Infidelity / Broken trust

❌ **Too vague:** "Storms pass; roofs still leak."

✅ **Clear but kind:** "Trust is broken. Repair would require full honesty and time. We need to build this from the ground up. If that cannot happen, protecting your heart is the way forward."

Phrase bank: compassionate clarity

No / Release

- "I cannot meet you in the way you deserve."
- "This love is complete. I'm closing the door with gratitude."
- "Please don't wait for me. Choose what chooses you."

Not yet

- "My heart isn't ready, and that matters. If readiness comes, it will be clear and consistent."
- "The timing is closed right now; healing must come first."

Conditional yes

- "Yes—if we honor boundaries and tell the truth even when it's hard."
- "Possible—only with steadiness, not with sparks that vanish."

Empowerment close

- "Your agency is sacred. Take only what returns you to yourself."
- "Let the answer guide your steps, not chain your heart."

Keep the poetry, sharpen the meaning

The beauty of the Love Letter Voice lies in its tenderness and lyric quality—it feels like the cards are whispering straight into the querent's heart. But poetry without clarity risks leaving someone guessing, or worse, clinging to false hope. The goal is to keep the lush, emotional flow while making the meaning unmistakable.

Here are the five golden practices to balance art and truth:

1. Use Plain Verbs

Words like *can / cannot, will / won't, is / isn't* bring clarity into the most poetic phrases. They act like anchors in the flowery current. Without them, you risk spinning in metaphor without ever answering the question.

✘ **Vague:** "Perhaps one day the door will swing open."

☑ **Clear with plain verb:** "The door is closed right now. It may open with honesty, but at this moment it remains shut."

2. Avoid Future Guarantees

Promise energy, not dates. Desire is safe to voice—guarantees are not.

✘ **Unethical promise:** "I'll marry you next year."

☑ **Ethical poetic longing:** "I dream of building a life with you. Whether I can step into that dream depends on the choices I make in honesty."

By naming possibilities rather than fixed outcomes, you stay in integrity while still giving the querent the intimacy they crave.

3. One Metaphor per Message

Poetry sings best when it's simple. Layering metaphor on metaphor creates fog. Choose one image and let it breathe.

✘ **Overloaded:** "I am the ship, the tide, the anchor, and the storm."

☑ **Sharpened:** "I am the tide, pulling away. It hurts, but I cannot stay."

If your line would make someone pause and puzzle over it rather than feel it, it's too much.

4. Cut the Passive Voice

Passive phrasing hides responsibility and makes the message slippery. Active voice makes the letter honest and accountable.

✘ **Passive:** "Mistakes were made, and things fell apart."

✔ **Active:** "I hurt you, and I cannot rebuild what was lost."

Even when the message is painful, clear ownership honors the querent far more than vague phrasing ever could.

5. Test for Paraphrase

A simple gut-check: could someone repeat your poetic line in plain words without guessing? If not, clarify it.

✘ **Too cryptic:** "I am smoke through your fingers."

✔ **Clarity check:** "I cannot stay. The bond fades when I try to hold it."

If your metaphor holds up to paraphrase, you know it's strong. If it collapses into confusion, rewrite.

Poetry should *illuminate* the truth, not blur it. The goal is that the querent walks away not only touched but also **clear.** They should be able to rest in your words instead of spinning in them.

A good love letter line should feel like a hand on the heart: tender, steady, and unmistakably true.

The Traffic-Light Check: A Quick Self-Audit for Love Letters

When giving a reading in the Love Letter Voice, it's easy to get swept up in metaphor. The words feel tender, even magical—but if the meaning is fuzzy, the querent may walk away confused or clinging to a hope that the cards don't support. That's why it helps to pause and *audit your own writing for clarity.*

Think of it like a stoplight for your love letters:

Green → The querent could act on this today without guessing. The message is tender *and* clear.

Yellow → The words are lovely, but fuzzy. Add one plain sentence to ground the meaning.

Red → The message could be read as a hidden yes (when the answer is no) or as a guarantee you can't give. Rewrite until the truth is unmistakable.

This quick check keeps your letters compassionate without crossing into confusion or false promises.

EXAMPLE: THE FULL THREE-BEAT ARC

Cards Pulled: Eight of Cups, Devil, Star (for a release reading)

Letter:

"I am walking away. What binds us now is more habit than healing, and I won't keep you small with me. Carry the light we found and give it back to yourself—your next dawn begins when you do."

Here, the clarity is unmistakable. The Eight of Cups speaks to leaving, the Devil acknowledges unhealthy bonds, and the Star offers healing and renewal. The message is poetic, but it doesn't hide the truth: this is a goodbye.

Clarity doesn't cancel tenderness—it delivers it. A compassionate no is always kinder than a confusing maybe, because it allows the heart to do what it knows how to do: honor, grieve, and then move toward what truly meets it.

Every Love Letter is a translation. You're not channeling someone's diary; you're translating energy, archetype, or higher wisdom into a voice that feels personal. Always keep that distinction clear in your own mind—it will naturally keep your boundaries strong.

A good mantra to hold close:

"This is love speaking, not a person. This is truth in tenderness, not a promise of behavior."

Far from limiting you, these guardrails actually deepen the practice. They make the letter *trustworthy*. When a querent reads or hears your words, they can relax into the intimacy, knowing you are not dangling false hope or manipulation. The safety you create is part of the healing.

Because at the end of the day, the Love Letter Voice is not about fantasy—it's about reflection. It's not about telling someone what they want to hear; it's about giving the heart a message it can trust, dressed in the tenderness it deserves.

CHAPTER 63
the anatomy of a love-letter reading

A love-letter reading isn't just pretty words—it's a carefully guided experience. The arc matters as much as the message, because it carries the querent from the ache of their question into the clarity of their next step. Think of it like writing a song: the verses build intimacy, the chorus delivers truth, and the final note lingers in the heart.

Here's how the structure works in practice:

1. Opening Attunement — Instant Intimacy

Begin by drawing the reader close. This is the first breath of connection, the moment where the cards' voice says, *I see you.* The opening should feel personal, gentle, and grounding.

Example: *"Beloved, I've watched you carry too much on a brave, quiet heart."*

Purpose: It signals safety. Whatever comes next, the querent knows they are met with tenderness, not judgment.

2. Truth — The Core Message of the Cards

This is where clarity enters. Poetry must serve meaning. Deliver the essence of the spread without hedging or hiding. If the energy is unsteady, say so. If it's promising, name that too.

Example: *"This connection flickers hot and cold; longing fills the gaps where presence should be."*

Purpose: It anchors the letter in honesty, showing the querent that tarot sees what they feel but may not have named aloud.

3. Tenderness — Validation Without Indulgence

Here, the tone softens again. Acknowledge the pain, hope, or vulnerability revealed by the cards. Validation does not mean indulging fantasy—it means affirming that their feelings make sense.

Example: *"Your yearning is not foolish; it's proof that you love deeply."*

Purpose: It keeps the letter from being clinical or cold. Even hard truths are easier to hold when wrapped in recognition of the querent's humanity.

4. Guidance — One Clear Step

Every letter should offer the querent something actionable. Not a rigid directive, but an invitation to move toward healing, empowerment, or alignment.

Example: *"Choose the pace that keeps your nervous system soft; love will meet you there."*

Purpose: To shift the querent from passive waiting into active co-creation. Guidance turns the reading into a compass instead of just a mirror.

5. Blessing / Release — A Closing Chord

Endings matter. The final lines should seal the reading with hope, affirmation, or loving closure. Whether the answer is yes, no, or not yet, close with words that leave the querent feeling cared for.

Example: *"What is meant for you will not require you to beg."*

Purpose: This ensures the querent leaves not with heaviness, but with a sense of peace and trust in themselves and their path.

Length & Flow

For a single card reading, 5–10 sentences can carry the full arc from attunement to blessing. For multi-card spreads, each card can hold its own paragraph, with the closing section weaving them together into a unified love letter. The rhythm should always feel conversational, lyrical, and flowing—never rushed or abrupt.

CHAPTER 64

converting third-person to love letter

MINI WALK-THROUGH

A love-letter reading transforms abstract guidance into intimate dialogue. The shift isn't just about words—it's about perspective. Instead of the cards speaking about the querent, they speak *to* them. Below are some examples of how that shift feels in practice.

Card: Eight of Cups (moving on, soul-seeking)

Third-person: "The Eight of Cups suggests leaving behind what no longer fulfills you."

Love Letter: "I love you enough to tell the truth: this place we built together can't hold the size of your spirit anymore. I won't keep you small. Take the path that calls your name in the night; I will bless your steps."

> *Notice the move:* The neutral language of "suggests leaving behind" becomes an intimate voice that affirms the querent's courage and grants permission. The card's imagery of departure is reframed as blessing.

Card: Knight of Swords (impulsive pursuit)

Third-person: "Fast, head-driven energy; be mindful of rushing."

Love Letter: "I feel your urgency, the way you want to sprint toward answers. Breathe with me. What's real won't vanish if you slow down."

> *Notice the move:* Instead of a cautionary warning ("be mindful"), the voice validates the urgency, then gently coaxes it into balance. It becomes less about control and more about companionship.

Card: The Star (healing, hope)

Third-person: "Renewal after difficulty; faith returns."

Love Letter: "Lay your heartbreak beside the water and let me rinse it clean. Your light is already returning; keep the night open with your trust."

> *Notice the move:* The dry reassurance of "faith returns" turns into an act of ritual intimacy. The voice offers to hold the querent's pain, transforming abstract "renewal" into a tender promise of cleansing.

Card: The Tower (sudden upheaval)

Third-person: "The Tower signals sudden change or disruption."

Love Letter: "I know the ground trembles beneath you and the walls are falling away. Let them. You were never meant to live in ruins disguised as safety. On the other side of collapse is the open air of your true life."

> *Notice the move:* Destruction becomes liberation, framed with compassion and courage.

Card: The Lovers (connection, choice)

Third-person: "The Lovers represent union, values, and decisions of the heart."

Love Letter: "Your heart already knows the vow it wants to make. Do not measure it against the world's expectations. Choose the hand that steadies your spirit, the bond that makes you feel like home."

> *Notice the move:* Neutral "values and decisions" becomes a sacred invitation to trust desire.

Card: Ten of Swords (painful ending)

Third-person: "The Ten of Swords shows defeat or painful endings."

Love Letter: "I see how sharp the pain is, how final it feels. But love, you are still breathing. Let this be the last time you carry blades in your back. Dawn is rising—you will rise with it."

> *Notice the move:* Finality becomes compassion, offering hope without denying the pain.

Card: Two of Cups (partnership, harmony)

Third-person: "The Two of Cups points to partnership and connection."

Love Letter: "Beloved, the way your soul mirrors another is no accident. Cherish the hand offered; let the flow between you remind you that love is holy when it's equal."

> *Notice the move:* A textbook phrase becomes a vow of intimacy and mutuality.

Card: The Hermit (solitude, inner wisdom)

Third-person: "The Hermit advises solitude and introspection."

Love Letter: "You are not lost for stepping away. I will walk with you into the quiet, lantern in hand, so you can hear the wisdom of your own heart again."

> *Notice the move:* Solitude shifts from isolation to a guided journey of self-return.

Card: Wheel of Fortune (cycles, fate)

Third-person: "The Wheel of Fortune reflects cycles and change beyond your control."

Love Letter: "Your story is turning to a new chapter, and I am here through every spin of the wheel. Trust that even in the chaos, the rhythm of life is carrying you where you are meant to be."

> *Notice the move:* Impersonal "change beyond control" becomes reassurance of companionship and destiny.

Card: Queen of Cups (intuition, compassion)

Third-person: "The Queen of Cups signifies empathy and intuition."

Love Letter: "Your sensitivity is not weakness—it is your gift. Trust the tides of your emotions; they are the language of your magic. Your heart knows the way."

> *Notice the move:* Flat "signifies empathy" becomes a direct affirmation of worth and power.

Third-person readings often sound like summaries. Love-letter readings open like a dialogue. They soften instruction into invitation, and prediction into presence. Every card becomes less "this means..." and more "I see you, I feel you, I walk beside you."

CHAPTER 65

choosing the narrator: four beautiful options

When shifting tarot into a love-letter voice, the *who* matters as much as the *what*. The narrator frames the entire message—turning a spread into intimacy, confession, or blessing depending on the lens you choose. Here are four narrator options, with their gifts, limitations, and when you might lean toward one over another.

1. The Beloved's Higher Self

What it is: The imagined voice of the person the querent is asking about—*not* their everyday ego, but the deeper, wiser version of them.

Tone: Tender, self-aware, sometimes conflicted but earnest.

Why use it:

- Helpful when the spread shows potential but also fear, resistance, or confusion.
- Brings compassion to situations where the "real" person might be unavailable, avoidant, or defensive.
- Gives voice to the longing and truth beneath surface behaviors.

Example: "I want to meet you bravely, but I'm learning how."

Caution: Can be soothing, but make clear to the querent this is *symbolic insight*, not literal telepathy.

2. The Connection Itself

What it is: The relationship, bond, or dynamic speaking as though it were a living thing.

Tone: Expansive, collective, lyrical—like waves, gravity, or a thread.

Why use it:

- Best for complicated dynamics, on-again-off-again ties, or situations that don't fit neatly into "yes/no."
- Helpful when both partners' energies show strongly in the spread—it honors the *between*.
- Keeps focus on the pattern rather than blaming one person.

Example: "Between us lives a tide: it ebbs when we avoid truth, it floods when we speak it."

Caution: This voice can be abstract; anchor it with clear imagery so it doesn't feel too vague.

3. The Querent's Future Love

What it is: A possible partner, love, or life that awaits—not necessarily a specific person, but the embodiment of future joy.

Tone: Encouraging, hopeful, beckoning forward.

Why use it:

- Powerful for openings and possibilities, especially if the spread leans toward growth, new beginnings, or healing from the past.
- Gives querents something to move *toward*, not just away from.
- Beautiful for clients who ask "Will I ever find love?" or "What's next for me?"

Example: "I'm walking toward a life that looks like us—meet me by choosing your joy now."

Caution: Keep it open-ended; this is an invitation, not a guarantee.

4. The Archetype

What it is: The card itself—or the Major Arcana figure—speaks directly as a living presence.

Tone: Mystical, wise, often larger-than-life.

Why use it:

- Deepens readings where the archetype is strong (especially with multiple Majors in a spread).
- Helps querents connect to the mythic or spiritual dimension of their question.
- Useful when the querent's own higher self needs to hear a sacred voice beyond "romance."

Example: (The High Priestess as narrator): "I will not answer your longing with simple facts; sit with me in the quiet until the truth ripens."

Caution: Can feel intense or cryptic; best for querents open to mythic language.

How to Decide

Gentle reassurance needed? → The *Beloved's Higher Self* can soothe without excusing bad behavior.

Tangled situation with both sides showing up? → Let the *Connection Itself* speak.

Querent stuck in grief or hopelessness? → Invite the *Future Love* to call them forward.

Deep, spiritual, or mythic spread? → Let the *Archetype* step into the role.

Each narrator opens a different door. Try on more than one—sometimes the shift from one voice to another is itself a revelation for the querent.

CHAPTER 66

introducing the narrator archetypes

Once you've chosen *who* is speaking (higher self, the bond itself, future love, or archetype), the next layer is *how* they speak. Each archetype carries its own emotional palette, like choosing a filter on the lens of the reading.

Some voices are tender, some are passionate, some are sharp as a blade. None are "better" than the others—they're tools for nuance. The right narrator can deliver the same truth in a way that either softens, emboldens, grounds, or awakens the querent.

Think of this as your voice palette, you can reach for different tones depending on the spread's mood and the querent's need. Below are quick cues to help you access the Major Arcana as living narrators.

Archetype Voice Cues

Tender – soothing, receptive, lyrical

- **The Fool:** "Take my hand. Let's learn as we go."
- **The High Priestess:** "Quiet yourself—your answer is already inside."
- **The Empress:** "Come rest; love grows where you're nourished."
- **Temperance:** "Let's blend gently; balance doesn't have to hurt."
- **The Star:** "Keep the window open; dawn is finding you."

Passionate – warm, emboldening, alive in the body

- **The Magician:** "Name what you want; I'll meet the clarity you speak."
- **Strength:** "Your softness is your roar. Trust it."

- **The Sun:** "Stand bare-faced in the light—joy wants to claim you."
- **The Lovers:** "Choose with your whole chest—value aligned or not at all."

Clear-edged – honest, precise, still kind

- **The Chariot:** "Focus your will. Where you aim, you'll arrive."
- **Justice:** "The truth is sharp, but it will set you steady."
- **The Devil:** "I'm intoxicating, but I will cost you. Is that your yes?"
- **The Tower:** "I broke what wasn't true so you could breathe."

Grounded – steady, practical, safety-forward

- **The Emperor:** "Safety is sexy. Let's build what lasts."
- **The Hierophant:** "Tradition has roots; choose which nourish you."
- **The Hermit:** "Walk with me into the quiet; your lantern is waiting."
- **Wheel of Fortune:** "Life turns. Stay centered; the spin won't throw you."

Sacred – devotional, spacious, luminous

- **The Hanged One:** "Pause. What shifts if you see upside down?"
- **Death:** "This door is closed. Honor it, and step forward."
- **Judgment:** "Wake up. Your life is calling you by your real name."
- **The World:** "This chapter is complete. Bow, and walk through."

Why choose one voice over another?

- **If the querent is fragile** → Lean tender or sacred.
- **If they're stuck or avoidant** → Clear-edged cuts through the fog.
- **If they need energy or courage** → Passionate wakes the blood.
- **If they crave stability** → Grounded offers safety and direction.

The art is not just in what you say, but in *whose voice* you let speak through you. Tarot becomes theatre of the heart—each archetype lending their tone to the love letter.

CHAPTER 67

Structuring full love-letter spreads

A love-letter reading is more than a card-by-card interpretation. It's an arc—like music, it needs a beginning, middle, and closing chord. Structuring your spreads as letters helps the message flow as one continuous voice rather than disjointed fragments.

SINGLE-CARD LOVE NOTE

Structure: One card, one paragraph, moving through the letter arc (attunement → truth → tenderness → guidance → blessing).

When to use:

- Daily draws (like pulling a "love note from the universe" each morning).
- As an add-on to a larger reading when a querent needs one distilled line of intimacy.
- For Instagram/TikTok "micro-letters" where brevity makes impact.

Tone: Sweet, concentrated, like a handwritten note slipped under the door.

EXAMPLE (THE LOVERS):

"Beloved, your heart already knows what it longs for. Do not weigh yourself against what others might approve—choose the vow that steadies your soul. The right love will always feel like returning home."

CHAPTER 68
three-card "past—present—invitation"

Structure: One paragraph per card, stitched together as a single flowing letter.

1. **Past** – What shaped the love or the querent's current question.
2. **Present** – The truth of the bond or heart-space right now.
3. **Invitation** – What opens with honesty, courage, or next steps.

When to use:

- Querents wanting clarity on an ongoing relationship.
- Situations where the arc of a story (how we got here, where we are, where we go) is key.
- To validate history while also pointing toward growth.

Tone: Reflective yet directional, like a letter written across time.

EXAMPLE (THREE OF CUPS – TWO OF SWORDS – THE STAR):

Past (Three of Cups)

"My beloved, I remember how we began in laughter, how the world felt wide open when we gathered joy like it was a language only we knew. There was lightness in those days—an ease, a celebration, as if love itself had chosen us for a dance. That foundation still lives in me, the memory of how it felt to be seen and cherished without question. Whatever else has come between us, let me first honor that joy. It was real. It still hums beneath my ribs."

Present (Two of Swords)

"But now, I confess, I stand at the crossroads. My heart strains under the weight of choices I do not want to make, truths I have avoided speaking out loud. The air between us feels still, heavy with silence, as though we are both waiting for the other to act. I feel the tension of what is unsaid, the fear that honesty might shatter what remains. And yet—what is harder still is this distance that grows in the absence of words."

Invitation (The Star)

"Even so, I write this with hope. If we dare to name the truth, if we place our fears beside the water and let them be washed clean, then healing will rush in like clear water at dawn. We do not need to know the entire path—only to keep the night open with our trust, to remember that faith is not naïve, but necessary. My invitation is this: let us begin again, with honesty as our guide and tenderness as our shield. Our light is already returning."

> See how this creates more space than a single-card love note? The three parts allow for memory, confession, and vision—all stitched as one voice.

CHAPTER 69
five-card soul letter

Structure: A longer spread that reads like a full page of confession and closure.

1. How I loved you.
2. What went wrong—or what went right.
3. What I can give.
4. What I cannot give.
5. Blessing for your path.

When to use:

- For deep relational work: breakups, reunions, or long-standing questions.
- When querents crave both clarity *and* tenderness—truth that doesn't dodge, but also doesn't wound.
- As a ritual reading (full-moon journaling, closing out a relationship, inviting a new one in).

Tone: Devastatingly tender, crystal clear—reads like someone's final or first honest letter.

EXAMPLE (SIX OF CUPS – TEN OF SWORDS – KNIGHT OF CUPS – FOUR OF PENTACLES – TEMPERANCE):

1. How I loved you (Six of Cups)

"I loved you with the innocence of memory, with the part of me that wanted to believe in forever. Being with you felt like returning to a place I already knew, as if our laughter had been echoing across lifetimes, waiting for us to step into it again. My love was childlike in its purity, unguarded in its trust, willing to believe that joy could last without condition. In those moments, nothing else mattered but the sweetness we found in each other."

2. What went wrong (Ten of Swords)

"But something broke between us. The pain was sharp, final, cutting deeper than I ever thought possible. I cannot pretend it didn't pierce me, that it didn't bring me to my knees. What went wrong wasn't just one thing—it was the accumulation of silences, of betrayals both spoken and unspoken, of truths too heavy to name until it was too late. There is no denying the ending; it happened, and it hurt. I carry the scars still."

3. What I can give (Knight of Cups)

"Even so, what I can give is this: my honesty, my tenderness, my heart as it is now—still beating, still capable of offering real feeling. I can offer sincerity without games, gestures of affection that are true and unhidden. I can give the kind of love that moves forward, not backward, love that isn't afraid to wear its heart on its sleeve. This is what remains within me to give, should you wish to receive it."

4. What I cannot give (Four of Pentacles)

"What I cannot give is ownership over me. I will not clutch myself small, nor can I surrender the freedom I've worked so hard to reclaim. I cannot offer love that cages or binds; I cannot live in fear that my worth depends on your grasp. What I withhold is not affection, but the part of me that belongs only to myself —my sovereignty, my wholeness, my safety."

5. Blessing for your path (Temperance)

"And so I leave you with this blessing: may your days stretch wide in balance, may you find the healing we could not create together. May your heart remember the sweetness and soften in forgiveness, even as it learns from the pain. I hope you find the alchemy that turns wounds into wisdom, and that you walk forward lighter, steadier, and at peace. Whatever we were, whatever we are no longer, I bless your steps with grace."

> Notice how this breathes—each position feels like its own "paragraph of the letter," giving space for both confession and closure. It reads like something you'd tuck into an envelope and leave on the table after a long night of truth-telling.

CHAPTER 70
seven-card "the whole love story"

SEVEN-CARD "THE WHOLE LOVE STORY"

Shape: A letter with chapters—sweeping, lyrical, cinematic.

1. The spark (what drew me to you).
2. The promise (what we dreamed).
3. The shadow (what haunts or blocks us).
4. The mirror (what we teach each other).
5. The choice (what must be faced).
6. The release (what to let go).
7. The vow (what I bless moving forward).

When to use:

- For querents wanting the *entire story arc* of a connection, not just fragments.
- Works beautifully for romantic partnerships, but also for friendships, family bonds, or even the querent's relationship with self.
- Best for readings where depth, memory, and closure are all desired—weddings, anniversaries, endings, or turning points.

Tone: Sweeping, story-driven—reads like a novel condensed into a letter, a love story in miniature.

Example Spread: Ace of Wands – Ten of Pentacles – The Moon – Justice – Two of Cups – Death – The World

FLUENT TAROT: MATTERS OF THE HEART

1. The Spark (Ace of Wands)

"My beloved, from the first moment, something ignited. You lit a fire in me I didn't know I carried. Desire rushed in like breath to flame, wild and undeniable. You were possibility incarnate—everything felt alive the moment you walked into my world."

2. The Promise (Ten of Pentacles)

"We dreamed in permanence, didn't we? We built castles in our minds, imagined a home, a legacy, a life that would stretch far beyond us. You felt like the promise of belonging, of roots twined together, of safety and abundance shared without end. That dream was our cathedral."

3. The Shadow (The Moon)

"But shadows crept in. Doubt slithered through the cracks, and illusions tangled our truth. I lost myself in uncertainties, in stories whispered by fear and half-light. Not everything was what it seemed, and we stumbled in the fog of unspoken worries. This haunted us, even as we tried to hold steady."

4. The Mirror (Justice)

"Yet you held up a mirror I could not avoid. You forced me to see myself—where I was fair, and where I was not. You taught me that love without truth is only pretense, and that balance is not a gift but a choice. Through you, I learned accountability, the sharp and holy kind."

5. The Choice (Two of Cups)

"So now, I must choose. Do I extend my hand to meet yours in full equality, heart to heart, soul to soul? Or do I walk away from the bond that once steadied me? This love demands a decision—not halfway, not hidden, but whole."

6. The Release (Death)

"I cannot cling to what is gone. I release the version of us that no longer breathes. I let the old patterns die so that something truer might live—whether together or apart. What we were must transform, and though grief bites, I honor this ending as a doorway."

7. The Vow (The World)

"So I bless you with this vow: may your life be full, may your circles complete, may you step through every ending into richer beginnings. Whether my hand is in yours or not, I bless you with wholeness, with triumph, with freedom. This is the end of one story, and the beginning of all that waits for you."

CHAPTER 71
nine-card "letter of reckoning"

Shape: A full-bodied confession, like the kind written but never sent.

Positions:

1. How I saw you.
2. How I misunderstood you.
3. How you saw me.
4. How you misunderstood me.
5. What kept us.
6. What broke us.
7. What remains between us.
8. What cannot remain.
9. What endures (the final truth/blessing).

When to use:

- For intense dynamics, karmic ties, or soulmate/break patterns where the querent needs the whole truth.
- Beautiful for closure rituals: burning, burying, or tucking into a journal.
- Best for relationships that shaped the querent profoundly, for better or worse.

Tone: Raw, surgical, unflinching—but still holding space for blessing.

EXAMPLE SPREAD: KING OF WANDS – SEVEN OF CUPS – QUEEN OF CUPS – FIVE OF PENTACLES – THE LOVERS – THE TOWER – EIGHT OF WANDS – FOUR OF PENTACLES – STRENGTH

1. How I saw you (King of Wands)

"I saw you as fire incarnate—magnetic, unstoppable, a leader with vision. You burned bright enough that I wanted to orbit you, to believe in your direction, to let your confidence steady my own trembling hands. You looked like power, and I was dazzled."

2. How I misunderstood you (Seven of Cups)

"But I misunderstood the haze around you. I thought your dreams were promises, that your many visions meant certainty. I didn't see that you lived in illusion as much as in clarity, that not every cup you offered was real or drinkable. I mistook possibility for devotion."

3. How you saw me (Queen of Cups)

"You saw me as tender, intuitive, endlessly receptive. You read my compassion as a well that would never run dry. To you, I was a vessel for feeling—a safe harbor where you could rest when the world's demands grew heavy. You weren't wrong, but you weren't complete, either."

4. How you misunderstood me (Five of Pentacles)

"You misunderstood the cost. You didn't see how lonely it was to hold you without being held, how abandoned I felt even while you stood beside me. You mistook my resilience for invulnerability, and so you left me out in the cold without knowing it."

5. What kept us (The Lovers)

"What kept us was the choice—the pull of something that felt fated, undeniable. The sense that our souls had recognized one another long before we did. The vow we kept making, silently or aloud, to try again and again, even when we were breaking each other."

6. What broke us (The Tower)

"What broke us was truth exploding through illusion. The structures we built on half-truths and avoidance could not stand. Everything crumbled—fast, devastating, beyond repair. It wasn't malice. It was inevitability. A tower cannot stay standing if its foundation is a lie."

7. What remains between us (Eight of Wands)

"What remains is momentum—the energy of all that moved between us, still humming in the air. Messages unsent, words still ringing, the velocity of our connection that carried us far and fast. That current lingers, even if the form of us has dissolved."

8. What cannot remain (Four of Pentacles)

"What cannot remain is my clutching. I will not hoard the memory of you, nor lock myself in the cage of what once was. I cannot keep living as though love is possession. What is mine will never have to be held so tightly. I release my grip."

9. What endures (Strength)

"And yet, this endures: I am stronger because of you. Softer, too. Loving you taught me the fierceness of gentleness, the courage of staying true to myself even when tempted to disappear. Even in parting, the truth is this—you made me braver than I was, and for that, I thank you."

> This spread reads like a reckoning—every corner of the relationship examined, every misunderstanding named, every gift and wound acknowledged. It's raw, but the blessing at the end keeps it from being despairing. It's closure in letter form.

CHAPTER 72
delivering love-letter readings

The cards may carry the message, but it's the delivery that determines how the words land. A raw truth can arrive as a comfort when spoken gently, while even the sweetest blessing can dissolve if rushed or cluttered. Each medium—written, audio, or video—creates its own kind of intimacy, and choosing the right one shapes the entire experience of the reading.

Written letters are lasting. On the page, love notes breathe best when you let them move slowly: short lines, plenty of white space, sentences that feel like an inhale and an exhale. The eye needs places to rest so the heart has time to absorb. A written reading can be returned to, underlined, tucked into a journal, even placed on an altar. Ending with a clear, actionable line gives the querent something they can carry with them—"Write the boundary you'll keep even if you're lonely," or "Say yes to the invitation that feels like sunlight." These simple sentences become vows.

Audio readings are intimate in a different way. To hear a voice, unadorned and close, is like receiving a late-night voice memo from someone you trust. Here, the pacing matters most. Speak slowly, letting silence do part of the work. A gentle pause after a truth lets it resonate. One strong image per card is enough, and one clear takeaway should linger after the recording ends. Warmth carries through tone, so even unseen, a soft smile will be felt.

Video, by contrast, is presence made visible. When you look into the camera with a soft gaze, when your shoulders stay open and your body language relaxed, the querent feels as though you are across the table. A love-letter reading in this form is less about performance than presence: speak as if you're reading a letter you adore, not reciting lines. Let pauses create space; let your eyes remind them they're being seen. The right body language—the tilt of the head, the lift of a hand—becomes part of the spell.

In any form, beauty must be clear. Mystery should never collapse into vagueness: if the cards say no, say no—kindly, unmistakably. Romance should never slip into fantasy; don't invent promises the cards cannot hold. And intimacy should never become intrusion. Always name the narrator—whether it's the beloved's higher self, the connection itself, a future love, or an archetype—so it's clear whose voice is speaking. We do not borrow words from another person's mind; we let the cards craft the voice.

When in doubt, return to one grounding line. It belongs anywhere, at any moment of intensity: *"Your agency is sacred; take only what returns you to yourself."*

This reminder is the heart of love-letter readings. No matter how tender, how lyrical, how piercing the truth may be, it always leads back to sovereignty. That's how we keep the work both poetic and empowering—beautiful words that open doors, not cages.

CHAPTER 73
practice assignments (fast and potent)

Love-letter tarot isn't just theory—it's craft that lives in the body. The following practices are designed to be short but powerful. Each one takes only a few minutes, yet they shift how you speak, how you listen, and how you hold the cards.

Third-Person vs. Love Letter

1. Pull one card. Write the classic third-person interpretation you might find in a guidebook or say to a querent—"The Eight of Pentacles shows dedication and growth through practice."
2. Now rewrite it as a love letter—"Beloved, every stroke of effort is shaping you. I see your devotion, and I promise the work is not wasted."
3. Read each version out loud. Notice how your body reacts. Do you sit taller with one, soften with the other? Pay attention to the *somatic difference*—it tells you why language matters.

Kind Goodbyes with Hard Cards

1. Choose a card often feared in readings—the Tower, Death, Eight of Cups, Ten of Swords.
2. Write a goodbye in love-letter voice. Make it kind, but unmistakable. No vague metaphors, no dodging the truth.
3. Example: "I cannot meet you there. What we were has already fallen

away. Step forward into the unknown—your spirit is bigger than this ending."
4. Hard truths soften when framed with blessing. This practice trains you to deliver closure that empowers rather than devastates.

Audio Letter in 60 Seconds

- Pull three cards and frame them as Past–Present–Invitation.
- Record yourself reading them aloud as a single flowing letter. Aim for one minute. Don't over-polish; let it sound like a voice memo.
- Keep one sentence crisp and actionable—the kind that sticks in the ear.
- Example takeaway: "Say yes to the invitation that feels like sunlight."
- Listen back. Did you rush, or did you pause enough to let each truth breathe? Practice until your pacing feels gentle, not hurried.

These fast drills aren't about perfection—they're about muscle memory. With repetition, you'll begin to *naturally* slip into love-letter voice, delivering clarity and tenderness without needing to force it.

CHAPTER 74

deep practice: the full love letter

This is your invitation to move beyond a quick exercise and create a letter that could live on someone's nightstand, folded into a journal, or spoken aloud at an altar. Choose either the five-card Soul Letter or the seven-card Whole Love Story as your framework. Give yourself a quiet hour, a notebook, and space to let the words arrive.

Draw the Spread

Lay the cards out and name each position clearly (e.g., *How I loved you, What went wrong, What I can give...*). Before you write, just sit with the imagery. Imagine the narrator you'll use: higher self, the bond itself, future love, or an archetype.

Write the Letter

Treat each card as a paragraph. Don't rush—write it as if you were truly addressing someone you once loved, or still do. Let it move through confession, tenderness, honesty, and blessing. Keep the voice consistent throughout.

Example opening:

"My beloved, I loved you with the innocence of memory, with the part of me that wanted to believe in forever..."

Speak the Letter Aloud

When your draft is complete, read it as though it were meant for an audience of one. Speak slowly. Pause after each truth. Notice how your voice changes as you move from shadow into blessing. This is where the love-letter style comes alive.

Reflection

- How did writing this letter feel different from a standard reading?
- Did any part of you resist being so direct, or so tender?
- What shifted in your body when you spoke the blessing out loud?

This deep practice isn't just about honing your reader's voice. It's about learning that tarot doesn't stop at interpretation—it becomes ceremony, art, and healing.

CHAPTER 75
why this style works

Tarot can be read a thousand ways, but love-letter style readings strike a chord that ordinary interpretation rarely reaches. They touch not only the intellect but also the heart, weaving truth into language that feels like it belongs to the querent. To understand why this approach works, it helps to look at what shifts when we move from analysis into intimacy.

Empathy

Traditional tarot language often creates distance: *"The Eight of Cups suggests it's time to move on."* This phrasing is safe, but clinical—it leaves the querent watching their own life from the outside. In love-letter style, we step inside the experience and speak as though love itself is addressing them: *"Beloved, this place cannot hold your spirit anymore. I bless your steps forward."* Suddenly the reading isn't about them—it's to them. The language bypasses defensiveness and analysis, going straight to empathy. The querent feels seen, not studied.

Intimacy

Love readings are tender territory. They so often touch longing, vulnerability, heartbreak—the places we rarely show in daylight. Speaking in first-person ("I want you to know..." or "I bless your path...") gives the querent a sense of intimacy that a detached tone cannot provide. It feels like a confession whispered across the table, like a note tucked into their palm. That intimacy allows difficult truths to land without cruelty. A clear "no" spoken in love-letter voice carries compassion instead of rejection.

Poetic Flow

Love itself is not linear; it doesn't move in bullet points. It lives in metaphor, in the way we reach for symbols when plain words fall short. Love-letter style mirrors that reality. We say, *"Lay your heartbreak beside the water and let me rinse it clean,"* rather than, *"This card suggests healing is possible."* The poetic flow creates resonance. It allows the querent to feel the truth in their body, not just process it in their mind. And because poetry is elastic, it leaves room for the querent's own meaning to arise alongside yours.

Memory Anchor

Most querents will forget the technical breakdown of a spread within hours. But they will remember how they felt when the words landed. Love-letter readings linger because they activate memory through emotion. A querent might not recall that they pulled *The Star*, but they will remember: *"The letter told me to keep the window open; dawn is finding me."* This is the difference between advice and imprint. Technical language informs; love-letter language anchors.

Love-letter readings work because they collapse the gap between reader and querent, between card and heart. They do not replace technical skill—they *translate* it into language that heals. This style turns tarot into more than prediction or analysis: it becomes art, confession, and blessing, delivered in the voice of love itself.

But Does It Still Count as Tarot?

Whenever a new style emerges, someone will ask if it still "counts." Love-letter tarot, with its first-person voice and lyrical tone, can sound so different from traditional card-reading that it raises questions. If you're speaking as though the card itself—or love itself—is addressing the querent, is it still tarot? The answer is yes. In fact, it's tarot at its most essential.

Tarot Has Always Been Translation

At its core, tarot is a language of symbols. The reader's role has never been to simply state what a card "means," but to translate its image and energy into words that make sense for the querent. Whether you phrase that translation as *"The Tower signals upheaval"* or *"Beloved, I broke what wasn't true so you could breathe,"* you are still reading the same card. The difference lies in delivery, not in substance.

Tradition Meets Evolution

Tarot has always evolved. What began as a Renaissance game became an esoteric system, then a tool of psychological insight, and now a practice woven into coaching, therapy, and art. Each generation reshapes tarot to meet its own needs. Love-letter style is part of that continuum: not a rejection of tradition, but a new vessel for its wisdom. Just as the Rider–Waite deck once gave fresh imagery to ancient archetypes, this approach gives fresh voice to timeless truths.

Accuracy Is Not Lost

Some worry that speaking in love-letter form risks drifting into fantasy. But the practice only works if it remains tethered to the cards. The Eight of Cups still names departure; the Knight of Swords still warns of urgency; the Star still promises renewal. What changes is not the message, but the tone. Instead of delivering these truths like diagnoses, we offer them like confessions. Accuracy is not sacrificed; it's softened into intimacy.

The Reader's Responsibility

Love-letter tarot is not an excuse to invent stories that the cards do not support. It requires the same discipline as any reading: clarity, honesty, respect for the querent's agency. In some ways, it demands *more* discipline, because metaphor and poetry can so easily run away from truth. The reader's role is to hold the line—to let beauty illuminate the message, not obscure it.

Why It Matters

Tarot has always been about meeting people where they are. And when people come to the cards with matters of the heart—grief, longing, vulnerability—they are already cracked open. Love-letter style honors that fragility by giving the message in a form they can hold. It doesn't just inform; it nourishes. It doesn't just interpret; it blesses.

So yes, this is still tarot. It is tarot spoken in a different register: not the voice of the scholar or the analyst, but the voice of the lover, the poet, the confidant. If tarot is a mirror, love-letter tarot is that same mirror draped in tenderness—still true, but easier to face.

CHAPTER 76

when not to use this style

Love-letter tarot is tender, lyrical, and deeply moving—but not every reading calls for it. Just as poetry doesn't fit every conversation, this style shines in some contexts and strains in others. Part of being a responsible reader is knowing when to step out of the love-letter voice and into another mode of clarity.

When the Querent Needs Straight Facts

Some querents come with very practical questions: *Should I take this job? How can I budget better?* These are moments when love-letter language can feel like fluff instead of guidance. In such cases, give them the data first—timelines, choices, consequences. If you still want to bring the letter voice, save it for a closing blessing, not the bulk of the message.

When Trauma Is Fresh

If someone is actively in shock, grief, or crisis, a love-letter reading can feel overwhelming—too lyrical, too emotional, almost invasive. What they may need first is grounding: a steady voice that names reality without ornament. Later, when they are ready to process more deeply, the love-letter form can hold them. But in the acute moment, gentleness means simplicity.

When It Crosses Ethical Boundaries

Love-letter voice can be misused if readers slip into speaking *for* someone else—"He says he loves you, he just can't show it." This is not only intrusive, it's harmful. Remember: the narrator must always be named. If you're using the voice of the beloved's higher self, the connection, or an archetype, say so clearly. Never claim access to a real person's mind.

When the Cards Themselves Ask for Precision

Not every spread wants to sing. Some cards—Justice, Seven of Swords, Five of Pentacles—arrive sharp, precise, almost clinical. Forcing them into flowery lines can dilute their medicine. In these moments, let the cards speak plainly first, then layer in tenderness after.

When You Feel Strained

Finally, don't force the style if it doesn't feel natural in the moment. If you're tired, distracted, or uninspired, it's better to give a clean, clear third-person reading than a clumsy love letter. This practice requires presence. If you can't enter that space authentically, wait until you can.

Love-letter tarot is powerful because it feels *chosen*. It's not the default for every situation. Think of it as a special register you reach for when the querent is tender enough to receive it and the cards open enough to carry it. The artistry lies in knowing when to pick up this voice, and when to set it down.

CHAPTER 77

how and when to use love-letter style

The beauty of love-letter tarot isn't that it replaces other approaches—it's that it expands your toolkit. Sometimes the querent needs clarity; sometimes they need comfort. The art is in knowing when to let the cards speak like an analyst, and when to let them sing like a lover.

How to Transition Between Styles

A reading rarely needs to stay in one voice from beginning to end. In fact, blending voices often creates the richest experience:

Start in Third-Person for Orientation

Begin with clarity: *"The Two of Swords shows indecision, a heart caught between choices."* This grounds the querent and establishes credibility.

Shift into Love-Letter Voice for Heart Impact

Then translate: *"Beloved, I feel the weight of your silence. The road won't choose you back until you choose it first."* This is where the message pierces deeper.

Return to Neutral for Action Steps

Close with plain guidance: *"So, your invitation is to name the decision, even if it scares you. That's where your next step lies."*

The rhythm becomes: **fact → feeling → forward.** Each voice serves a purpose, and together they create a layered, memorable reading.

When to Use Love-Letter Style

Love-letter readings are most powerful in certain contexts:

Matters of the Heart

Any spread about love, loss, intimacy, or longing comes alive in this style. It mirrors the language of the question itself.

Moments of Vulnerability

When the querent is cracked open—heartbreak, transition, healing—the tenderness of a love letter can soothe where a blunt statement might sting.

Closing Notes or Blessings

Even in a practical spread, the love-letter voice is perfect for the last lines. You can give clear bullet-point advice, then close with: *"Your agency is sacred; take only what returns you to yourself."*

Ritual and Journaling

When a reading is part of ceremony—a full moon, a breakup ritual, a birthday reflection—this style transforms the cards into art the querent may keep, reread, or even burn as release.

Self-Readings for the Soul

Pulling a daily card? Try framing it as a love letter to yourself. Over time, this builds not only understanding of the cards but also compassion for your own journey.

You don't need to use love-letter style every time. Its magic lies in being intentional: choosing it when intimacy, tenderness, or memory will serve best. By learning to flow between voices, you create readings that are not only accurate but also unforgettable—readings that live in the heart long after the cards are shuffled away.

PART SEVEN

writing poetic yet clear readings

CHAPTER 78

why balance matters

When we step into the Love Letter voice, it's tempting to let the language sweep us away. The words want to turn lush, dripping with metaphor and imagery—and that's part of the magic. But a tarot reading isn't a poem for its own sake. It's guidance. The querent comes not just to be moved, but to be anchored.

Lean too far into poetry, and the message risks dissolving into mist. The querent may leave thinking, *"That was beautiful... but what does it mean for me?"* On the other hand, lean too far into bluntness, and the intimacy is lost. The querent may feel as though they received a weather report instead of a love letter: precise, but cold.

The sweet spot lies in the middle—language that sings and shines *and* delivers truth plainly enough to be lived. A love-letter reading should read like art, but function like a compass.

Why Too Poetic Can Fail

Poetry without clarity can leave the querent enchanted but uncertain. A line like *"The Tower is thunder in your veins, a lightning strike across your sky"* might sound gorgeous, but if it never grounds into *"This card signals a necessary ending you must walk through,"* the querent walks away dazzled but directionless. Beauty alone can blur the message.

The risk is that the reading becomes performance instead of guidance—something admired, but not lived. Querents may even misinterpret, projecting fantasies onto metaphors. Without clarity, the reading fails its purpose: to empower choice. Tarot should never leave someone spellbound but powerless.

Why Too Blunt Can Fail

At the other extreme, bluntness can flatten intimacy. A line like *"The Two of Swords means you're indecisive"* may be technically correct, but it strips the nuance from the card and the tenderness from the message. Delivered without care, blunt truths can feel like accusations.

Love readings, in particular, ask for softness. When the querent comes with their heart in their hands, they don't just need information—they need compassion. A blunt reading risks leaving them feeling scolded, judged, or dismissed, as if they've been handed a weather report instead of a love letter. Accuracy without tenderness can wound instead of heal.

The Dance Between the Two

The artistry of love-letter tarot lies in weaving clarity and poetry together.

Clarity names the truth. It gives the querent something solid to grasp—an orientation, a direction, a clear step forward.

Poetry carries that truth into the heart. It softens sharp edges, adds resonance, and makes the message memorable.

Together, they create language that is both useful and unforgettable. A good reading should feel like art that guides, a love letter that also happens to be a map.

For example:

Blunt: *"The Tower means your relationship is ending."*

Poetic: *"The Tower is thunder in your veins."*

Balanced: *"Beloved, the walls you built together are crumbling. Let them. This ending is painful, but it frees you to breathe again."*

In the balanced version, the querent knows exactly what the card means *and* feels held by the way it's spoken. This is the dance: truth made tender, guidance made beautiful.

CHAPTER 79

tips for balancing beauty with accuracy

Finding the sweet spot between poetry and clarity is an art, but it can be practiced. Here are tools you can use to keep your readings romantic *and* useful—lyrical, but never lost in mist.

Pair Every Image with a Plain Line

Metaphor opens the heart, but without grounding it can drift. For each poetic line you write, add one sentence that names the truth directly.

Poetic: *"The Tower splits the sky with lightning."*

Plain: *"This signals a sudden ending you cannot avoid."*

Balanced: *"Beloved, the lightning has struck. This chapter ends whether you're ready or not, but endings make space for your breath again."*

This pairing keeps the beauty intact while ensuring the querent knows exactly what it means.

2Anchor Each Reading with One Action Step

A love letter can soar in metaphor, but the querent needs something to *do* with it. After you've spoken the beauty, close each card (or the whole spread) with a single clear invitation.

Example: *"Say yes to the invitation that feels like sunlight."*

Example: *"Write the boundary you'll keep, even if you're lonely."*

This final step grounds the poetry in the querent's everyday life.

Limit the Metaphors

It's tempting to layer image upon image, but too many can feel cluttered. One strong metaphor per card is often more powerful than three. Choose the image that resonates most and let it breathe.

Instead of: *"The Moon is fog, shadow, tides, illusion, a dream you can't touch..."*

Try: *"The Moon is fog; you must learn to walk by trust, not by sight."*

Clean images carry farther.

Speak to the Body as Well as the Mind

Clarity names what's happening; poetry tells the querent where they'll feel it. A balanced reading often includes both.

Clear: *"This is a crossroads; you need to choose."*

Poetic: *"Your chest tightens because the silence between paths has grown too heavy."*

Together, they help the querent both understand and *feel seen*.

Use White Space and Pauses as Part of the Message

Balance isn't only about the words—it's also about pacing. In written readings, break lines often. In spoken readings, pause after the truth. The space lets the message land.

Without pause: *"The Tower is collapse but collapse is freedom."*

With pause: *"The Tower is collapse. (pause) But collapse is also freedom."*

That silence becomes part of the medicine.

Always Return to Agency

The most powerful balance comes when you pair beauty with sovereignty. No matter how lyrical the message, anchor it in choice.

Example: *"Beloved, the path that calls is not the one that cages you. Your agency is sacred; take only what returns you to yourself."*

This ensures the poetry doesn't sweep the querent into helplessness—it brings them back to their own power.

Putting It Together

Think of it this way: Clarity is the compass, Poetry is the song. One tells you where to go; the other makes the journey worth walking. Together, they turn tarot into both map and music—guidance that is lived, and language that is remembered.

CHAPTER 80

archetype voices in love-letter style

MAJORS

The best way to understand the love-letter approach is to see it in action. Below are three cards rendered in this style, each one showing how an archetype can speak as a living voice. Notice how the *Archetype Voice* frames the personality of the card, and how the *Love Letter Line* delivers that essence in a way that feels both intimate and clear.

0. THE FOOL

Archetype Voice: *The Beginner*

Why this voice: The Fool embodies openness, innocence, and risk. As archetype, it's the one who leaps without fear, inviting you to trust the unknown.

Love Letter Line: *"Take my hand. Let's learn as we go."*

How it lands: This line captures the wonder and risk of beginnings. It reassures the querent that not knowing is part of the beauty.

I. THE MAGICIAN

Archetype Voice: *The Creator*

Why this voice: The Magician channels power, focus, and manifestation. In archetype voice, it becomes the one who says, *you already have what you need.*

Love Letter Line: *"Name what you want; I'll meet the clarity you speak."*

How it lands: The card affirms agency. It transforms abstract potential into invitation, urging the querent to claim their desire.

II. THE HIGH PRIESTESS

Archetype Voice: *The Oracle*

Why this voice: The High Priestess is mystery, intuition, inner knowing. As archetype, it's the keeper of secrets who offers truth only when you're ready.

Love Letter Line: *"Quiet yourself—your answer is already inside."*

How it lands: The message feels both mystical and practical. It empowers the querent to trust their own intuition instead of looking outside themselves.

III. THE EMPRESS

Archetype Voice: *The Nurturer*

Why this voice: The Empress embodies abundance, care, and creation. In archetype voice, it becomes the lover who makes space for growth.

Love Letter Line: *"Come rest; love grows where you're nourished."*

How it lands: The line offers comfort without passivity. It makes love feel safe and generative, rooted in care.

IV. THE EMPEROR

Archetype Voice: *The Protector*

Why this voice: The Emperor stands for structure, safety, and grounded authority. As archetype, it becomes the one who steadies and secures.

Love Letter Line: *"Safety is sexy. Let's build what lasts."*

How it lands: The message reframes boundaries and responsibility as acts of devotion. It turns discipline into intimacy.

V. THE HIEROPHANT

Archetype Voice: *The Teacher*

Why this voice: The Hierophant is tradition, wisdom, and ritual. In archetype voice, it's the guide who roots you in lineage and asks what you'll carry forward.

Love Letter Line: *"There is wisdom in what came before—choose which roots will nourish you."*

How it lands: This line dignifies tradition while affirming choice. The querent feels connected to history, but not trapped by it.

VI. THE LOVERS

Archetype Voice: *The Union*

Why this voice: The Lovers embody choice, alignment, and intimacy. As archetype, it speaks as the vow itself—the commitment that asks for all of you.

Love Letter Line: *"Choose with your whole chest—value aligned or not at all."*

How it lands: The card becomes a mirror of integrity. It affirms that real love is whole-hearted and uncompromising in truth.

VII. THE CHARIOT

Archetype Voice: *The Driver*

Why this voice: The Chariot is willpower, momentum, and direction. In archetype voice, it becomes the one urging you to focus and claim the road.

Love Letter Line: *"Focus your will. Where you aim, you'll arrive."*

How it lands: The line sharpens determination. It reassures the querent that they have control, but only if they choose where to steer.

VIII. STRENGTH

Archetype Voice: *The Gentle Power*

Why this voice: Strength embodies courage through softness, resilience through tenderness. As archetype, it becomes the one who tames by love, not force.

Love Letter Line: *"Your softness is your roar. Trust it."*

How it lands: The line reframes vulnerability as strength, giving the querent permission to lead with compassion instead of control.

IX. THE HERMIT

Archetype Voice: *The Lantern-Bearer*

Why this voice: The Hermit holds solitude, wisdom, and reflection. In archetype voice, it's the guide who walks with you into the quiet.

Love Letter Line: *"Walk with me into the silence; your lantern is waiting."*

How it lands: This message removes the sting of isolation and reframes solitude as companionship with one's own wisdom.

X. WHEEL OF FORTUNE

Archetype Voice: *The Spinner of Cycles*

Why this voice: The Wheel embodies change, destiny, and the turning of seasons. As archetype, it's the voice of life's rhythm itself.

Love Letter Line: *"The wheel turns, beloved. Trust that the motion carries you where you're meant to be."*

How it lands: The line reminds the querent that change is inevitable, but not hostile—it's part of the pattern.

XI. JUSTICE

Archetype Voice: *The Truth-Teller*

Why this voice: Justice embodies fairness, clarity, and cause-and-effect. In archetype voice, it speaks sharp but kind, naming what cannot be avoided.

Love Letter Line: *"The truth is sharp, but it steadies you."*

How it lands: This message delivers accountability without cruelty, affirming that clarity brings freedom even when it cuts.

XII. THE HANGED ONE

Archetype Voice: *The Surrenderer*

Why this voice: The Hanged One teaches pause, surrender, and new perspective. As archetype, it's the voice that asks you to see differently by waiting.

Love Letter Line: *"Pause here with me; the world looks new when you're upside down."*

How it lands: This reframes delay as gift, inviting the querent to shift perspective rather than resist suspension.

XIII. DEATH

Archetype Voice: *The Releaser*

Why this voice: Death embodies endings, transformation, and rebirth. As archetype, it's the one who clears space for what must come next.

Love Letter Line: *"I had to let go of who I was, to be reborn into who we might become."*

How it lands: The line dignifies endings, naming them as part of transformation, not as annihilation.

XIV. TEMPERANCE

Archetype Voice: *The Alchemist*

Why this voice: Temperance holds balance, blending, and healing integration. As archetype, it becomes the patient guide who teaches harmony.

Love Letter Line: *"Let us blend gently; balance doesn't have to hurt."*

How it lands: The line softens the idea of compromise, reframing it as a healing act of mixing what belongs together.

XV. THE DEVIL

Archetype Voice: *The Temptation*

Why this voice: The Devil embodies desire, compulsion, and entanglement. As archetype, it becomes the seducer—the one who knows it costs you, but beckons anyway.

Love Letter Line: *"I burn for you in ways I shouldn't, but I can't let go."*

How it lands: This doesn't soften the Devil's grip; it names it. The card speaks as temptation itself, making the danger clear while showing why it feels irresistible.

XVI. THE TOWER

Archetype Voice: *The Breaker*

Why this voice: The Tower embodies disruption, collapse, and revelation. As archetype, it's the force that shatters illusions so truth can breathe.

Love Letter Line: *"I broke what wasn't true so you could finally breathe."*

How it lands: The line names the devastation without cruelty, framing collapse as a violent but liberating act.

XVII. THE STAR

Archetype Voice: *The Healer*

Why this voice: The Star carries hope, renewal, and faith after difficulty. In archetype voice, it's the gentle hand that pours light back into the night.

Love Letter Line: *"Keep the window open; dawn is finding you."*

How it lands: The message is tender and luminous, reminding the querent that hope is already on its way.

XVIII. THE MOON

Archetype Voice: *The Dreamer*

Why this voice: The Moon embodies illusion, mystery, and the pull of the unconscious. As archetype, it becomes the whisper of fog and shadow.

Love Letter Line: *"Walk with me through the fog; trust your feet more than your sight."*

How it lands: The line acknowledges uncertainty but turns it into invitation, urging trust over fear.

XIX. THE SUN

Archetype Voice: *The Radiance*

Why this voice: The Sun embodies joy, warmth, and clarity. In archetype voice, it's the lover who insists on light and celebration.

Love Letter Line: *"Stand bare-faced in the light—joy wants to claim you."*

How it lands: This line feels like blessing and permission. It turns happiness into something the querent is allowed to receive fully.

XX. JUDGMENT

Archetype Voice: *The Awakener*

Why this voice: Judgment embodies revelation, reckoning, and renewal. As archetype, it's the trumpet call that demands you rise.

Love Letter Line: *"Wake up. Your life is calling you by your real name."*

How it lands: The line is sharp but liberating—it frames accountability as the path to freedom.

XXI. THE WORLD

Archetype Voice: *The Completer*

Why this voice: The World represents wholeness, completion, and integration. In archetype voice, it's the one who blesses the end of the cycle.

Love Letter Line: *"This chapter is complete. Bow, and walk through."*

How it lands: The line gives closure with dignity, turning endings into initiations for what comes next.

CHAPTER 81

Archetype Voices in Love-Letter Style

SWORDS

Suit of Swords in Love-Letter Style

ACE OF SWORDS

Archetype Voice: *The Clarifier*

Why this voice: The Ace of Swords cuts through confusion, offering truth and mental clarity.

Love Letter Line: *"I cut the air clean—I am the moment you finally know."*

How it lands: This line gives the querent permission to claim certainty as liberation, not cruelty.

TWO OF SWORDS

Archetype Voice: *The Crossroads*

Why this voice: The Two of Swords embodies indecision and avoidance, the tension of silence.

Love Letter Line: *"Beloved, you cannot wait forever—choose the road that chooses you back."*

How it lands: It names the paralysis clearly while offering an empowering call to act.

THREE OF SWORDS

Archetype Voice: *The Wound*

Why this voice: The Three of Swords reveals heartbreak, grief, betrayal.

Love Letter Line: *"I will not pretend it doesn't hurt—you are pierced, but you will heal."*

How it lands: It validates pain honestly without leaving the querent in despair.

FOUR OF SWORDS

Archetype Voice: *The Rest*

Why this voice: The Four of Swords embodies recovery, pause, and stillness.

Love Letter Line: *"Lay your weapons down; rest is the only way forward."*

How it lands: It reframes rest as active healing, not weakness.

FIVE OF SWORDS

Archetype Voice: *The Conflict*

Why this voice: The Five of Swords is tension, hollow victory, and ego battle.

Love Letter Line: *"You could win, but at what cost? Walk away before the triumph poisons you."*

How it lands: It offers the querent agency to disengage instead of staying trapped in conflict.

SIX OF SWORDS

Archetype Voice: *The Passage*

Why this voice: The Six of Swords speaks of transition, leaving behind pain to seek calmer waters.

Love Letter Line: *"I'll carry you across—leave what hurt you on the shore."*

How it lands: It softens the sorrow of leaving with the reassurance of arrival.

SEVEN OF SWORDS

Archetype Voice: *The Trickster*

Why this voice: The Seven of Swords reveals secrecy, deception, or acting alone.

Love Letter Line: *"I slip through shadows, but secrets weigh more than truth."*

How it lands: It names the hidden act while hinting at the cost of concealment.

EIGHT OF SWORDS

Archetype Voice: *The Captive*

Why this voice: The Eight of Swords is restriction, self-limitation, entrapment.

Love Letter Line: *"Beloved, the cage isn't locked—your freedom waits when you lift your eyes."*

How it lands: It exposes the illusion of helplessness and hands power back to the querent.

NINE OF SWORDS

Archetype Voice: *The Nightmare*

Why this voice: The Nine of Swords embodies anxiety, sleepless nights, mental anguish.

Love Letter Line: *"I know the hour is dark and heavy, but morning will still come."*

How it lands: It acknowledges the torment but anchors hope without minimizing pain.

TEN OF SWORDS

Archetype Voice: *The Ending*

Why this voice: The Ten of Swords represents collapse, finality, the bottom of suffering.

Love Letter Line: *"This is the last blade, beloved—dawn is already rising."*

How it lands: It names the devastation honestly but insists on renewal.

PAGE OF SWORDS

Archetype Voice: *The Inquirer*

Why this voice: The Page of Swords embodies curiosity, restless energy, and sharp observation.

Love Letter Line: *"Your questions are your wings—follow them, even if you stumble."*

How it lands: It reframes uncertainty as courage in motion.

KNIGHT OF SWORDS

Archetype Voice: *The Pursuer*

Why this voice: The Knight of Swords is urgency, action, and sometimes recklessness.

Love Letter Line: *"I rush with you, but remember—truth won't vanish if you breathe."*

How it lands: It validates urgency while urging steadiness.

QUEEN OF SWORDS

Archetype Voice: *The Truth-Keeper*

Why this voice: The Queen of Swords is clarity, honesty, and boundary with compassion.

Love Letter Line: *"My words are sharp, but they cut only lies away."*

How it lands: It assures the querent that truth is protection, not cruelty.

KING OF SWORDS

Archetype Voice: *The Judge*

Why this voice: The King of Swords rules with intellect, fairness, and strategy.

Love Letter Line: *"I see the whole field—trust me to rule with reason and truth."*

How it lands: It frames authority not as dominance, but as clarity in service of justice.

CHAPTER 82

archetype voices in love-letter style

WANDS

Suit of Wands in Love-Letter Style

ACE OF WANDS

Archetype Voice: *The Spark*

Why this voice: The Ace of Wands ignites beginnings, creativity, passion, and raw desire.

Love Letter Line: *"I am the flame in your chest—say yes, and let me catch."*

How it lands: This line captures urgency and inspiration, empowering the querent to act on passion.

TWO OF WANDS

Archetype Voice: *The Visionary*

Why this voice: The Two of Wands is planning, dreaming, and standing at the threshold of expansion.

Love Letter Line: *"Look out across the horizon; your future waits when you dare to step."*

How it lands: It reframes hesitation as opportunity, reminding the querent they already hold the power to choose.

THREE OF WANDS

Archetype Voice: *The Explorer*

Why this voice: The Three of Wands speaks of progress, opportunity, and the journey unfolding.

Love Letter Line: *"Your ships are coming in—trust the horizon you've set your eyes on."*

How it lands: The message affirms patience while keeping the energy expansive and forward-looking.

FOUR OF WANDS

Archetype Voice: *The Celebration*

Why this voice: The Four of Wands is homecoming, joy, and shared milestones.

Love Letter Line: *"Come dance with me—here, you are safe and seen."*

How it lands: It offers reassurance of belonging, anchoring the querent in community and stability.

FIVE OF WANDS

Archetype Voice: *The Challenger*

Why this voice: The Five of Wands is competition, conflict, and clashing wills.

Love Letter Line: *"I push you not to wound you, but to sharpen your flame."*

How it lands: It reframes conflict as growth, acknowledging tension without making it destructive.

SIX OF WANDS

Archetype Voice: *The Victor*

Why this voice: The Six of Wands represents recognition, triumph, and confidence.

Love Letter Line: *"Stand tall, beloved—your light is seen, your victory deserved."*

How it lands: The card becomes a moment of affirmation, allowing the querent to bask in acknowledgment.

SEVEN OF WANDS

Archetype Voice: *The Defender*

Why this voice: The Seven of Wands is resilience, holding ground, and standing firm under pressure.

Love Letter Line: *"Hold your ground; your fire is worth protecting."*

How it lands: The line empowers boundaries and perseverance without glorifying struggle.

EIGHT OF WANDS

Archetype Voice: *The Messenger*

Why this voice: The Eight of Wands is speed, movement, communication, and rapid change.

Love Letter Line: *"I come rushing—let momentum carry you where you're meant to fly."*

How it lands: It frames urgency as natural flow, encouraging trust in movement.

NINE OF WANDS

Archetype Voice: *The Survivor*

Why this voice: The Nine of Wands represents perseverance, grit, and boundaries earned through struggle.

Love Letter Line: *"I see your scars—they are proof you're still standing."*

How it lands: It validates resilience, offering compassion while affirming strength.

TEN OF WANDS

Archetype Voice: *The Burden-Bearer*

Why this voice: The Ten of Wands embodies responsibility, exhaustion, and overwhelm.

Love Letter Line: *"You've carried enough—lay some of it down."*

How it lands: It releases the querent from obligation, turning weariness into permission to let go.

PAGE OF WANDS

Archetype Voice: *The Enthusiast*

Why this voice: The Page of Wands is curiosity, spark, and a call to adventure.

Love Letter Line: *"Follow your spark—it doesn't matter if you don't know the way."*

How it lands: It validates experimentation, encouraging joy and exploration over certainty.

KNIGHT OF WANDS

Archetype Voice: *The Adventurer*

Why this voice: The Knight of Wands is boldness, passion, and sometimes recklessness.

Love Letter Line: *"I ride fast and hot—are you ready to keep pace?"*

How it lands: It celebrates daring energy while warning gently against burnout.

QUEEN OF WANDS

Archetype Voice: *The Radiant Flame*

Why this voice: The Queen of Wands embodies charisma, confidence, and magnetic warmth.

Love Letter Line: *"Your fire lights the room—trust your glow."*

How it lands: It affirms self-worth and presence, empowering the querent to own their brilliance.

KING OF WANDS

Archetype Voice: *The Visionary Leader*

Why this voice: The King of Wands is mastery, influence, and bold vision brought to life.

Love Letter Line: *"I see farther than most; follow me, and we'll build what lasts."*

How it lands: It frames leadership as inspired guidance, giving permission to dream boldly and act decisively.

CHAPTER 83

archetype voices in love-letter style

CUPS

Suit of Cups in Love-Letter Style

ACE OF CUPS

Archetype Voice: *The Overflow*

Why this voice: The Ace of Cups is new love, emotional renewal, and sacred outpouring.

Love Letter Line: *"My heart spills over; let yourself drink."*

How it lands: It feels like an opening blessing—abundant, generous, and alive.

TWO OF CUPS

Archetype Voice: *The Mirror*

Why this voice: The Two of Cups embodies partnership, harmony, and sacred connection.

Love Letter Line: *"In you, I see myself—and in us, I see something greater."*

How it lands: It affirms both intimacy and expansion, the holiness of reciprocity.

THREE OF CUPS

Archetype Voice: *The Celebration*

Why this voice: The Three of Cups is joy, friendship, and belonging.

Love Letter Line: *"Raise your glass with me; love multiplies when shared."*

How it lands: It centers community and joy as love's fertile soil.

FOUR OF CUPS

Archetype Voice: *The Withholder*

Why this voice: The Four of Cups is apathy, disconnection, and missed opportunity.

Love Letter Line: *"I sit before abundance, but my eyes refuse to lift."*

How it lands: It names the numbness directly while nudging awareness back to gratitude.

FIVE OF CUPS

Archetype Voice: *The Mourner*

Why this voice: The Five of Cups is grief, regret, and sorrow for what's lost.

Love Letter Line: *"I bow to what is spilled, but love, don't forget what still stands."*

How it lands: It validates heartbreak while gently turning the querent toward what remains.

SIX OF CUPS

Archetype Voice: *The Memory*

Why this voice: The Six of Cups is nostalgia, innocence, and the sweetness of the past.

Love Letter Line: *"Come sit with me in the garden of before; let tenderness remind you who you were."*

How it lands: It offers comfort without trapping the querent in nostalgia.

SEVEN OF CUPS

Archetype Voice: *The Dreamer*

Why this voice: The Seven of Cups is fantasy, options, and illusion.

Love Letter Line: *"So many visions, beloved—but not all are real. Choose what your soul can touch."*

How it lands: It acknowledges the pull of possibility while urging discernment.

EIGHT OF CUPS

Archetype Voice: *The Seeker*

Why this voice: The Eight of Cups is leaving behind what no longer fulfills, walking toward soul truth.

Love Letter Line: *"I love you enough to say: this place cannot hold your spirit anymore. Walk on."*

How it lands: It blesses departure, giving courage for endings without bitterness.

NINE OF CUPS

Archetype Voice: *The Contented One*

Why this voice: The Nine of Cups is satisfaction, joy, and fulfillment of desire.

Love Letter Line: *"Look—what you wished for is here. Let yourself feel the feast."*

How it lands: It centers gratitude and permission to enjoy abundance without guilt.

TEN OF CUPS

Archetype Voice: *The Beloved Community*

Why this voice: The Ten of Cups is harmony, family, and emotional fulfillment.

Love Letter Line: *"This is love woven wide—here, you are home."*

How it lands: It feels like a blessing of belonging, making love communal and lasting.

PAGE OF CUPS

Archetype Voice: *The Dreamchild*

Why this voice: The Page of Cups is innocence, curiosity, and emotional openness.

Love Letter Line: *"My heart is wide as the sea; I bring you beginnings wrapped in wonder."*

How it lands: It offers innocence and hope, reminding the querent of love's playful side.

KNIGHT OF CUPS

Archetype Voice: *The Romantic*

Why this voice: The Knight of Cups is charm, pursuit, and emotional invitation.

Love Letter Line: *"I come with flowers and a promise—will you ride with me into the dream?"*

How it lands: It feels sweeping and romantic, but slightly idealized—perfectly true to the Knight's energy.

QUEEN OF CUPS

Archetype Voice: *The Empath*

Why this voice: The Queen of Cups embodies intuition, compassion, and deep emotional wisdom.

Love Letter Line: *"Your feelings are sacred—I hold them with both hands."*

How it lands: It validates emotional depth and turns vulnerability into holy ground.

KING OF CUPS

Archetype Voice: *The Steady Heart*

Why this voice: The King of Cups is emotional mastery, stability, and mature compassion.

Love Letter Line: *"I feel it all, but I will not drown—I will hold us steady."*

How it lands: It conveys maturity and responsibility without losing tenderness.

CHAPTER 84

archetype voices in love-letter style

PENTACLES

Suit of Pentacles in Love-Letter Style

ACE OF PENTACLES

Archetype Voice: *The Seed*

Why this voice: The Ace of Pentacles represents new beginnings in the material realm—security, abundance, and opportunity.

Love Letter Line: *"I am the seed in your palm—plant me, and I'll grow into forever."*

How it lands: It turns potential into invitation, showing the querent the tangible gift they already hold.

TWO OF PENTACLES

Archetype Voice: *The Juggler*

Why this voice: The Two of Pentacles embodies balance, adaptability, and handling multiple responsibilities.

Love Letter Line: *"Yes, it's a dance—keep moving, and you won't drop what matters."*

How it lands: It reframes struggle as rhythm, empowering the querent to trust their balance.

THREE OF PENTACLES

Archetype Voice: *The Builder*

Why this voice: The Three of Pentacles is teamwork, collaboration, and creating something lasting.

Love Letter Line: *"We build best when we build together."*

How it lands: It emphasizes partnership as strength, turning love into craft and cooperation.

FOUR OF PENTACLES

Archetype Voice: *The Keeper*

Why this voice: The Four of Pentacles represents security, control, and sometimes possessiveness.

Love Letter Line: *"I hold tight, but too much grasping can strangle what I love."*

How it lands: It acknowledges fear of loss while gently warning against clinging.

FIVE OF PENTACLES

Archetype Voice: *The Outcast*

Why this voice: The Five of Pentacles embodies hardship, exclusion, and lack.

Love Letter Line: *"I know the cold, but love—there's still light in the window."*

How it lands: It names the pain of being left out, but offers hope of shelter and belonging.

SIX OF PENTACLES

Archetype Voice: *The Giver*

Why this voice: The Six of Pentacles is generosity, balance in giving and receiving.

Love Letter Line: *"Take my hand—we rise by lifting each other."*

How it lands: It frames love as reciprocal, showing abundance as something to be shared.

SEVEN OF PENTACLES

Archetype Voice: *The Gardener*

Why this voice: The Seven of Pentacles is patience, reflection, and slow growth.

Love Letter Line: *"The fruit is coming—your waiting is not wasted."*

How it lands: It reassures the querent that patience and investment will bear results.

EIGHT OF PENTACLES

Archetype Voice: *The Apprentice*

Why this voice: The Eight of Pentacles is mastery through practice, devotion to craft.

Love Letter Line: *"Every careful stroke shapes us; love is the work we return to daily."*

How it lands: It shows love as an active practice, not just a feeling.

NINE OF PENTACLES

Archetype Voice: *The Sovereign*

Why this voice: The Nine of Pentacles is independence, abundance, and self-respect.

Love Letter Line: *"I stand in my own garden, and still—I welcome you to walk with me."*

How it lands: It validates self-sufficiency while leaving space for connection.

TEN OF PENTACLES

Archetype Voice: *The Legacy*

Why this voice: The Ten of Pentacles is wealth, family, roots, and long-term stability.

Love Letter Line: *"This is the love that outlives us—woven into home, lineage, forever."*

How it lands: It grounds the querent in the power of shared history and future.

PAGE OF PENTACLES

Archetype Voice: *The Student*

Why this voice: The Page of Pentacles is curiosity, learning, and small beginnings.

Love Letter Line: *"I hold the first coin of devotion—will you learn with me?"*

How it lands: It frames love as exploration, humble but sincere.

KNIGHT OF PENTACLES

Archetype Voice: *The Steadfast One*

Why this voice: The Knight of Pentacles is reliability, patience, and quiet devotion.

Love Letter Line: *"I'll take every step—slow, steady, but always toward you."*

How it lands: It reassures the querent of loyalty and consistency, even if romance comes without flash.

QUEEN OF PENTACLES

Archetype Voice: *The Nurturer of Home*

Why this voice: The Queen of Pentacles embodies care, provision, and grounded abundance.

Love Letter Line: *"I make warmth from what we have—your safety is my joy."*

How it lands: It makes love practical and nourishing, offering security without conditions.

KING OF PENTACLES

Archetype Voice: *The Provider*

Why this voice: The King of Pentacles is stability, prosperity, and responsibility.

Love Letter Line: *"I build what lasts—I will not waver."*

How it lands: It grounds the querent in reliability, turning love into a lasting foundation.

CHAPTER 85

practice: the love letter voice lab

This exercise helps you practice moving between archetype voice and love-letter lines until the style becomes second nature. Think of it like vocal training for your tarot.

Draw a Card at Random

Pull one card from your deck. Before checking the guide, sit with the image. Ask:

- If this card spoke as a person, who would they be?
- What mood or role do they carry? (temptation, nurturer, dreamer, judge, etc.)

Write down your instinct before looking at the library.

Speak the Archetype Voice

Read the Archetype Voice aloud from your notes or the library. Example:

- The Devil as The Temptation.
- Say it in character: seductive, magnetic, a little dangerous.

Notice how your tone shifts when you take on that archetype.

Write Your Own Love Letter Line

Before peeking at the example line, write one yourself in love-letter style. Use "I" statements and speak directly to the querent.

Example (Two of Cups): *"I reach for you, because in your eyes I finally recognize myself."*

Then compare it with the example from the library: *"In you, I see myself—and in us, I see something greater."* Notice what's similar, what's different, and where your own voice wants to come through.

Balance Poetry and Clarity

Take your line and refine it. Add one clear, grounding sentence.

- Poetic: *"I burn for you in ways I shouldn't, but I can't let go."*
- Grounded: *"This desire has a cost—ask if it's one you're willing to pay."*

Now you have a balanced message: lyrical + usable.

Embody the Delivery

Choose your medium:

- **Written:** Write it as a short paragraph, leaving space between lines.
- **Audio:** Record yourself reading the line slowly, with pauses.
- **Video:** Speak it looking into the camera with open posture.

Compare how the *same card* feels different depending on the delivery.

Reflection

After three cards, journal:

> Which archetypes came most naturally to you?
>
> Where did you get stuck—poetry, clarity, or delivery?
>
> Which style (written, audio, video) felt most alive in your body?

PART EIGHT

examples of love letter readings

CHAPTER 86

single card love note

EXAMPLES

A single card can be a quick "note from the heart." Perfect for daily practice, journaling, or giving a querent a message to carry with them. The trick is to frame the card as though a lover, soul, or guiding presence is writing directly to the querent—short, but emotionally rich.

EXAMPLE 1: ACE OF CUPS

Querent's Question: *"Am I ready to open myself to love again after heartbreak?"*

Love Letter Response:

"My beloved, my heart overflows the moment I think of you. I am brimming with beginnings, with tenderness waiting to be poured. You fear that love will undo you, but I promise it will rebuild you instead. You don't have to leap all at once—just let one drop at a time soften your spirit. I am here, overflowing, patient, certain that your heart still knows how to bloom."

How it lands: The Ace speaks as a lover offering renewal, giving hope without pressure.

EXAMPLE 2: NINE OF SWORDS

Querent's Question: *"Why do I keep replaying the past in my head at night?"*

Love Letter Response:

"I know the hours you lie awake haunted by the shadows of what you've lost. The fears circle you, whispering that you failed, that you will never be free. But listen—those voices are only echoes of your pain, not truth. Even in your nightmares, I stay with you, holding the light that morning will bring. You are not defined by what torments you. You are the dream I chase, and I will not let you vanish into the dark."

How it lands: The Nine speaks as both witness and comforter, validating the struggle while promising dawn.

EXAMPLE 3: STRENGTH

Querent's Question: *"How can I face the challenges ahead without falling apart?"*

Love Letter Response:

"You are braver than you know. The world may roar against you, but my love rises to meet your courage. I see the gentleness with which you hold your own fears, and that gentleness is your power. You do not need to crush what frightens you—only to steady it with your hand. Every tremble, every scar, every quiet breath is proof: your softness is your strength, and nothing can take that from you."

How it lands: Strength speaks as encouragement and empowerment, turning vulnerability into resilience.

> Each example shows how **one card** can answer a specific question while still feeling like a note from love itself: short, lyrical, clear, and emotionally charged.

CHAPTER 87

3-card love letter

EXAMPLES

A three-card love-letter spread gives enough room for a story to unfold. It validates where the querent has been, names the truth of the moment, and offers a blessing or next step. Each card becomes a paragraph, stitched into one flowing letter.

EXAMPLE 1: QUESTION ON LOVE

Querent's Question: *"Is there still hope for me in love, or am I too broken?"*

Cards: Six of Cups – Five of Pentacles – The Star

Love Letter Response:

Past (Six of Cups)

"My beloved, I remember the sweetness of your love, how innocence and joy once filled your days like sunlight. Love came easily then—tender, playful, alive. That memory still beats within you, proof that your heart has always known how to give and receive."

Present (Five of Pentacles)

"But now I see you standing in the cold, feeling left out of the feast of others' joy. You press your face against the window of love, believing you are unworthy to step inside. The loneliness stings, I know. Yet the door has never been locked—it waits for you."

Invitation (The Star)

"So here is my blessing: lay your sorrow beside the water, and let me rinse it clean. Your heart is not broken beyond repair. Hope is rising again, a soft light pulling you forward. Trust it. Walk toward it. Love is still waiting for you, and you are not too late."

Letter

My beloved,

I remember the sweetness of your love, how innocence and joy once filled your days like sunlight. There was a time when laughter came easily, when you trusted that affection was simple, safe, and yours by birthright. Love felt playful, alive, and unafraid. That memory still beats within you—it has not vanished, no matter what has happened since. It is proof that your heart has always known how to give and receive.

But now, I see you standing in the cold, feeling left out of the feast of others' joy. You press your face against the window, watching warmth flicker for everyone else, believing you are unworthy to step inside. Loneliness stings, I know. It whispers that you have been forgotten, that you are too broken to belong again. Yet hear me: the door has never been locked. The table has always had space for you. What keeps you outside is not the world's refusal, but the walls sorrow has built around your own heart.

And so here is my blessing: lay your sorrow beside the water and let me rinse it clean. You are not beyond repair. Your heart, though scarred, still shines, still beats, still longs. Hope is already rising for you, soft and certain as the dawn. Trust it. Walk toward it. When you do, you will find that love is not gone—it has been waiting for you, patient and steady, calling you forward.

You are not too late. You never were.

With all tenderness,

—Your Star

EXAMPLE 2: QUESTION ON CAREER/PATH

Querent's Question: *"Should I keep chasing my dream, or is it time to give up?"*

Cards: Eight of Cups – Two of Swords – Ace of Wands

Love Letter Response:

Past (Eight of Cups)

"My love, you've walked away before—leaving what no longer fed your spirit, trusting there was more meant for you. You've been brave enough to release comfort in order to seek meaning, and that courage lives in you still."

Present (Two of Swords)

"Now you sit at a crossroads, heart heavy with indecision. Fear whispers that choosing wrong will ruin everything. But silence cannot protect you forever; the only wrong choice is refusing to choose at all. You already know what calls your spirit—you've just been afraid to name it."

Invitation (Ace of Wands)

"So take this spark in your hands. Let it catch, let it blaze. This dream is not done with you—it wants you to say yes again. Begin anew, even trembling. Creation will meet you once more."

Letter

My beloved,

I see the paths you've already walked away from—the jobs, the projects, the spaces that no longer fed your spirit. You knew, even when it hurt, that staying would have starved your soul. You were brave enough to leave behind comfort in order to seek meaning, and that courage still lives in you. It has not vanished; it waits quietly, ready to rise again when you call on it.

And now you sit at a crossroads, heart heavy with indecision. Fear whispers that choosing wrong will ruin everything, that one false step will undo all your efforts. So you sit in silence, hoping the road will choose you instead. But beloved, silence cannot protect you forever. The only wrong choice is refusing to choose at all. Deep down, you already know what calls your spirit—you've simply been afraid to name it aloud, because naming it means committing yourself to it.

So take this spark in your hands. Let it catch. Let it blaze. This dream is not done with you; it has been patient, waiting for you to believe in it again. Begin anew, even trembling. You do not need to be fearless—you only need to begin. Creation will meet you the moment you say yes, and together you will build something bright enough to light your way.

With unwavering faith in you,

—Your Wand

EXAMPLE 3: QUESTION ON HEALING/CLOSURE

Querent's Question: *"How do I release the pain of this breakup and move forward?"*

Cards: Three of Swords – The Hermit – Ten of Cups

Love Letter Response:

Past (Three of Swords)

"I will not deny the wound—you were pierced, heart split open by loss. The grief was sharp, undeniable, and it cut deep. To pretend otherwise would dishonor your pain, and I love you too much to look away."

Present (The Hermit)

"Now you walk the quiet road alone. It feels isolating at times, but this solitude is not punishment—it is sanctuary. In the lantern you carry is wisdom, and in the silence, your own soul waits to speak. Stay with yourself long enough to hear it."

Invitation (Ten of Cups)

"And when you are ready, love will not only return—it will expand. A wider home, a fuller joy, a belonging that feels like family will rise to meet you. Release what is gone, and step forward into a future woven with harmony and wholeness."

Letter

My beloved,

I will not deny the wound—you were pierced, heart split open by loss. The grief was sharp, undeniable, and it cut deep. To pretend otherwise would dishonor your pain, and I love you too much to look away. I see the tears you did not let fall, the silence you tried to keep, the weight of absence pressing against your chest. What you lost mattered, and so the ache matters too.

Now you walk the quiet road alone. At times it feels like punishment, as though you've been abandoned in the dark. But hear me: this solitude is not exile—it is sanctuary. The lantern you carry glows with a wisdom only you can kindle. In this silence, your soul is whispering truths you could never hear in the noise of love's clamor. Stay with yourself long enough to listen. This is not emptiness; it is sacred space.

And when you are ready, love will not only return—it will expand. What waits for you is wider than what was lost: a home, a harmony, a joy that feels like family. The Ten Cups are not just romance, but belonging in its truest form, woven with laughter, safety, and shared light. Release what has already gone, and step forward, trembling if you must, into a future rich with wholeness. You will not walk it alone forever.

With infinite tenderness,

—Your Cups

These three examples show how a three-card spread becomes a mini love letter: part confession, part truth-telling, part blessing. Enough detail to feel cinematic, but short enough to carry in the heart.

CHAPTER 88

5-card soul letter

Spread Positions

1. How I see you
2. What I feel for you
3. What holds me back
4. What I long for
5. What I promise

EXAMPLE ONE

Queen of Cups – How I see you

"My beloved, I see you as someone whose heart holds oceans—vast, deep, unafraid to feel. You have always been tender, intuitive, the kind of soul who can sit with another's pain and still find beauty in it. Your love has never been shallow. To me, you are water itself: nourishing, gentle, and strong enough to carve stone."

Two of Cups – What I feel for you

"What I feel when I think of you is not simple affection—it is reflection. You were the mirror where I first saw my truest self, and in our bond I recognized something sacred. You were not just a partner; you were the other half of a vow my spirit whispered long before I could name it. My love for you still feels holy, as though in loving you I was closer to something greater than both of us."

The Moon – What holds me back

"And yet, I am lost in shadows. The Moon confuses me, filling my nights with illusions I cannot tell from truths. I am haunted by uncertainty, afraid of what I might find if I look too closely. My memories blur with my longings, my fears with my desires. I do not always trust myself to know whether I miss you or the dream of you."

Four of Pentacles – What I long for

"Still, part of me longs to hold on. I clutch the memory of you as though letting go would mean losing myself. I want to keep you, to protect what was ours, to believe that what I once claimed could still belong to me. I know there is danger in grasping too tightly, but the longing to preserve even a fragment of what we shared is hard to release."

Temperance – What I promise

"And so I promise this: to find balance, even if it takes me years. To learn how to blend what was with what is, to temper the ache with patience and grace. I cannot promise to stop loving you, but I can promise not to let that love poison me or bind you. I vow to let healing guide me, to soften what is raw, until all that remains is gentleness between us."

The Combined Love Letter

My beloved,

I see you as someone whose heart holds oceans—vast and unafraid to feel. You have always been tender, intuitive, the kind of soul who can cradle pain without breaking under its weight. To me, you are water itself: nourishing, gentle, and strong enough to carve stone. (Queen of Cups)

When I think of you, I still feel the bond that made me whole. You were the mirror where I first saw myself clearly, the vow my spirit kept even when my body faltered. Our love was not ordinary—it was sacred, and in its reflection I felt closer to the divine. (Two of Cups)

And yet, I stumble in shadows. My nights are filled with illusions I cannot untangle—dreams that blur with memory, fears that masquerade as truth. The Moon clouds me, and I cannot always tell if I miss you, or only the dream of you. (The Moon)

Still, I long to hold on. I clutch the memory of you like a coin pressed in my fist, unwilling to release what once felt like mine. I know that love cannot be preserved by grasping, and yet my spirit aches to keep even a fragment of what we were. (Four of Pentacles)

And so I promise this: to seek balance, to walk with patience and grace. I promise to let healing weave between us until the sharp edges soften. I cannot promise to stop loving you, but I can promise to let that love evolve into something gentler—no longer a chain, but a blessing. (Temperance)

You are still my mirror, still my ocean, still the echo that calls me forward. If love has a memory, then know this: I remember you. And I carry you, even as I learn how to release you.

With enduring tenderness,

—Your Soul

EXAMPLE TWO

Querent's Question: *"What is the truth of this new relationship beginning in my life?"*

Cards: The Fool – Ace of Wands – Nine of Swords – Lovers – World

The Fool – How I see you

"My love, I see you as the beginning of everything—fresh, open, willing to leap into the unknown with me. You carry a lightness that makes the future feel less like a burden and more like an adventure. You are possibility itself, a companion in risk and wonder. Being with you feels like standing on the edge of a cliff, terrified and exhilarated, knowing the only way forward is to jump."

Ace of Wands – What I feel for you

"When I think of you, fire catches. My whole spirit blazes with the spark you bring. You awaken a desire in me to create, to begin, to build something that has never existed before. My passion is restless, rushing to meet you, burning hot enough to light the path ahead. To feel for you is to be alive in every nerve, every breath, every dream."

Nine of Swords – What holds me back

"And yet, as much as I burn for you, fear presses in on me. I lie awake with questions I cannot silence, haunted by the thought that it could all collapse before it truly begins. Doubt scratches at the edges of my joy, whispering every possible failure. I worry that I will ruin it, or that it will ruin me. My mind circles shadows, even as my heart longs for light."

Lovers – What I long for

"Still, what I long for is simple and holy: to choose you with my whole chest, to align with you in truth, to make no vow smaller than everything. I crave a love that is more than passion—that is integrity, choice, and devotion. I want to stand with you in clarity, knowing that this is not just desire but alignment, the deep and honest yes of soul to soul."

World – What I promise

"And so this I promise: if we walk this path together, I will see it through to fullness. No half-measures. No false endings. I vow to complete the cycle, to stay until the work of love becomes wholeness. With you, I will step into completion, not as two halves searching for more, but as two whole beings weaving a greater whole together."

The Combined Love Letter

My beloved,

I see you as the beginning of everything—fresh, open, willing to leap into the unknown with me (The Fool). You make the future feel less like a weight and more like an invitation. To stand beside you is to feel the world open like a door, daring me to step through.

When I think of you, fire catches. My body and spirit blaze with the spark you bring (Ace of Wands). You awaken creation itself in me—the urge to dream, to act, to build a life that is not ordinary but extraordinary. Desire becomes more than a feeling in your presence; it becomes momentum.

And yet, fear does not leave me. I lie awake at night, haunted by the thought that it could all collapse, that what begins so brightly might still end in ashes (Nine of Swords). My mind circles shadows, whispering every failure before it happens. The more I long for you, the more fragile it feels.

Still, my heart insists: what I long for is to choose you with my whole chest (Lovers). I want a love that is both passion and alignment, both fire and vow. To look at you and say yes, fully, without hesitation, without compromise. To love you not just with feeling, but with truth.

And so this I promise: if we walk this path, I will see it through (World). I will not vanish halfway, nor fracture the vow. With you, I will step into completion —no longer wandering, no longer uncertain. Only whole. Only home.

With everything in me,

—Your Soul

> Both examples show how five cards become a *complete letter*: layered, confessional, and deeply human. Each paragraph is a heartbeat, together creating something the querent can hold onto long after the reading.

CHAPTER 89

tones & variations

ONE SPREAD, MANY VOICES

One of the most powerful truths of tarot is that the same set of cards can hold many different layers. A spread is never locked into a single interpretation—it breathes, it bends, it adapts to what the querent most needs. The reader's intuition becomes the lens that focuses the light.

This is especially true in love-letter style readings. A card like the Eight of Cups may speak of heartbreak and endings, but it may also bless the courage of moving on. The Two of Swords may reveal painful indecision, or it may dignify the pause before clarity. The Ace of Wands may be the spark of a new romance, or it may remind the querent that they carry their own fire. None of these perspectives are "wrong." Each is a facet, and the artistry of the reader is knowing which facet to bring forward.

Tone is everything. The same three cards can become a romantic promise, a sobering warning, or a love note to the self. Choosing which note to strike doesn't mean inventing new meanings—it means leaning into one current of truth that already flows through the cards.

In the pages ahead, you'll see how a single three-card spread can transform into three very different letters: one hopeful and romantic, one shadowed with truth, and one empowering the querent to return to themselves. These examples show that tarot isn't static—it's a living language, and you as the reader get to choose which voice speaks loudest.

Example: Three Tones from the Same Spread

ROMANTIC, POSITIVE EMPHASIS

Querent's Question: "Should I keep chasing my dream of love?"

Love Letter Response:

My beloved,

You have already been so brave. I see the paths you've walked away from, the loves and lives you left behind because they no longer fed your spirit (Eight of Cups). That choice took courage. It showed the world—and yourself—that you will not settle for crumbs when your soul longs for a feast. That moment of departure was not failure; it was a declaration of your worth.

Now you stand at a crossroads, heart heavy with silence (Two of Swords). You feel the weight of choosing, afraid that one road might bring joy and the other regret. But hear me: this is not punishment, it is a sacred pause. The space before clarity is part of the unfolding. Even in your uncertainty, you are gathering strength. Trust that the decision you make will rise from truth, not fear.

And when you are ready to step forward, the fire will catch (Ace of Wands). A new beginning already waits for you—bright, passionate, alive. This is not the echo of an old story but the first breath of a new one. Desire, joy, connection: they are not behind you, they are waiting just ahead. Love has not abandoned you; it is circling closer, ready to blaze the moment you open your hands to receive it.

So yes, my love, keep chasing. Not with desperation, but with the same courage that has already carried you this far. What you seek is seeking you. Step forward, and let the flame rise to meet you.

With all tenderness,

—Your Soul

Tone: Encouraging, romantic, hopeful. The cards become affirmations of new love on the horizon.

ROMANTIC, NEGATIVE/SHADOW EMPHASIS

Querent's Question: "Does this connection have a future?"

Love Letter Response:

My beloved,

I see the trail of loves left behind you (Eight of Cups). I see the ache of searching for what could never hold your spirit, the disappointments that taught you what love should feel like by showing you what it is not. You have been brave enough to walk away before, even when it broke your heart, and that courage still lingers in you now. It whispers quietly that you cannot stay in what starves your soul.

And yet, here you stand in silence, caught between choices you cannot name (Two of Swords). Your heart already knows there is a decision waiting, but fear has wrapped itself around you like a blindfold. You hope that if you delay long enough, the answer will reveal itself without the cost of action. But love does not choose for us—waiting too long is its own kind of loss. Silence becomes its own answer, and it is rarely the one we long for.

Yes, I see the passion that flares hot and bright between you (Ace of Wands). Desire sparks quickly, fierce enough to consume you for a night, maybe even a season. The flame warms you, yes—it thrills, it excites, it reminds you that you are still alive. But beloved, ask yourself: does it light your way forward? A flame without roots can dazzle but not endure. It burns brightly, but without fuel, it will fade into smoke.

So I will not lie to you. This connection may carry heat, but heat alone does not promise a future. Only you can decide if the spark you hold is worth tending—or if your spirit deserves a fire that will keep you warm long after the first blaze has dimmed.

With clarity and compassion,

—Your Soul

Tone: Honest, sobering. The cards tilt toward endings, warnings, or instability.

EMPOWERING / SELF-LOVE FOCUS

Querent's Question: "What do I most need to know for myself right now?"

Love Letter Response:

My beloved,

I honor your courage in leaving behind what no longer fed your soul (Eight of Cups). Walking away is never easy, even from what hurts us, and yet you chose growth over comfort. You chose truth over familiarity. That was an act of self-love so profound that even if no one else applauded it, the universe took notice. You proved to yourself that you can say no when your spirit whispers that it deserves more. That choice still echoes in your bones as proof of your strength.

Now you stand in the space between—two paths stretched before you, silence pressing for an answer (Two of Swords). It feels heavy, I know. The weight of decision presses on your heart. But hear me: this moment is not weakness. This pause is power. You are not failing by hesitating; you are gathering yourself, listening, waiting for the inner yes that feels steady and whole. No one else can choose this for you, and that is your gift. You are the one who decides.

And when you choose, your spirit will blaze with creation once more (Ace of Wands). The spark is already in your hands, waiting. It is not a gift someone else must bestow, not a permission slip from the outside world. It is yours, burning inside you, longing to be claimed. You are the fire. You are the passion. You are the beginning you've been waiting for.

So trust yourself. You are not broken, not behind, not lost. You are on the edge of your own becoming, and the only step left is the one you will choose.

With all faith in your fire,

—Your Soul

Tone: Empowering, self-focused, resilient. The cards become about self-worth, choice, and agency.

SEE HOW THE SAME CARDS BECOME:

Romantic & hopeful (positive focus)

Romantic but sobering (shadow focus)

Empowering & self-love (agency focus)

This is the heart of intuitive reading: the spread doesn't *force* a message; it *offers a range*, and the reader chooses what serves the querent best.

CHAPTER 90

practice prompts

These exercises are designed to help you embody the love-letter voice in real time. Think of them as training the "muscle" of intuition and language—each one stretches you in a different way.

1. SINGLE-CARD, THREE TONES

Prompt: Pull one card and write three different love notes with it—one romantic, one bittersweet, one empowering.

A single card is never flat. The Fool can be a tender invitation to leap, a bittersweet reminder of risks taken, or an empowering declaration that freedom is your birthright. Practicing tonal shifts teaches you flexibility. It also helps you notice what the querent most needs—hope, truth, or agency.

- Romantic → Let the card speak as a lover calling the querent closer.
- Bittersweet → Lean into what is tender, lost, or difficult, but write it with compassion.
- Empowering → Center the querent's agency, reminding them they hold the power.

No card has only one "note." You are the musician who chooses the melody.

2. THREE-CARD PAST/PRESENT/FUTURE LOVE LETTER

Prompt: Pull three cards and write a love letter that flows in time:

- Past: What shaped the love or the heart.
- Present: The truth of the bond now.
- Future: The invitation or opening ahead.

This spread helps you practice *narrative flow*. Instead of reading cards as isolated, you weave them into a story. Love-letter style is strongest when it feels like a single voice unfolding, not three separate bullet points.

- Give each card its own paragraph.
- Use transitions ("But now… / Still, I write this…") to make the letter seamless.
- Imagine the letter as something the querent could fold into a pocket and read again.

Practice stitching multiple cards into one continuous, emotional arc.

3. FIVE-CARD FULL SOUL LETTER

Prompt: Pull five cards and assign them roles such as: *How I see you, What I feel, What holds me back, What I long for, What I promise.* Then write a full-page love letter from start to finish.

Five cards are enough to create depth, complexity, and closure. This spread asks you to move from simple notes to a layered confession—something that feels like an actual letter, complete with beginning, middle, and end.

- Let each card become a paragraph.
- Keep the voice consistent (lover, higher self, archetype, etc.).
- End with a line of blessing or promise—a "closing chord" that resonates.

This exercise trains you to handle longer readings without losing intimacy or clarity.

> **Pro Tip for All Three Exercises:** Read your letters aloud after writing them. Notice how they feel in your body—do they sound like truth? Do they land like intimacy? Your voice will tell you when you've found the balance.

CHAPTER 91

reflection

Love Letter readings live in a wide spectrum. Sometimes they are just a breath—a single card whispering one tender sentence, like a note tucked into a pocket. Other times they expand into something lush and lyrical, pages long, where five or more cards pour out a confession that feels as intimate as a handwritten letter sealed with wax. Both are equally true, equally powerful. The art is not in the length, but in the feeling it leaves behind.

This style of reading shifts tarot from being *about* someone to being *for* them. It transforms analysis into intimacy. A card is no longer a distant signpost but a voice speaking directly to the querent's heart: *I see you. I want you to know this. I bless your next step.* It isn't just information—it's devotion in words.

The more you practice, the more fluid this voice becomes. At first, it may feel like translating: you'll pull a card, pause, and think, *What would the lover say here? What would the soul whisper?* Over time, the voice will arrive more quickly, as though the cards themselves are dictating the letter through your hands. You'll find that the High Priestess doesn't need interpretation—she will simply say, *"Quiet yourself, the answer is already inside."* The Tower will sigh, *"I broke what wasn't true so you could finally breathe."* The words will flow with less effort because you've trained your ear to listen in this way.

One of the unexpected gifts of this style is how much it lingers. Querents may forget the exact cards you pulled, or even the structure of the spread, but they will remember how the letter made them feel. They'll carry a line with them for days, weeks, sometimes years: *"Your softness is your roar." "You are the fire." "What you seek is seeking you."* Love-letter tarot doesn't just deliver a reading—

it leaves a memory, a touchstone of language they can return to when their courage falters.

And perhaps the most beautiful part: this practice isn't only for querents. As you work with it, you'll find the voice begins to speak to you as well. The cards will write you love letters when you pull for yourself, reminding you of your own strength, your own tenderness, your own agency. The line that moves your querent to tears may also be the one you needed to hear. In this way, the practice becomes reciprocal—you are not only writing for others, but being written through.

So whether it is a quick daily pull or a full soul confession, let yourself enter the voice fully. Trust the mix of clarity and poetry, of tenderness and truth. Let the cards speak as a lover, as a guide, as the higher self who blesses without judgment. And when you close a letter, remind both yourself and your querent:

Your agency is sacred. Take only what returns you to yourself.

Because in the end, that's what a love letter truly is—not a command, not a forecast, but a reminder that you are already worthy of the love you seek.

CHAPTER 92

reflection exercise

WRITING A LOVE LETTER TO YOURSELF

This practice is simple, but profound. You are not only the reader—you are also the beloved. The voice you've been channeling for others can also be a mirror for your own heart.

Pull a Card

Choose one card from your deck. Trust what rises. This card will act as the narrator of your love letter.

- If you pull the **High Priestess**, let her speak as the quiet inner voice.
- If you pull the **Strength**, let her remind you of the power in your tenderness.
- If you pull the **Eight of Cups**, let her bless your courage in walking away.

Write as the Voice of Love

Without overthinking, let the card speak directly to you. Begin with:

"My beloved, I see you..."

Let the words flow for a few minutes. Don't worry about being perfect—let it be messy, lyrical, raw. This is a letter, not a report.

Read it Aloud

Give the words back to yourself with your own voice. Notice how they land in your body. Do you feel relief? Softness? Power? A tear rising? That's how you know the letter found its mark.

Keep or Release

If the letter feels like a blessing you want to carry, tuck it somewhere safe (journal, altar, wallet, mirror).

If the letter feels like closure, burn it, tear it, or release it to water. Trust the ritual to hold it for you.

> This practice shows that the love-letter voice isn't just a tool for readings—it's also a form of self-tending. When the cards write through you to you, they become both mirror and balm.

PART NINE

tarot & music in love readings

CHAPTER 93

why music works in love readings

Love and music are inseparable. From the moment we first hum along to the radio, we're steeped in it—every ballad, anthem, or late-night song is about love in some form: longing, heartbreak, passion, devotion. Even the tracks that aren't "love songs" still brush up against it—loneliness, freedom, desire, loss. Music bypasses logic. It doesn't ask you to analyze—it sweeps you up, slips under the skin, and goes straight to the body, the memory, the heart.

Tarot works in much the same way. A card isn't only an intellectual symbol; it's an emotional trigger. The Tower doesn't simply "signify disruption." It feels like a crashing chord in your chest, a sound that shakes your ribs. The Lovers aren't just about "choice." They echo like a duet you can't stop singing—two voices weaving into harmony or pulling apart in tension. Tarot, like music, is an experience as much as it is a message.

This is why the pairing is so natural. When you bring music into a love reading, you add resonance. A querent may forget your technical breakdown of the Seven of Cups—but they'll never forget when you smiled and said, *"This feels like that lyric—too many choices, too many voices, I can't decide."* Suddenly, the card doesn't sit flat on the table. It vibrates in their body, looping in their mind like a song they can't shake. The card becomes unforgettable.

Because music is sticky. It attaches emotion to experience. One melody can carry us back ten years in a heartbeat. One chorus can remind us of a person we've tried to forget. One verse can make us ache for someone we haven't met yet. Songs are containers for memory and feeling, and when we link them to tarot, we're not only interpreting—we're anchoring. We're giving our querents a way to carry the reading with them long after the cards are shuffled back into the deck.

Music makes tarot sing. It turns archetypes into ballads, spreads into playlists, and readings into soundtracks. And just as every relationship has its playlist—the songs you claimed together, the ones you can't listen to without tears, the ones that still make you laugh—every tarot card carries a song of its own, waiting to be heard.

To weave music into tarot is to remind us that love is never just an idea. It is rhythm and pulse. It is melody and harmony. It is the way a lyric lodges in your chest the same way a lover's touch once did. And when you bring those echoes into your readings, you create an experience that doesn't just tell a querent what love means—it lets them *feel* it.

CHAPTER 94

practical ways to weave music into readings

1. ASSIGN SONGS TO CARDS

Once we understand that music and tarot move through the heart in the same way, the next step is learning how to weave them together. There's no single formula—you don't need to be a musician or know every lyric by heart. All you need is curiosity and a willingness to let songs become another language in your readings. Here are some ways to invite music into your tarot practice:

1. Assign Songs to Cards

Every tarot card has a voice, and many of them already echo in the songs we know by heart. The Three of Swords is a breakup ballad—the kind you scream-sing in the car when you can't stop replaying what went wrong. The Six of Cups could be a nostalgic oldie, the song that takes you back to summer nights and first crushes. The Strength card? That's the anthem you play when you need to remind yourself that tenderness is still power.

When you start linking songs to cards, something clicks—the archetype gains a soundtrack. The next time you pull that card, you may hear the chorus in your head, and so will your querent when you share it. Suddenly the message isn't just intellectual—it's embodied. It has rhythm, tone, and memory attached to it.

This works because songs carry emotional shorthand. One lyric can tell the whole story of a card. One beat can pull a querent into the mood before you've even explained. By giving the card a soundtrack, you make it unforgettable.

Examples:

Seven of Cups → *"Should I Stay or Should I Go?"* by The Clash (indecision, too many choices, restless energy).

The Star → *"Fix You"* by Coldplay (healing, hope, light returning after loss).

Knight of Wands → any wild road-trip anthem—fast, reckless, irresistible, here for the thrill.

Ten of Cups → *"Home"* by Edward Sharpe and the Magnetic Zeros (belonging, joy, love that feels like family).

The Devil → a dark, addictive track with heavy bass—the kind that makes you want to dance even though you know it might break you.

Wheel of Fortune → *"You Can't Always Get What You Want"* by The Rolling Stones (cycles, fate, and the bittersweetness of change).

How to Practice:

- Pick a single card and ask yourself: *If this were a track on a soundtrack, what would it sound like?*
- Think of the mood first (joyful? heartbreaking? chaotic?) and then match it with a song that makes you feel the same way.
- Over time, build your own "tarot playlist" deck—78 songs you can use as shorthand in your readings.

The point isn't to get the "perfect" song. It's to capture the *feeling* of the card. The song becomes a bridge between the card's meaning and the querent's body.

CHAPTER 95

tarot playlist starter kit: the majors

The Fool → *"Born to Run"* – Bruce Springsteen
(Leaping into the unknown, reckless joy, freedom calling.)

The Magician → *"I've Got the Power"* – Snap!
(Resourcefulness, charm, the thrill of making things happen.)

The High Priestess → *"Breathe Me"* – Sia
(Intuition, mystery, the quiet pull inward.)

The Empress → *"Halo"* – Beyoncé
(Nurture, abundance, the overwhelming beauty of love.)

The Emperor → *"Respect"* – Aretha Franklin
(Authority, stability, the demand to be seen and honored.)

The Hierophant → *"Like a Prayer"* – Madonna
(Tradition, ritual, faith expressed through devotion.)

The Lovers → *"I Choose You"* – Sara Bareilles
(Aligned love, conscious choice, the joy of devotion.)

The Chariot → *"Don't Stop Me Now"* – Queen
(Momentum, willpower, the unstoppable forward drive.)

Strength → *"Fight Song"* – Rachel Platten

(Gentle power, courage, finding strength in tenderness.)

The Hermit → *"Sound of Silence"* – Simon & Garfunkel

(Solitude, wisdom, the voice you only hear in quiet.)

Wheel of Fortune → *"You Can't Always Get What You Want"* – The Rolling Stones

(Change, cycles, the bittersweet truth of fate.)

Justice → *"Man in the Mirror"* – Michael Jackson

(Clarity, truth, responsibility, facing oneself.)

The Hanged One → *"Let It Be"* – The Beatles

(Surrender, stillness, release into what is.)

Death → *"The End of the World"* – Skeeter Davis

(Transformation, endings that break and remake us.)

Temperance → *"Landslide"* – Fleetwood Mac

(Balance, integration, the gentle flow of time and healing.)

The Devil → *"Toxic"* – Britney Spears

(Temptation, obsession, the sweet trap you can't resist.)

The Tower → *"It's the End of the World As We Know It"* – R.E.M.

(Collapse, shock, the chaos that clears space for renewal.)

The Star → *"Fix You"* – Coldplay

(Hope, faith, the light that returns after loss.)

The Moon → *"Boulevard of Broken Dreams"* – Green Day

(Illusion, longing, walking through confusion and shadow.)

The Sun → *"Here Comes the Sun"* – The Beatles

(Joy, clarity, renewal, warmth you can trust.)

Judgment → *"Shake It Out"* – Florence + The Machine

(Reckoning, awakening, the call to rise and release the past.)

The World → *"Circle of Life"* – Elton John

(Completion, wholeness, the cycle that brings you home again.)

CHAPTER 96

practical ways to weave music into readings

2. BUILD PLAYLISTS FOR SPREADS

Think of a spread as a playlist. Each card becomes a track, and together they create the mood of the reading. A three-card "past/present/future" spread isn't just three cards—it's three movements of one song: the opening verse that sets the tone, the chorus that hits the heart of the story, and the bridge that carries us into what's next. A five-card soul letter might read like a carefully sequenced album, where every track matters, each one layering onto the last until the story feels whole.

When you work this way, you're not just interpreting cards—you're curating an *experience*. Just as a playlist can carry us through grief, hype us up for a new chapter, or hold us steady during heartbreak, a tarot spread becomes not just information, but a soundtrack for the querent's life.

This practice can live in metaphor—*"These three cards feel like three tracks on the same record"*—or it can be literal. After a session, you might create an actual playlist for your querent: five songs that echo the messages in their reading. They can return to it whenever they need to reconnect with what came through in the cards.

It's one thing to say, *"You're stepping into new beginnings."* It's another to say, *"This moment in your life feels like the song 'Dog Days Are Over.' Play it when you forget what's rising for you."* Suddenly, the reading doesn't vanish the moment the querent leaves. It lives on in sound, in rhythm, in memory.

Example: A three-card "Past–Present–Future" spread might sound like this:

Past (Six of Cups): *"Summer of '69"* by Bryan Adams (nostalgia, memory, first loves).

Present (Five of Cups): *"Someone Like You"* by Adele (heartbreak, loss, mourning).

Future (The Star): *"Unwritten"* by Natasha Bedingfield (healing, renewal, hope).

Together, these aren't just three cards. They're a playlist—a mini love story told in sound.

Playlists are deeply personal. We already use them to mark seasons of our lives: the breakup playlist, the road trip playlist, the falling-in-love playlist. By framing a tarot spread as a playlist, you tap into that existing relationship with music. You're giving your querent not only interpretation, but something they can press play on whenever they need reminding.

> Pro tip: Encourage querents to add *their own songs* to the playlist after the reading. The deck may start it, but their heart completes it. That way, the reading keeps growing long after the cards are put away.

CHAPTER 97
the love story playlist spread ♪♫♪

Map the emotional arc of a love connection through music and tarot, turning the reading into a living soundtrack.

CARD POSITIONS

Card 1 Track One – The Opening Verse

How this story began. The first notes of attraction, the spark that set everything in motion.

Card 2 Track Two – The Chorus

The heartbeat of the relationship. What keeps repeating, what the core rhythm really is.

Card 3 Track Three – The Bridge

The turning point. What shifted, challenged, or redefined the connection.

Card 4 Track Four – The Breakdown

What threatens harmony. The dissonance, the conflict, the shadow side that can't be ignored.

Card 5 Track Five – The Outro

Where this love is leading. The closing notes, the invitation to carry forward.

HOW TO READ IT

Musical Frame: Treat each card as if it were a song. Ask yourself: *If this card were on a soundtrack, what would it sound like? What lyrics would it sing?*

Literal Layer: You can assign an actual song to each card (from your tarot playlist or intuitively in the moment).

Querent's Input: Invite them to add their own songs—maybe one that already feels like "their song" as a couple, or one that captures how they're feeling now.

EXAMPLE READING

Querent's Question: *"What's the soundtrack of my relationship with Sam?"*

Track One (Ace of Cups): *"At Last"* – Etta James (the feeling of new love pouring over).

Track Two (Two of Pentacles): *"Love is a Battlefield"* – Pat Benatar (the rhythm of juggling, love as both joy and struggle).

Track Three (Tower): *"Back to Black"* – Amy Winehouse (the turning point of heartbreak and collapse).

Track Four (Devil): *"Toxic"* – Britney Spears (desire and entanglement, knowing it's unhealthy but hard to let go).

Track Five (Temperance): *"Landslide"* – Fleetwood Mac (a softer balance, integration, healing as the final note).

How it lands: The querent walks away not only with a card interpretation but with a *playlist* they can return to—an echo of their love story captured in sound.

> Pro tip: After the spread, encourage the querent to literally put these songs into a playlist. That way, the reading doesn't end with the cards—it keeps playing, reminding them of the message every time they press "repeat."

CHAPTER 98

practical ways to weave music into readings

3. INVITE THE QUERENT'S SONG

Sometimes the most powerful music in a tarot reading isn't the track you choose—it's the song the querent brings with them. Music is personal in a way few other things are. A melody that makes one person cry might feel neutral to another. A chorus that sounds like heartbreak to you might sound like triumph to them. By inviting the querent's own soundtrack into the reading, you give them agency in shaping the story, and you tap into an emotional shorthand already alive in their body.

You can begin simply. Ask: *"What's the song that feels like this relationship right now?"* or *"What's the track you've had on repeat this week?"* Their answer becomes a lens through which every card in the spread can be read. If they name a heartbreak anthem—say Adele's *"Someone Like You"*—then the **Five of Cups** no longer carries only symbolic weight. It vibrates with the ache of that ballad, the lyric that haunts them, the nights they've sat with that song on loop. If they name an upbeat love song—like *"Walking on Sunshine"*—then the **Two of Cups** doesn't just mean partnership. It radiates with the lighthearted joy of dancing in the kitchen, of love as celebration.

This practice does more than personalize the reading—it deepens it. You may know the language of tarot inside out, but the song gives you access to *their* language of feeling. A single lyric can crack open a truth they've been holding tight. A familiar melody can surface emotions they didn't realize were still present. Suddenly, the spread isn't just symbolic—it's alive, pulsing with memory, echoing their lived experience.

The beauty of this approach is how participatory it becomes. Instead of tarot being something *done to* them, it becomes something *done with* them. The querent brings their song, their emotional truth, and you weave it with the cards. The reading becomes a duet: your interpretation, their soundtrack. And afterward, when they return to that song, it will no longer sound the same. It will carry the echo of the spread—the insight, the blessing, the moment of recognition they felt when the card and lyric fused.

In this way, music extends the life of the reading. It becomes memory. Memory becomes anchor. And tarot becomes not just an intellectual tool but a living exchange—reader and querent, card and song, heart and heart.

Because love already has a soundtrack. All we're doing is inviting it to play.

CHAPTER 99

music prompts for tarot readings

Tarot already has rhythm. Shuffle the deck and you'll hear it: the soft percussion of cards against cards, the breath before one is turned, the silence that follows when an image speaks louder than words. Like music, tarot bypasses logic and moves straight into the body. It doesn't just tell you something—it makes you *feel* something.

And love? Love has always had a soundtrack. From the ballads that break us open, to the anthems that carry us through, to the quiet songs that remind us who we are, music has always been the language of the heart. It lingers in ways words alone cannot. One lyric can hold an entire memory. One chorus can remind you of someone you'd rather forget—or someone you hope to find.

This is why music and tarot pair so naturally, especially in love readings. Both speak in symbols, both awaken memory, and both stir the emotions that live just beneath the surface. When we bring them together, readings become not only intellectual but visceral. Cards don't just give guidance—they sing it.

FOR HEARTBREAK OR CLOSURE

"What's the song you've been playing when you miss them most?"

"If this breakup had a soundtrack, what track would be on repeat?"

"Which song feels like the ache you can't put into words?"

The chosen song reveals where they are in their grief cycle—mourning, release, or lingering attachment.

FOR NEW LOVE

"What song feels like the beginning of this connection?"

"If your new partner were a track, what would they sound like?"

"What's the song that makes you blush when you hear it now?"

The song becomes a playful mirror of their excitement, infatuation, or fears about diving in.

FOR SELF-LOVE AND EMPOWERMENT

"What's the anthem that makes you feel like yourself again?"

"If your soul wrote you a playlist right now, what's track one?"

"What song reminds you of your own strength?"

The chosen song sets the tone for empowerment readings—turning the spread into a pep talk and a mirror of their agency.

FOR DESTINY OR FUTURE-ORIENTED READINGS

"What's the song that makes you feel like you're moving forward?"

"If your life right now were a movie, what's playing over the opening credits?"

"What's the track you hear when you imagine your best future?"

The song becomes an anchor for visioning—letting the querent emotionally *feel* their path, not just think about it.

FOR COMPLICATED LOVE / ON-AND-OFF RELATIONSHIPS

"If this relationship were an album, what track are you on right now?"

"What's the song you'd dedicate to them, honestly?"

"Which track do you avoid because it hurts too much?"

The song reveals the dynamic—whether they're stuck in longing, denial, intensity, or cycles they're ready to break.

> **Pro tip:** After the reading, invite the querent to *make a playlist* that includes both the songs they brought and the songs the cards suggested. It becomes a living soundtrack for their love story—and a tool they can return to when they need to reconnect with the reading's truth.

CHAPTER 100

practical ways to weave music into readings

4. USE LYRICS AS ANCHORS

Sometimes the most powerful interpretation of a tarot card isn't a long explanation—it's a single lyric. Music has a way of distilling emotion into a handful of words that hit harder than paragraphs ever could. When you borrow a lyric, you're not just borrowing meaning—you're borrowing rhythm, memory, and the emotional punch that comes with it.

Think of the Tower. You could spend ten minutes explaining sudden change, collapse, and the breaking down of structures that no longer serve. Or you could look your querent in the eye and say, *"And the walls came tumbling down."* Immediately, they feel it. The lyric carries the weight of history, memory, and sound. The card is no longer an abstract archetype—it's a visceral moment.

The Lovers can be just as simple. Instead of circling around choice and alignment, you might quote: *"I choose you, in a hundred lifetimes."* The lyric doesn't erase nuance, but it gives the heart something to hold. Suddenly, the querent isn't thinking about definitions—they're feeling the truth of devotion in their chest.

Why does this work so well? Because lyrics are sticky. They loop in our minds. They carry rhythm that makes meaning easier to remember. And most importantly, they come with emotional resonance already built in. A song that once made someone cry, or fall in love, or dance under the stars—when you quote even a fragment, the memory comes rushing back. That's the kind of depth no textbook definition can reach.

When you use lyrics in a reading, you also offer a bridge between tarot and the querent's lived experience. You're not just saying, *"This card means heartbreak."*

You're saying, *"This heartbreak sounds like Adele, or Fleetwood Mac, or the chorus that's been haunting you for years."* It's not only information—it's recognition.

This technique doesn't mean you abandon clarity. A lyric can stand as the opening line, the anchor, and then you can expand if needed. But sometimes, especially in love readings, the lyric is enough. It lands in the body, not just the mind. The querent walks away not with a string of key terms, but with a line they'll hum to themselves on the way home.

Because that's the gift of tarot paired with music: it doesn't just inform, it *lingers*. And sometimes, the most powerful thing you can give someone isn't a paragraph—it's a lyric that stays with them like a heartbeat.

CHAPTER 101

lyric bank for love readings

MAJORS

The Fool — "Take my hand—let's fall before we fly."

The Magician — "Say the word, and I'll make it real."

The High Priestess — "The answer was inside you all along."

The Empress — "Where you rest, love grows."

The Emperor — "What we build together will last."

The Hierophant — "Sacred words hold us when we falter."

The Lovers — "I choose you, in a hundred lifetimes."

The Chariot — "Nothing can stop us if we move as one."

Strength — "Your softness is your roar."

The Hermit — "In silence, I hear your soul."

Wheel of Fortune — "Round and round we go—this time, say yes."

Justice — "Truth will not betray you."

The Hanged One — "I let go, and I finally see."

Death — "To begin again, I had to end."

Temperance — "In your arms, I find my balance."

The Devil — "I crave you, even as it costs me."

The Tower — "And the walls came tumbling down."

The Star — "You are the light I kept alive."

The Moon — "I'm lost in you, and I don't know what's real."

The Sun — "Here comes the warmth—I can breathe again."

Judgment — "Wake up—your real life is calling."

The World — "This is the chapter that sets me free."

CUPS

Ace of Cups — "My heart runs wild the moment I see you."

Two of Cups — "In your eyes, I find myself."

Three of Cups — "We dance and the world disappears."

Four of Cups — "I miss what's here because I'm staring at what's gone."

Five of Cups — "I'm haunted by the empty glass."

Six of Cups — "I remember the sweetness of before."

Seven of Cups — "Too many dreams—tell me which one is ours."

Eight of Cups — "I walk away, though my heart still lingers."

Nine of Cups — "For this moment, I have everything."

Ten of Cups — "Home is wherever we're together."

Page of Cups — "What if I wrote you a love note in the margins?"

Knight of Cups — "I'll follow my heart straight to you."

Queen of Cups — "My love is an ocean—you can drown or heal in it."

King of Cups — "I steady the waves so you can rest in me."

WANDS

Ace of Wands — "You set me on fire."

Two of Wands — "The horizon calls, and I ache to follow."

Three of Wands — "I see our future rising."

Four of Wands — "Here's to the love we made a home in."

Five of Wands — "We clash because our fire won't stay contained."

Six of Wands — "I win, and I want you to see me."

Seven of Wands — "I'll protect what burns inside me."

Eight of Wands — "Your name is already on the wind."

Nine of Wands — "I'll fight for this, even bruised."

Ten of Wands — "I carry love like a weight across my shoulders."

Page of Wands — "Adventure begins the moment I say yes."

Knight of Wands — "I want you, now, before the flame goes out."

Queen of Wands — "I shine because I dare to."

King of Wands — "My passion leads, and I will not be ignored."

SWORDS

Ace of Swords — "Here is the truth—sharp, clean, undeniable."

Two of Swords — "I'm standing at the crossroads, afraid to choose."

Three of Swords — "My heart broke, but it still beats for you."

Four of Swords — "Let me lay this love down for a while."

Five of Swords — "We win, but at what cost?"

Six of Swords — "I'm rowing us toward calmer waters."

Seven of Swords — "I hide what I fear you'll take away."

Eight of Swords — "I'm trapped in a cage of my own making."

Nine of Swords — "You're the thought that keeps me awake."

Ten of Swords — "It's over, and it cut me to the bone."

Page of Swords — "I watch, I wonder, I'm not ready to speak."

Knight of Swords — "I'm already halfway there—catch me if you can."

Queen of Swords — "I love you enough to tell the truth."

King of Swords — "I rule with reason, not with yearning."

PENTACLES

Ace of Pentacles — "Plant this love, and watch it grow."

Two of Pentacles — "I dance to keep it all from falling."

Three of Pentacles — "Together, we build what lasts."

Four of Pentacles — "I hold too tightly—I'm afraid to lose you."

Five of Pentacles — "Love left me in the cold."

Six of Pentacles — "I give because I want us to rise together."

Seven of Pentacles — "Patience, beloved—growth takes time."

Eight of Pentacles — "Love is in the practice, not just the promise."

Nine of Pentacles — "I bloom because I claimed myself."

Ten of Pentacles — "This is the legacy of our love."

Page of Pentacles — "Teach me how to love in small, steady steps."

Knight of Pentacles — "I'll show up, slow but sure."

Queen of Pentacles — "My devotion is in the details."

King of Pentacles — "I build the ground we stand on."

CHAPTER 102

the song deck

Music and tarot are such natural partners that I created a deck built entirely around this concept: a Song Deck, where each card is a song, complete with lyrics. Instead of pulling The Lovers, you might draw *"At Last"* by Etta James—soulful, timeless, a declaration of finally finding the one. Instead of Death, you might see *"Nothing Compares 2 U"* by Sinéad O'Connor—raw, aching, a song about endings that also leaves space for transformation. Or perhaps the Tower shows up not as rubble but as *"Smells Like Teen Spirit"* by Nirvana—chaotic, loud, the sound of everything breaking apart so something new can be born.

Suddenly the spread doesn't just speak—it sings. Each card comes with a soundtrack, turning the reading into a lyrical mixtape of the soul. When a querent leaves, they don't only carry your words; they carry a song they can press play on whenever they need to feel the reading again.

And here's the beauty—you don't need to wait for a published deck to start experimenting. You can make your own. Music is endlessly personal, and curating a Song Deck lets you bring your own emotional history and favorite soundtracks into the reading space. The Star might be *"Dog Days Are Over"* by Florence + the Machine for you, while someone else might hear *"Rise Up"* by Andra Day. The Devil might not be Britney's *"Toxic"* this time but Nine Inch Nails' *"Closer."* The Chariot could be Jay-Z's *"99 Problems"* or Fleetwood Mac's *"Go Your Own Way."* There is no wrong answer—only the song that vibrates closest to how the card feels in your body.

When you build your own Song Deck, you're not just writing down titles. You're building a deeply intimate map of how love, heartbreak, joy, and growth sound to you. And when you share it in readings, that intimacy transfers—the querent feels not only the message of the card but the emotion of the song. It's tarot as a mixtape, tarot as a love letter set to music.

How to Make Your Own Song Deck

Pick up a blank tarot deck, a simple deck of playing cards, or even just slips of paper. On each card, write down the name of a song that captures a particular feeling, memory, or archetype. Keep it simple: one card, one song. If you don't want to commit to handwriting on a deck, jot titles on small pieces of paper and drop them into a bowl, a jar, or a cup. When you draw one, it becomes the "card" for your reading.

Over time, your song deck will grow—like a living playlist in physical form. You might start with obvious choices: heartbreak ballads for the Three of Swords, anthems of empowerment for Strength, hopeful tracks for The Star. But as you keep going, you'll find songs that don't just match tarot archetypes but reflect your personal story. That's where the magic lives—because every pull carries not only collective meaning, but your own resonance.

Weaving Multiple Decks Together

Song decks don't have to replace tarot—they can stand alongside it. Try pulling a tarot card and a song card together. The interplay is often uncanny. A Two of Cups paired with *"Lucky"* by Jason Mraz and Colbie Caillat? Partnership with harmony. A **Tower** paired with *"Rolling in the Deep"* by Adele? Heartbreak that tears down illusions.

You can also weave decks you've made yourself with ones already published. A lyric card pulled next to a traditional tarot card expands the reading, giving the querent both a symbolic anchor *and* a musical echo to carry with them.

The Emotional Impact

Creating your own song deck invites you to slow down and consider: *What music carries the weight of this archetype for me?* In that way, you're not just interpreting tarot—you're building a personal library of emotional shorthand. Every card becomes more memorable because it's tied to a melody. Every spread becomes more immersive because it's scored like a soundtrack.

And here's the real magic: when you hand a querent a song from your deck, you're not just giving them a message—you're giving them something they can return to again and again. The song will live with them long after the reading ends, replaying the insight whenever it plays.

A Taylor Swift On my own site, you'll even find my **Taylor Swift-themed Song Deck**—because let's be real, her discography is practically an oracle on its own. Pulling *"All Too Well"* hits differently than pulling *"Begin Again."* Her catalog captures the full spectrum of love readings: longing, passion, heartbreak, rebirth. And having those songs in card form makes every draw feel like being handed the next track in your own personal breakup-to-make-up playlist.

A song deck—whether homemade, themed, or purchased—bridges the gap between tarot's symbols and music's emotions. It transforms the reading into a living mixtape, something both mystical and deeply human.

CHAPTER 103
create your own song deck ♪♪♪

PRACTICE ASSIGNMENT

Practice Assignment: Create Your Own Song Deck ♪♪

Gather Your Materials

You don't need anything fancy. Choose one of the following:

- A blank tarot deck or playing cards you don't mind writing on.
- Slips of paper you can fold and drop into a jar, bowl, or cup.
- Index cards, sticky notes, or even a digital notes app if you prefer.

The point is simply to create a physical (or digital) stack of songs you can pull from.

Choose 10 Songs

Pick ten songs (or 78, it's up to you!) that carry strong emotion for you. Think about love, heartbreak, longing, joy, endings, or empowerment. These can be classics, guilty pleasures, or tracks that always make you cry or dance. Write one song title per card or slip of paper. Don't overthink—trust the ones that pop into your head first.

Do a Three-Card Reading

Shuffle your tarot deck. Lay out three cards for the spread:

1. Past (what shaped the love or question)
2. Present (truth of the bond or heart-space now).
3. Future (the invitation or what opens ahead).

Then shuffle your Song Deck and draw one song to pair with each tarot card.

Weave the Story

Now comes the fun. Read each card as usual, but let the song deepen or shift its meaning. For example:

- If the Five of Cups comes up with *"Back to Black"* by Amy Winehouse, the grief feels raw, lingering, hard to shake.
- If the Two of Cups comes up with *"Lucky"* by Jason Mraz and Colbie Caillat, the relationship feels playful, sweet, and mutually uplifting.
- If the The Star comes up with *"Rise Up"* by Andra Day, the message becomes a rallying cry for hope, not just a whisper.

Reflect

Ask yourself:

> How did the songs change or deepen the card's message?
>
> Did the lyrics bring up emotions or memories that clarified the reading?
>
> What surprised you about the pairings?

Keep Growing Your Deck

Add new songs over time. Let your deck evolve. Maybe each suit eventually gets its own genre (Cups = ballads, Wands = anthems, Swords = break-up songs, Pentacles = grounding tracks). Maybe you create multiple themed Song Decks: one for romance, one for self-love, one for closure.

By making and using your own Song Deck, you'll see just how much music can add motional depth to your practice. A single lyric can make a card unforgettable, and a playlist can turn a reading into a memory that lingers.

PART TEN

tarot + oracles in love

CHAPTER 104

why use oracles with tarot in romance readings

Tarot and oracle cards share a common intention: to help us listen more deeply to ourselves, to spirit, or to love itself. But while tarot has a very specific structure, oracle decks are wide open—each one as unique as the creator who made it. To understand why they pair so well with tarot, especially in romance readings, it helps to know what they are (and what they aren't).

What Oracle Decks Are

Oracle decks are free-form divination tools. They don't follow the 78-card system of tarot, nor do they share a universal structure. Instead, each oracle deck has its own theme, number of cards, and style of messages. Some decks might have 44 cards, others 52, or any number at all.

They can be focused on almost anything:

- **Love and relationships** (affirmations, blessings, invitations)
- **Spiritual guidance** (angels, deities, ascended masters)
- **Nature themes** (plants, animals, elements)
- **Shadow work** (healing, release, self-reflection)
- **Empowerment** (confidence, clarity, personal growth)

Where tarot asks you to interpret layers of symbolism, oracle cards usually speak more directly. A card might simply say *"Healing Heart"* or *"Forgiveness."* Others might have short passages, affirmations, or even single words like *"Trust"* or *"Patience."* This directness makes them easy to use, even for beginners.

What Oracle Decks Are Not

They are not bound by a universal system like tarot. You won't find a shared archetype called "The Fool" across every oracle deck, nor a fixed sequence of suits. Because of this, oracle decks are less about memorization and more about intuition. They don't replace tarot—they complement it.

They also aren't fortune-telling machines that will give you one rigid "right" answer. Oracle cards are more like gentle companions, nudging you toward clarity, reassurance, or a shift in perspective. Where tarot can feel like the bones of a story, oracles are more like the breath that animates it.

How Oracle Decks Look and Feel

Physically, oracle decks can vary just as much as their messages. Some are large, oversized cards with lush illustrations and long affirmations. Others are small, pocket-sized, with simple keywords. The artwork can range from whimsical watercolor to moody gothic photography to minimal black-and-white design.

What matters is the vibe. Oracle decks often feel softer, more approachable, and more conversational. If tarot speaks in archetypes and symbols, oracles speak in whispers, blessings, or straight talk.

Why They Work in Love Readings

This makes them a natural fit for romance readings. Tarot reveals the structure—the repeating patterns, the choices, the energies at play. Oracle cards add emotional texture: they tell the querent what the heart needs to hear. Tarot says, *"Here's what's happening."* Oracle says, *"Here's how to hold it with grace."*

Together, they create a duet: tarot as the map, oracle as the love letter. The querent leaves with both clarity and comfort, both the bones and the breath of their story.

That's why oracle cards pair so seamlessly with tarot in matters of the heart. One grounds. The other uplifts. Together, they make the reading whole.

CHAPTER 105

how to use oracle decks with tarot in love readings

Once you know what oracle decks are, the next question is: *how do you bring them into tarot practice?* The good news is that there are no rigid rules—only creative options. Because oracles are flexible, they slip into readings like breath into the body. Here are some of the most powerful ways to pair them with tarot in romance work.

Use Oracles to Open the Reading

Before you lay down any tarot cards, pull a single oracle. Let it set the tone.

Example: A querent asks, *"What's next in my relationship?"* You draw an oracle that says *"Trust the Timing."* Suddenly the tarot reading that follows is framed within patience, divine timing, and surrender. The oracle acts like the overture to a love story, preparing the querent's heart for what's to come.

Use Oracles to Close the Reading

Tarot can sometimes feel heavy—especially if the spread reveals conflict, endings, or hard truths. Closing with an oracle card brings the blessing, the reassurance, or the takeaway.

Example: A tarot spread shows the Tower (disruption) and Five of Cups (grief). You close by pulling an oracle that says *"New Horizons."* It doesn't erase the pain, but it offers hope, softening the edges and reminding the querent that endings always lead to openings.

Use Oracles Beside Each Tarot Card

For a truly lyrical spread, pair each tarot card with an oracle. This creates a "call and response" effect: tarot shows the structure, oracle shows the heart.

Example: You pull the Two of Swords (indecision) and place beside it an oracle card that says *"Choose With Love."* The combination makes the message unmissable: stop choosing with fear, start choosing with heart.

Use Oracles as Clarifiers

When a tarot card feels murky, let an oracle card sharpen it.

Example: The Moon comes up, full of illusions and uncertainty. You pull an oracle that says *"Boundaries."* Suddenly, the meaning is clearer: the confusion isn't just emotional—it's about where the querent needs to draw a line.

Use Oracles as Daily Love Notes

For self-love practice, oracles can stand alone—or accompany a single tarot card. They're perfect for journaling, affirmations, and daily pulls.

Example: Pull The Star for the day, then draw an oracle card that says *"Tenderness."* You write: *"My hope isn't just about big dreams. Today it's about treating myself tenderly, holding my own heart with care."*

The synergy is simple, tarot speaks in archetypes and complexity, while oracle speaks in plain language. Tarot tells you *what's happening.* Oracle tells you *what to remember as you live through it.* Tarot digs into the bones of the relationship. Oracle offers the breath that keeps it alive.

Used together, they create a reading that feels both grounded and soulful. A querent walks away not only with clarity but also with comfort. They have both the map and the blessing.

And in love readings especially, this pairing is gold. Romance isn't only about decisions and patterns—it's about how those truths land in the heart. Tarot shows the structure. Oracles give the song.

CHAPTER 106

why oracles work so well in love readings

Love readings are among the most tender and vulnerable sessions we offer as tarot readers. When someone asks about their heart, they're often carrying hope, fear, and longing all at once. Tarot provides incredible depth for exploring these questions—it shows the structure, patterns, and energies at play in a relationship.

But sometimes, tarot's precision can feel sharp. Its imagery and archetypes cut straight to the core, which can be exactly what's needed... or it can feel overwhelming to someone who's already raw. This is where oracle cards shine.

When paired with tarot, oracle decks add softness, affirmation, and a different kind of language. They don't replace tarot—they complement it, creating balance in readings where the stakes are deeply emotional.

Tarot can sometimes feel like a blunt truth-teller. The Three of Swords doesn't hide its message. The Tower doesn't sugarcoat upheaval. These cards are powerful teachers, but they can also hit hard—especially if a querent is in the middle of heartbreak or confusion.

Oracle cards bring in a gentler voice. Many oracle decks are designed to speak in affirmations, imagery, or single words that land softly. Instead of a direct symbol of heartbreak, an oracle might offer a card that says *"Healing"* or *"Release."*

These messages don't avoid the truth—they hold it with compassion. When layered into a love reading, oracle cards act like a soft hand on the shoulder, helping the querent hear the harder messages of tarot without feeling crushed by them.

For example:

- The Tower might appear in tarot, signaling a painful breakup or sudden shift.
- Alongside it, an oracle card reading *"New Beginnings"* reminds the querent that while this chapter is ending, a new one is waiting.

The result is balance—truth paired with hope.

Oracles Are Flexible

Tarot has a defined structure: 78 cards, four suits, and a clear symbolic system. This structure is part of what makes tarot so rich and layered, but it also means there are limits to the language it uses.

Oracle decks are limitless. Each one is unique, often built around a theme. Some focus on self-care, others on relationships, spirituality, animal guides, or even specific ideas like "sacred boundaries" or "inner child healing."

In love readings, this flexibility is invaluable. Oracle cards can give words to concepts that tarot only hints at.

For instance, a querent might be struggling with co-dependency or communication issues. While tarot can reflect that tension, an oracle card that literally says *"Boundaries"* or *"Speak Your Truth"* makes the message crystal clear.

Examples of themes oracle decks can cover that tarot doesn't name outright:

- Twin Flames or Soulmates
- Forgiveness and letting go
- Relationship patterns like avoidance or attachment
- Specific advice like *"Self-Worth," "Rebuild,"* or *"Wait."*

This directness gives you more tools to reflect what's really happening in the querent's emotional world.

Oracles Are Empowering

Love readings can leave querents feeling vulnerable. They're often looking for clarity about another person's feelings or actions, which can easily slip into a dynamic of helplessness, *"Do they love me? Will they stay? What will happen to me?"*

Tarot shows patterns and truths, but without care, it can accidentally reinforce that feeling of passivity—especially if the cards reveal a challenging dynamic.

Oracle cards bring empowerment back to the table. Many decks use affirmations or direct, uplifting language that reminds the querent of their own agency and strength.

For example:

- Tarot might reveal the Ten of Swords, signaling an ending.
- Alongside it, an oracle card could say *"You Are Enough."*

The message shifts from *"This is over"* to *"This may be ending, but you are whole and worthy regardless."*

These cards give the querent something to hold onto, a mantra or reminder they can carry with them long after the reading ends. Instead of leaving them with just insight, you leave them with a tangible sense of hope.

Blending Tarot and Oracle Cards

When you weave tarot and oracle cards together, you create a dynamic balance:

Tarot gives structure, clarity, and the story of what's happening.

Oracles add compassion, nuance, and practical guidance.

A love reading might start with a classic tarot spread to uncover the relationship's dynamics, followed by one or two oracle cards to clarify, soothe, or inspire.

For example:

- Tarot shows conflict and miscommunication in the relationship.
- Oracle cards add messages like *"Speak With Love"* and *"Trust the Timing."*

The combination deepens the reading, giving both insight and comfort.

Love is one of the most vulnerable spaces we explore as tarot readers. By layering oracle cards into these readings, we create a more supportive experience—one that acknowledges both the challenges and the beauty of the querent's journey.

Tarot shows the bones of the relationship—the patterns, choices, and truths. Oracle cards breathe life into those bones, offering hope, healing, and heart.

Together, they remind the querent that love is never just about answers. It's about growth, courage, and the endless possibilities that come with an open heart.

CHAPTER 107

Cautions & Ethics — Using Oracle Cards with Integrity

Oracle cards can bring magic, beauty, and emotional resonance to your readings, especially in matters of the heart. But like any powerful tool, they require care. Without mindful boundaries, oracle cards can create confusion, dilute the message of the tarot, or even unintentionally mislead a querent.

This is where ethics come in. Ethics are not rules meant to limit you—they are the framework that keeps readings safe, empowering, and respectful for everyone involved. When you approach oracle cards with integrity, you create a reading that honors both the querent's journey and your role as a guide.

Oracle Cards Should Complement, Not Replace Tarot

Tarot is a structured system. Its 78 cards have a deep, interconnected framework that provides context and clarity. Oracle cards, on the other hand, are limitless—they can cover anything from angels and affirmations to animal spirits and specific relationship themes.

Because of this, it's easy to get swept away by the simplicity of oracle cards and let them take over the reading entirely.

While oracles add depth, they should never overshadow the foundation tarot provides. Think of tarot as the story's bones and oracle cards as the color and texture that bring it to life.

For example:

- Tarot might show the Lovers, Five of Wands, and The Star in a love reading.

- Oracle cards like *"Boundaries"* and *"Healing"* could then be layered in to highlight key themes without replacing the interpretation of the tarot cards themselves.

If you find yourself leaning on oracle cards because they feel easier or more direct, pause and return to the tarot. Tarot is the structure. Oracle cards are the echoes, the whispers, the clarifying brushstrokes that support the story—not the whole picture.

Avoid the "Fortune Cookie" Trap

It can be tempting to pull an oracle card at the end of a reading and simply toss it on top as a final flourish. While it may look pretty, this habit risks reducing the oracle deck to a gimmick—like cracking open a fortune cookie for a quick one-liner.

Oracle cards deserve more depth than that. They're not meant to stand alone without context. Each oracle card should be integrated into the flow of the reading, woven thoughtfully into the narrative already unfolding through tarot.

For example, instead of simply pulling an oracle card and saying, *"Oh, it says 'Forgiveness,' so you need to forgive someone,"* try connecting it to the tarot spread:

"Your tarot cards showed conflict and misunderstanding in this relationship. This oracle card about forgiveness highlights how healing can only move forward if resentment is addressed. What would forgiveness look like for you in this situation?"

By grounding the oracle message in the larger story, you avoid vague or surface-level interpretations. The card becomes meaningful rather than random.

Be Careful with Claims of Fate or Destiny

Many oracle decks use language that feels big, sweeping, and absolute. Cards might say things like *"Twin Flame," "Destiny,"* or *"This is Your Person."* These words are powerful—and they can deeply impact a querent, especially if they're in a vulnerable place.

While these cards can open up fascinating conversations, they should always be framed as **guidance, not guarantees**. Tarot and oracle readings are tools for reflection and insight—not declarations carved in stone.

For instance:

If a "Soulmate" card appears, avoid saying, ✗ *"This is your one true soulmate forever."*

Instead, try framing it like this:

☑ *"This card suggests there's a strong soul connection here. It invites us to explore the depth and meaning of this bond, and what lessons it might be bringing into your life right now."*

The difference is subtle but profound. One approach locks the querent into a fixed fate; the other empowers them to engage with the relationship as an evolving experience.

Remember, when we make absolute claims about someone else's future or relationships, we take away their agency. Ethical readings do the opposite—they give agency back.

Stay Grounded in Your Role as a Guide

As readers, we're not here to play the role of prophet, judge, or unquestionable authority. We are guides. We hold space. We help the querent uncover their own truth through conversation with the cards.

When you work with oracle cards—especially ones with bold or dramatic imagery—it's vital to keep your role clear. You're not telling someone what will *definitely* happen. You're helping them explore possibilities, themes, and choices.

Boundaries protect everyone involved:

For the querent: They leave feeling empowered, not dependent on you for every decision.

For you as the reader: You avoid burnout and the heavy weight of feeling responsible for someone's future.

For the reading itself: It stays clean, clear, and meaningful instead of chaotic or manipulative.

A simple phrase can make all the difference:

- "These cards show patterns and energies at play right now. They point to what's possible, but the future is shaped by your choices."
- This keeps the reading rooted in empowerment rather than fear or dependency.

When used with care, oracle cards can elevate a reading, bringing softness, clarity, and inspiration to even the most complex love questions. But without mindful practice, they risk becoming confusing or even harmful.

By:

- Letting tarot remain the foundation,
- Avoiding "fortune cookie" shortcuts,
- And framing every oracle message as guidance rather than guarantee,

...you create a reading that is both magical and ethical.

Oracle cards are a bridge between worlds—the known and the mysterious, the personal and the universal. When you honor that bridge with integrity, you give your querent something far more valuable than predictions: you give them clarity, hope, and the power to choose their own path forward.

CHAPTER 108

blending tarot and oracle cards

The best way to learn how to integrate oracle cards with tarot is through hands-on exploration. These prompts are designed to help you experience the difference between tarot's structured storytelling and oracle's free-flowing guidance. By experimenting with both, you'll discover how the two systems can complement each other—and where their unique voices shine on their own.

Set aside time for these exercises in a quiet space. Keep a journal nearby to capture your spreads, your reflections, and any patterns you notice over time. These practice prompts will be best served with both a tarot deck and an oracle deck. If you don't have an oracle deck, google and find an image of one, incorporate it into your readings as if you'd pulled the card.

PROMPT 1: THE FINAL BLESSING

How an oracle card can soften or sharpen a tarot message.

Shuffle your tarot deck and pull **three cards** for a relationship reading. These cards represent:

Card 1: The current state of the relationship.

Card 2: The challenge or tension that needs attention.

Card 3: The path forward or advice for growth.

Interpret the tarot spread first, noting the key themes and messages that arise.

Ask yourself:

> How do these cards speak to each other?
>
> What story are they telling?

Now, shuffle your oracle deck and pull **one card only**. This card acts as the "final blessing" or overarching insight.

Journal about how the oracle card interacts with the tarot spread:

> Does it soften a difficult message? (For example, a harsh Five of Swords story eased by an oracle card like "Forgiveness" or "Healing.")
>
> Does it sharpen the focus, making the tarot message feel even clearer or more urgent?
>
> Does it introduce a new theme or perspective you hadn't considered?

Reflection Questions:

> What did the oracle add that the tarot alone didn't reveal?
>
> Did it feel supportive, challenging, or both?
>
> How might you explain this layered reading to a querent in a compassionate way?

PROMPT 2: TAROT & ORACLE CONVERSATION

Let the decks "speak" to one another like characters in a dialogue.

Choose **one card from your tarot deck** and **one card from your oracle deck**.

These can be drawn randomly or chosen intentionally based on a current situation in your life.

Imagine these two cards as characters meeting for the first time.

> If your tarot card were a person, what would they sound like?
>
> What about your oracle card?

Journal a **conversation between the two cards**.

> Write it out like a dialogue scene, alternating their voices.

Example:

The Chariot (Tarot): "I am ready to move forward, focused and determined. Nothing will stand in my way."

Healing (Oracle): "Your pace is admirable, but you need to tend to your wounds before you charge ahead."

The Chariot: "If I stop now, I might lose my momentum."

Healing: "Momentum without restoration leads to collapse."

Once the dialogue feels complete, read it back to yourself. Look for insights hidden in their exchange.

Reflection Questions:

> Which card felt dominant in the conversation—tarot or oracle?
>
> Did the oracle challenge, support, or redirect the tarot card's energy?
>
> What does this reveal about the relationship between the two systems?

This exercise helps you *feel* the dynamic energy between tarot and oracle rather than only think about it. It also strengthens your intuitive storytelling skills.

PROMPT 3: MIRROR READING — TAROT VS. ORACLE

Exploring the unique voices of each system.

Choose a focus for this reading: **self-love.**

Ask a guiding question like:

"What do I need to nurture and honor myself right now?"

First, do the reading **using only oracle cards.**

- Pull three to five cards, interpreting them as a collective message.

Notice how the oracle deck frames its guidance.

> Does it speak in broad themes, affirmations, or direct advice?

Next, repeat the reading **using only tarot cards.**

Pull the same number of cards and interpret them with tarot's structure and symbolism.

Observe the difference in tone and detail compared to the oracle reading.

Finally, journal a comparison between the two readings:

> What did the oracle emphasize that the tarot didn't?
>
> What depth or structure did the tarot add to the topic?
>
> If you were giving this reading to a querent, how might you combine both systems for the clearest, most supportive message?

Bonus Step:

Layer the two readings together into a single spread by placing the oracle cards above the tarot cards. See how they complement or contrast with one another.

INTEGRATING THE PRACTICE

These exercises aren't just about technique—they're about relationship building.

Tarot offers the **skeleton** of the reading: structured, detailed, interconnected.

Oracle cards bring **color and texture**: emotional resonance, affirmation, and intuitive symbolism.

Through these prompts, you'll learn to weave both voices into a unified whole, creating readings that are rich, balanced, and deeply meaningful.

As you repeat these exercises over time, you'll start to notice your own preferences:

> Do you reach for oracles when you need softness or clarity?
>
> Do you prefer tarot's structure when seeking depth and detail?
>
> Or do you find your magic in the way they sing together?

Write down these observations. They will guide you toward a style of reading that is uniquely yours—a blend of tarot and oracle woven with care and integrity.

Tarot is the architecture of a love reading—detailed, structured, and precise. Oracle cards are the poetry—intuitive, emotional, and lyrical. Together, they create a reading that feels like both a map and a love song.

This small addition makes your readings richer, more flexible, and more deeply resonant—especially in matters of the heart.

PART ELEVEN

tarot & storytelling —

archetypes in romance

CHAPTER 109

why storytelling matters in love readings

Love is the oldest story we tell.

Before humans wrote history, they sang of love and longing around fires. They painted passion and heartbreak on cave walls, wove it into myths, poems, ballads, and epics. Even now, every romance novel, movie, or pop song carries echoes of these timeless patterns. At its core, tarot speaks the same language. Each card is a fragment of that universal story, representing archetypes of desire, connection, choice, and transformation.

When you read tarot through the lens of story, you aren't just interpreting symbols—you're helping your querent see themselves inside an unfolding narrative. Love readings are never just about one moment or one partner. They're chapters in a living, breathing tale of the human heart.

THE POWER OF ARCHETYPES

Archetypes are the universal characters and themes that show up across all cultures and stories. They are the lovers who can't be together, the hero on a quest, the wise guide, the shadow villain. Tarot is built entirely out of these archetypal roles.

When you connect a card to a familiar love story or character, two powerful things happen, the Cards become unforgettable and the reading comes alive.

Tarot can feel abstract when you're first encountering it. A single card may hold dozens of meanings, and it's easy to get lost in lists of keywords or complex symbolism. This is especially true in love readings, where emotions run high and every interpretation matters. By connecting tarot cards to familiar stories and characters, you transform that abstraction into something vivid, emotional, and deeply memorable.

Think about *The Lovers* card. On its own, it represents choice, connection, harmony, and passion—but for many people, those concepts are still theoretical. When you link *The Lovers* to a famous love story like Romeo and Juliet, the card immediately comes alive. Suddenly, it's not just a symbol on a piece of cardstock. It's star-crossed lovers standing under a balcony, whispering promises while the world tries to keep them apart.

This connection doesn't just make the card easier to understand in the moment—it makes it unforgettable. The next time someone sees *The Lovers*, they won't have to recall a keyword list. Instead, they'll remember the urgency of forbidden love, the thrill of first passion, and the heartbreak of choices that can't be undone. The story cements the meaning in a way pure memorization never could.

The same is true for other cards, especially the emotionally complex ones. Consider the *Two of Cups*. You could explain it as mutual attraction, harmony, and partnership, and that would be correct—but it's far more evocative to say, *"This is Elizabeth Bennet and Mr. Darcy in Pride and Prejudice, finally coming together after misunderstandings and pride have been stripped away. It's that moment when two people see each other clearly and choose to connect."*

By grounding the card in a cultural touchstone, you create instant resonance. The querent doesn't just understand what you're saying—they feel it. They've seen this moment play out before in books and movies, and now they can see it reflected in their own life through the spread on the table.

This approach is especially powerful with cards that carry shadow energy, like *The Devil*. For many people, *The Devil* can be difficult to interpret because it holds such intense, layered meanings: desire, obsession, entrapment, temptation. It can represent both the thrill of passion and the danger of losing yourself inside it. Explaining that complexity with only abstract words can leave a querent confused or even frightened.

But when you say, *"The Devil is the passionate, toxic energy of Wuthering Heights—love that burns so hot it leaves scars,"* the meaning lands instantly. You've painted a picture of a relationship that's magnetic but destructive, one that feels fated even as it consumes both people involved. The archetype gives the querent an immediate emotional reference point. They don't just understand *The Devil* intellectually—they recognize its energy in their own life experience.

This is the magic of archetypes: they take something intangible and make it personal and visceral. They speak directly to the heart.

A card like *The Tower* might simply mean "sudden upheaval" in a textbook. But when you compare it to a dramatic scene in a movie where everything changes in a single moment—a proposal gone wrong, a shocking betrayal, a life turned upside down—the querent sees themselves in that story.

They don't just think, *"Oh, this card is about endings."*

They feel the collapse, the rush of adrenaline, and the space for renewal that comes afterward.

Archetypes work because they're universal. Love, heartbreak, longing, jealousy, reunion—these are experiences every human has felt in some form. By tying a tarot card to a familiar story, you help the querent recognize that they are not alone in what they're going through. They are part of a larger narrative that has been told for centuries, in countless ways.

For the reader, this technique also deepens connection to the cards. It shifts tarot from being a static tool to a living, breathing library of human experience. Instead of memorizing isolated meanings, you begin to see the cards as characters, each with their own motives, desires, and arcs. This not only makes readings more engaging, but it also sharpens your intuition. When you see *The Knight of Cups*, you might think of a romantic hero—charming, dreamy, perhaps a little impulsive. When you see *The Queen of Swords*, you might imagine a wise, clear-eyed mentor who cuts through lies with precision.

These associations make it easier to weave cards together into a cohesive story. They give you a language of emotion and imagery that both you and your querent can understand. Tarot stops being a puzzle to solve and becomes a story to tell—a story the querent recognizes as their own.

Instead of a flat interpretation, you invite the querent into a story. The reading becomes cinematic—characters with motives, desires, flaws, and victories. You aren't just telling them, *"This person may have mixed feelings."*

Instead, you might say, *"They're standing at a crossroads like Tristan and Isolde—deep passion pulling them one way, duty pulling them another."*

When readings shift into story, querents engage with the narrative on a deeper level. They stop seeing the cards as random predictions and start recognizing themselves as an active participant in their love story.

Tarot is a Storybook of the Heart. The tarot deck is like a library of romance novels waiting to be opened.

The Majors are the sweeping epic—grand gestures, soul-level choices, once-in-a-lifetime love stories.

The Minors are the quieter chapters—misunderstandings, daily joys, shared work, and the tender moments that sustain a relationship.

The Court Cards are the cast of characters—the people who enter the querent's life, bringing their own roles, lessons, and arcs.

Each card represents a recurring theme that we've seen a thousand times before in books and films:

- *The Fool* leaping into new love like the opening chapter of a rom-com.
- *The Lovers* making a fateful choice like Romeo and Juliet on the balcony.
- *The Tower* crashing down like a dramatic breakup scene.
- *The Star* glimmering with hope after heartbreak, like the soft reunion in the final pages of a novel.

When you think in terms of story, you stop delivering isolated definitions and start weaving a tale that resonates deeply.

CHAPTER 110

major arcana as romance archetypes

0. The Fool – The Adventurer, The Innocent

- Archetype: The start of a new romance, naïve but full of possibility.
- Pop Culture: Rapunzel (*Tangled*), Bridget Jones, Ted Mosby (*How I Met Your Mother*).

I. The Magician – The Charmer, The Seducer

- Archetype: Words like spells, attraction through wit, charisma, and confidence.
- Pop Culture: Don Juan, Gatsby (*The Great Gatsby*), Howl (*Howl's Moving Castle*).

II. The High Priestess – The Mystery, The Untouchable

- Archetype: Alluring but distant, holding secrets, representing forbidden knowledge or hidden desires.
- Pop Culture: Morticia Addams, Galadriel (*Lord of the Rings*).

III. The Empress – The Nurturer, The Beloved

- Archetype: Abundance, sensuality, and unconditional love. The archetypal "wife/mother/earth goddess."
- Pop Culture: Molly Weasley (*Harry Potter*), Demeter (myth), Padmé Amidala (*Star Wars*).

IV. The Emperor – The Protector, The Authority

- Archetype: Stability, structure, protective but sometimes controlling.
- Pop Culture: Mr. Darcy (*Pride & Prejudice*), Aragorn (*Lord of the Rings*).

V. The Hierophant – The Traditionalist, The Bound Lover

- Archetype: Marriage, vows, tradition, or restriction. Could symbolize conventional romance or the pressure of family/culture.
- Pop Culture: arranged marriage tropes, Edward Cullen (*Twilight*) in his moral restraint.

VI. The Lovers – The Soulmates, The Star-Crossed

- Archetype: Passion, choice, and fated romance. Sometimes harmony, sometimes forbidden love.
- Pop Culture: Romeo & Juliet, Jack & Rose (*Titanic*), Hazel & Gus (*The Fault in Our Stars*).

VII. The Chariot – The Pursuer, The Determined Lover

- Archetype: Willpower, conquest, the chase. The one who *won't stop* until they win love.
- Pop Culture: Westley (*The Princess Bride*), Noah (*The Notebook*).

VIII. Strength – The Gentle Protector, The Patient Lover

- Archetype: Love that tames the beast, patience that transforms passion into trust.
- Pop Culture: Belle (*Beauty & the Beast*), Katniss with Peeta (*Hunger Games*).

IX. The Hermit – The Withdrawn Lover, The Wise One

- Archetype: Solitude, self-reflection, absence, or spiritual connection. Sometimes the one who needs space.
- Pop Culture: Edward Rochester (*Jane Eyre*), Shadowhunters' Magnus Bane in isolation mode.

X. Wheel of Fortune – The Fated Lovers, The Twist of Destiny

- Archetype: Serendipity, chance encounters, karmic timing.
- Pop Culture: Serendipity (film), Amélie (*Amélie*).

XI. Justice – The Truth Teller, The Equal Partner

- Archetype: Balance, fairness, the weighing of hearts. Love based on equality or difficult truths.
- Pop Culture: Elizabeth Bennet (*Pride & Prejudice*), Atticus Finch (*To Kill a Mockingbird* as moral love).

XII. The Hanged Man – The Self-Sacrificing Lover

- Archetype: Sacrifice for love, waiting, surrender.
- Pop Culture: Jack Dawson (*Titanic*), Sidney Carton (*A Tale of Two Cities*).

XIII. Death – The Transformer, The Phoenix Love

- Archetype: Endings that create beginnings, heartbreak that births new love.
- Pop Culture: Buffy & Angel (*Buffy the Vampire Slayer*), Elizabeth Gilbert (*Eat Pray Love*).

XIV. Temperance – The Healer, The Harmonizer

- Archetype: Balance, patience, gentle blending of opposites.
- Pop Culture: Samwise Gamgee (*Lord of the Rings*), Jim Halpert (*The Office*).

XV. The Devil – The Forbidden Lover, The Intoxicating Affair

- Archetype: Obsession, lust, control, unhealthy attraction.
- Pop Culture: Christian Grey (*Fifty Shades*), Damon (*The Vampire Diaries*), Harley Quinn & Joker.

XVI. The Tower – The Shattering Relationship

- Archetype: Sudden endings, betrayal, shocking revelations.
- Pop Culture: Anna Karenina, Gatsby & Daisy's collapse (*The Great Gatsby*).

XVII. The Star – The Healing Love, The Guiding Light

- Archetype: Hope after heartbreak, the soulmate who helps you believe again.
- Pop Culture: Augustus Waters (*Fault in Our Stars*), Peeta (*Hunger Games*).

XVIII. The Moon – The Illusion, The Dream Lover

- Archetype: Mystery, fantasy, confusion, or longing. Love that feels unreal, dreamlike, or deceptive.
- Pop Culture: Phantom (*Phantom of the Opera*), Jay Gatsby (*The Great Gatsby*).

XIX. The Sun – The Joyful Love, The Childlike Romance

- Archetype: Innocence, joy, pure happiness.
- Pop Culture: Anna (*Frozen*), Sam & Suzy (*Moonrise Kingdom*).

XX. Judgement – The Returned Lover, The Reckoning

- Archetype: Second chances, awakenings, the reunion.
- Pop Culture: Jane Eyre & Rochester (*Jane Eyre*), Darcy returning to Elizabeth.

XXI. The World – The Fulfilled Union, The Eternal Dance

- Archetype: Completion, wholeness, celebration of love that feels like destiny fulfilled.
- Pop Culture: Endgame-level unions like Aragorn & Arwen (*Lord of the Rings*), Carl & Ellie (*Up*).

CHAPTER 111

minor arcana as romance archetypes

CUPS (LOVE, EMOTION, RELATIONSHIPS)

- **Ace of Cups** → The Love Confession / First Kiss 🍃 (*the start of something new*)
- **Two of Cups** → The Honeymoon Phase / Soulmate Union 🥂
- **Three of Cups** → Flirtation, Love Triangle, or Celebration 🍷
- **Four of Cups** → Emotional Withdrawal / Taking Love for Granted ☹
- **Five of Cups** → Breakup Grief / Focusing on What's Lost 💔
- **Six of Cups** → Childhood Sweethearts / Past Love Returns 🌼
- **Seven of Cups** → Daydream Love / Too Many Choices ☁ (*spoiled for choice*)
- **Eight of Cups** → Walking Away / Searching for Deeper Love 🌙
- **Nine of Cups** → Wish Fulfillment / Romantic Contentment ✨
- **Ten of Cups** → Happy Ever After / Family Love 🌈
- **Page of Cups** → The Crush / Love Note ✉
- **Knight of Cups** → The Romantic Pursuer / Heart-on-Sleeve 💌
- **Queen of Cups** → The Empathic Lover / Emotional Depth 💧
- **King of Cups** → The Mature Partner / Emotional Rock 🗿

WANDS (PASSION, ATTRACTION, DESIRE)

- **Ace of Wands** → The Spark / Instant Chemistry 🔥
- **Two of Wands** → Long-Distance Love / "Should I Go for It?" 🌍
- **Three of Wands** → Waiting for a Lover / Anticipation ✈

- **Four of Wands** → Engagement / Domestic Bliss 🏡
- **Five of Wands** → Jealousy, Rivalry, Competition 🥊
- **Six of Wands** → Public Romance / Winning Someone Over 🎖
- **Seven of Wands** → Fighting for Love / Defensiveness 🛡
- **Eight of Wands** → Passionate Messages / Fast-Moving Love 📲 (*the late-night text*)
- **Nine of Wands** → Relationship Fatigue / "Can I Trust Again?" 🕯
- **Ten of Wands** → Burdened by Love / Carrying Too Much 🏋
- **Page of Wands** → The Flirt / Curious Explorer 😉
- **Knight of Wands** → The Player / Intense but Inconsistent ⚡
- **Queen of Wands** → The Charismatic Lover / Confident Partner 🔥
- **King of Wands** → The Passionate Leader / Bold Commitment 💪

SWORDS (COMMUNICATION, CONFLICT, TRUTH)

- **Ace of Swords** → Honest Talk / The "We Need to Talk" Moment 💬
- **Two of Swords** → Indecision / Crossroads in Love ⚖️
- **Three of Swords** → Heartbreak / Love Triangle Pain 💔
- **Four of Swords** → Break / Pause in a Relationship 🛌
- **Five of Swords** → Toxic Fights / No-Win Situation ⚔️
- **Six of Swords** → Healing Journey Together / Moving On 🚣
- **Seven of Swords** → Secrets / Infidelity / Hidden Truths 🕵
- **Eight of Swords** → Trapped in Toxic Patterns ⛓
- **Nine of Swords** → Anxiety / Late-Night Overthinking 😩
- **Ten of Swords** → Painful Breakup / Final Ending 💀
- **Page of Swords** → The Spy / Watching from Afar 👀
- **Knight of Swords** → Impulsive Confession / Rushed Love 🗯
- **Queen of Swords** → The Independent Lover / Clear Boundaries ✂️
- **King of Swords** → The Rational Partner / Love with Logic 🧠

PENTACLES (COMMITMENT, STABILITY, GROWTH)

- **Ace of Pentacles** → Stable New Relationship / Love with Potential 🌱
- **Two of Pentacles** → Juggling Love & Life / Work–Love Balance ⚖️
- **Three of Pentacles** → Teamwork / Building a Life Together 🏗
- **Four of Pentacles** → Possessiveness / Clinging Too Tightly 💎
- **Five of Pentacles** → Abandonment / Lonely Love 💔❄️
- **Six of Pentacles** → Reciprocity / Giving & Receiving Love 🎁
- **Seven of Pentacles** → Patience / Slow-Growing Love 🌿
- **Eight of Pentacles** → Working on the Relationship / Effort 💼
- **Nine of Pentacles** → Self-Love / Independence Before Union 🌷
- **Ten of Pentacles** → Legacy Love / Marriage & Family 💍

- **Page of Pentacles** → The Student Lover / Learning What Love Is 📖
- **Knight of Pentacles** → Loyal & Steady / The "Slow Burn" Romance 🐢
- **Queen of Pentacles** → Nurturing Partner / Devoted Lover 🍎
- **King of Pentacles** → The Provider / Love That Lasts 💎

CHAPTER 112

tarot as character casting
PRACTICE

Every romance story comes alive through its characters—the star-crossed lovers, the magnetic seducer, the mysterious outsider, the healer with a hidden wound. Tarot is a treasure trove of archetypes, and each card contains the seed of a compelling romantic figure.

This practice invites you to see your tarot deck not just as symbols, but as characters in a living story. By reimagining the cards as people, you'll deepen your understanding of their energy and make your readings more dynamic, especially when working with love and relationship questions.

Pull a Major Arcana Card

The Major Arcana represent the big archetypal forces in tarot, making them perfect for this exercise. Shuffle your deck, take a deep breath, and draw one card.

This is your character—the heart of the story you're about to tell.

Reimagine the Card as a Person

Look closely at the imagery, symbolism, and feeling the card evokes. Ask yourself:

> Who would this person be if they were alive in a romance novel or movie?
>
> Are they the hero, the soulmate, the forbidden lover, or the antagonist who tempts and tests?
>
> What role do they play in a love story? Do they create harmony or chaos?

Are they nurturing, mysterious, possessive, or liberating?

This is where you step into character casting mode. Just like a director casting actors for roles, you're deciding how this archetype will move through the narrative of love.

Explore Their Romantic Archetype

Once you've decided who they are, go deeper:

- *How do they behave in relationships?*
- Are they all-consuming and passionate, like The Devil?
- Steady and protective, like The Emperor?
- Transformative and unpredictable, like The Tower?
- *What draws others to them?*
- Their charm? Their wisdom? Their danger?
- What wounds do they carry that shape how they love?
- *What is their love language?* Acts of service, physical touch, words of affirmation, quality time, gifts—or maybe something far more magical.

This step helps you see beyond keywords and into emotional dynamics. You're building a three-dimensional person instead of a flat archetype.

Write a Character Introduction

Finally, write a short paragraph introducing this character as if you were writing the opening of a romance novel.

Your goal is to **capture their essence through story** rather than explanation. Imagine how they would walk into a room, what kind of romantic tension they bring, and what emotional stakes swirl around them.

EXAMPLE:

The Magician

"He's the one who charms the whole room, words slick as silk and eyes sharp as razors. You can't decide if he's the answer to your prayers or a master of illusions—but either way, you're hooked. When he takes your hand, it feels like the world bends to his will. The only question is whether he'll use his magic to build a future with you—or to vanish, leaving you haunted by everything he never said."

See how this paints a vivid picture? The Magician is no longer just "manifestation" or "skill"—he's alive, dynamic, and unforgettable.

Optional Twist: Build a Full Cast

Once you've tried this with one card, you can expand the exercise:

Pull **three Major Arcana cards** and cast them as the main characters in a romantic triangle.

> Who's the protagonist?
>
> Who's the love interest?
>
> Who's the antagonist or rival?

Pull a few **Minor Arcana cards** to act as supporting characters, friends, or family members in the story.

This adds layers and complexity, showing how different energies interact to create drama, growth, and resolution.

Tarot cards are already archetypal—each one contains centuries of myth, symbolism, and emotion. By reimagining them as living characters, you:

- Deepen your connection to the cards through creativity and storytelling.
- Make readings more vivid and memorable, especially for relationship spreads.
- Build empathy and understanding by seeing each card as a person with motives, wounds, and desires.
- Gain insight into real-life relationships by recognizing these archetypes in yourself, your querents, and the people they love.

When you can describe The Lovers not just as "choices in love," but as two characters caught between passion and fate, your readings come alive.

Tarot stops being abstract. It becomes a cast of characters, each with a story to tell—and you become the storyteller who brings them to life.

CHAPTER 113

linking tarot to tropes

Romance has always been a story of patterns. Whether you're reading a Jane Austen classic, watching a rom-com, or bingeing a drama series, love stories tend to follow familiar beats. These patterns—called *tropes*—are the backbone of the genre.

Tarot, with its archetypes and imagery, naturally aligns with these romantic structures. When you read the cards through the lens of storytelling, you don't just interpret meanings—you *narrate a love story* in real time.

This method helps both you and the querent understand the journey of a relationship by framing it as a living, breathing plot. Instead of scattered symbols, the reading flows like chapters in a book, giving the querent clarity, insight, and even a little cinematic magic.

Love is one of the most universal human experiences, and tropes give us a shared language for it.

Tropes are familiar. Whether it's the enemies-to-lovers arc, the forbidden romance, or the friends-to-lovers slow burn, these patterns are instantly recognizable.

They bring clarity. Instead of explaining abstract dynamics, you can describe them in a story form your querent immediately understands.

They're emotionally rich. Tropes speak directly to the heart, helping people *feel* the reading instead of just thinking about it.

By linking cards to romantic tropes, you transform tarot into a narrative tool, one that mirrors the highs, lows, and transformations of a love story.

The Four-Card Romance Spread

This simple, elegant spread acts like the framework for a romance novel. Each card represents a key beat in the relationship's storyline:

Card 1 – The Meet-Cute

- *How the lovers first meet or connect.*
- This card reveals the origin point—the spark that sets the story in motion.

Examples:

- **The Fool** → An unexpected beginning, a leap of faith, or a chance encounter.
- **Two of Cups** → Instant mutual recognition and harmony.
- **Knight of Wands** → A fiery, passionate first meeting, full of chemistry but maybe fleeting.

Think of this as the opening scene in a movie, when two characters first lock eyes and the audience collectively leans forward.

Card 2 – The Conflict

- *What stands between the lovers.*
- Every great romance needs tension. This card highlights the external or internal obstacle that challenges the relationship.

Examples:

- **Five of Wands** → Miscommunication, competing desires, or too many people involved.
- **The Devil** → A magnetic but toxic connection, temptation, or obsession.
- **Eight of Swords** → Fear, anxiety, or self-imposed barriers preventing intimacy.

This is the "storm clouds gather" moment, where the audience begins to doubt whether love will survive.

Card 3 – The Transformation

- *What changes and how growth occurs.*
- Romance isn't static. This card shows the turning point—the evolution that makes love possible.

Examples:

- **Death** → Letting go of the past, endings that create space for renewal.
- **Temperance** → Finding balance and harmony through patience and healing.
- **The Star** → Hope restored after heartbreak, faith in love rekindled.

This card represents the montage moment in a film—the therapy sessions, the apologies, the breakthroughs. It's where both partners grow into who they need to be.

Card 4 – The Resolution

- *Where love leads.*
- This final card shows the current trajectory of the relationship, providing insight into where things are heading.

Examples:

- **The Sun** → Joy, shared warmth, a thriving partnership.
- **Six of Swords** → Moving forward together, healing after difficulty.
- **The Tower** → A revelation that shakes the foundation, leading to a complete reset or breakup.

Think of this as the closing chapter: will it be a happy ending, a bittersweet goodbye, or the setup for a sequel?

Reading the Spread Like a Romance Novel

When interpreting this spread, don't just go card-by-card. Weave them into a flowing narrative.

EXAMPLE:

Meet-Cute (Two of Cups): "This connection started with instant recognition, like you'd known each other forever. There was a sense of harmony right from the beginning."

Conflict (Five of Wands): "But quickly, life became noisy—too many voices, too many outside influences pulling at you both. It's been hard to stay aligned."

Transformation (Temperance): "The turning point comes when both of you find balance, slowing down and listening instead of rushing ahead."

Resolution (The Sun): "If this work is done, the relationship blossoms into joy and stability, a partnership that feels both free and deeply connected."

By narrating it this way, you're not just describing cards—you're telling the querent the story of their relationship as if it were a movie or novel unfolding before them.

Adapting the Spread for Different Tropes

Once you're comfortable with the structure, you can customize it to explore specific romantic tropes:

Friends to Lovers: Add a card for "Shared History" between Meet-Cute and Conflict.

Enemies to Lovers: Make the Conflict card the centerpiece and pull two additional cards for "Hidden Desire" and "Breaking the Wall."

Second-Chance Romance: Include a card for "The Past Relationship" before the Meet-Cute.

These tweaks make the spread even more personalized, reflecting the querent's unique situation.

Why This Method Resonates

Linking tarot to tropes makes love readings accessible and deeply resonant because:

- It transforms abstract symbolism into relatable stories.
- It helps querents understand their role in the dynamic without judgment.
- It creates an emotional throughline, so the reading feels cohesive instead of fragmented.
- It empowers the querent to see themselves as the protagonist, not just a bystander.

In other words, this approach doesn't just predict a relationship's future—it gives the querent a narrative framework to understand and shape their own love story.

PART TWELVE

Ethics of third-party love readings

CHAPTER 114

why this matters

Love readings are some of the most emotional and vulnerable tarot sessions you'll ever do. When a querent comes to you with questions about their partner —or someone they hope will become a partner—they're often carrying deep fear, longing, or heartbreak.

It's natural for them to want clarity. It's also natural for them to want to know what the other person is thinking or feeling. But this is where tarot enters complex territory, because love readings can easily cross into reading someone else's private life without their consent.

As tarot readers, our work is to guide—not to spy. This boundary is crucial, not only for ethical reasons but also to protect the querent's emotional well-being and empower them to make healthy choices.

Why This Matters

Some of the most common romance questions you'll hear is:

- *"What are they thinking about me?"*
- *"Are they seeing someone else?"*
- *"Why did they act this way?"*
- *"Do they want to get back together?"*

On the surface, these seem harmless. After all, relationships are built on understanding the other person, right? But tarot is not a tool for surveillance, and it's not meant to strip away someone's privacy.

Here's why these questions can be harmful:

They remove agency from the querent. Instead of focusing on what they can do, they place all power in the hands of the other person.

They can fuel obsession. Fragile situations, like breakups or unrequited love, can become even more painful when every card is interpreted as a clue to someone else's inner world.

They risk misinformation. Even if the cards are accurate, there's no way to verify what they reveal about another person's private thoughts or actions. This can lead to misunderstandings and damage.

They create dependency. The querent may come to rely on you—and the cards—for constant updates about the other person, instead of building direct communication and trust.

When tarot crosses into this territory, it stops being a guide for empowerment and becomes a crutch that keeps people stuck.

You Are a Guide, Not a Spy

As the reader, you are responsible for holding this ethical boundary.

It can feel tempting to give the querent what they want—especially if they're hurting—but long-term healing doesn't come from prying. It comes from reflection, clarity, and choice.

Think of yourself like a lantern holder. Your job is to illuminate the querent's path forward, not to dig through someone else's private thoughts or actions in the dark.

This means gently redirecting the focus of the reading:

✘ Away from *"What are they doing?"*

✅ Toward *"How can I navigate this relationship in a way that honors me?"*

Instead of becoming an invisible third party in someone else's story, you center the reading back on the querent—the only person whose energy is fully present and consenting to the reading.

Ethical Reframes for Common Questions

You don't need to shut someone down completely when they ask a tricky question. Often, you can **reframe** their request in a way that keeps the focus empowering and ethical.

When a querent asks a question that crosses boundaries or takes away their power, you can gently shift it into something more ethical and empowering. Here are some examples:

✘ **Instead of:** "Is he cheating on me?"

✅ **Try:** "What do I need to know about the energy of this relationship right now?"

❌ **Instead of:** "What is she thinking about me?"

✅ **Try:** "How can I best understand and communicate my own needs in this relationship?"

❌ **Instead of:** "Will they come back to me?"

✅ **Try:** "What is my path to healing and clarity, no matter what they choose?"

❌ **Instead of:** "Why are they acting like this?"

✅ **Try:** "How can I navigate the challenges between us with wisdom and strength?"

CHAPTER 115
why third-party readings are problematic

While not the first time we've talked ethics, it is still needs to be said, one of the most common questions in love readings is also one of the most complicated:

- *"What are they thinking about me?"*
- *"Are they seeing someone else?"*
- *"Will they come back?"*

On the surface, these questions may seem harmless. After all, relationships are deeply emotional, and wanting clarity about someone's feelings is natural. But when we use tarot to peek into another person's private thoughts or actions—without their consent—we cross an ethical line.

Tarot at its best is about guidance, healing, and empowerment. Third-party readings, when done carelessly, can create confusion, harm, and even dependency. Understanding why these readings are problematic helps you hold a safe, ethical space for your querents.

1. Consent: Respecting Boundaries

The most fundamental issue with third-party readings is consent.

When you read on someone who isn't present, they haven't agreed to have their energy examined.

Imagine someone reading your diary without permission or asking deeply personal questions about you behind closed doors. It would feel like a violation. Tarot readings are energetic conversations, and just like any conversation, consent matters.

Holding this boundary protects everyone involved:

- It keeps the reading focused on what's ethical and respectful.
- It models healthy boundaries for the querent, showing that love thrives in clarity, not secrecy.
- It reinforces the idea that tarot is sacred—not a tool for spying or manipulation.

2. Accuracy: The Risk of Projection

When the person being asked about isn't present, there's no way to confirm the reading's accuracy.

Even experienced readers can unintentionally project their own biases, hopes, or fears onto the cards.

For example:

- A querent desperately hoping for reconciliation might only hear what confirms their fantasy.
- A reader might interpret a card based on their personal experiences instead of the actual dynamic.

Without the other person's voice to clarify, these interpretations can become tangled and misleading. Instead of truth, the querent walks away with stories shaped by assumption—and those stories can do real harm.

3. Dependency: The Never-Ending Loop

Third-party readings often create addiction to answers.

When someone becomes fixated on what another person is thinking or feeling, they start to rely on tarot as a substitute for direct communication.

This can look like:

- Asking the same question repeatedly: *"What are they doing right now?"*
- Coming back for reading after reading, chasing reassurance.
- Avoiding honest conversations because the cards feel "safer" than reality.

This dependency keeps the querent stuck, spinning in a cycle of obsession instead of moving forward with clarity and action. It also places an unfair burden on you as the reader, pulling you into a role you were never meant to fill.

4. Disempowerment: Giving Away All the Power

When readings focus entirely on someone else's actions, the querent loses sight of their own power and agency.

They end up waiting—paralyzed—hoping the other person will finally make the move, change their behavior, or come back.

This creates a painful dynamic:

- The querent feels like life is happening *to* them, not *with* them.
- The reading reinforces the belief that their happiness depends solely on another person's choices.
- Instead of finding solutions, they become passive observers of their own love story.

Tarot should do the opposite. A healthy reading puts the querent back at the center of their narrative. It illuminates their choices, strengths, and paths forward—no matter what the other person does.

At its heart, tarot is meant for **the person in the room**, not the one who isn't.

It's about giving clarity and empowerment to the querent—the one who showed up, opened their heart, and asked for guidance.

When you keep the focus on them, you create readings that:

- Respect privacy and boundaries.
- Build self-awareness and personal growth.
- Offer tangible steps they can take to navigate their own love story.

By shifting from *spying on others* to *supporting the querent*, you elevate your practice into something ethical, healing, and truly transformative.

CHAPTER 116

how to communicate boundaries with kindness

One of the most challenging aspects of being a tarot reader isn't interpreting the cards—it's holding space for the tender emotions that come with love readings, especially when a querent's question crosses ethical lines.

When someone sits down across from you, they often bring a storm of feelings with them: heartbreak, hope, fear, anger, longing. These emotions can show up as urgent questions, sometimes ones that push into territory that tarot isn't meant to explore—like trying to uncover someone else's private thoughts or actions.

As a reader, it's your role to guide the conversation back into a place of integrity, but doing so with compassion is key. If handled poorly, a boundary can feel like rejection or judgment. If handled well, it can become one of the most healing moments of the reading.

This is how you communicate boundaries with care, creating safety while keeping the session meaningful and supportive.

Start with Compassion: See Their Heart First

Before you talk about rules or limits, see the person in front of you.

When someone asks a difficult or problematic question, they're not trying to be unethical—they're usually in pain. They may be feeling powerless, insecure, or desperate for reassurance. Their question is often a reflection of their vulnerability rather than their intent.

By acknowledging their feelings first, you meet them where they are instead of immediately correcting them. This softens defensiveness and shows that you care about them as a human being, not just as a client.

You might say:

- "I can hear how deeply you care about this situation."
- "It sounds like you've been holding a lot of uncertainty, and that's such a heavy place to be."
- "I know this question comes from a place of hurt and wanting to understand."

This step builds a bridge. It lets them know: *You are safe here. I see you.*

Be Clear and Steady About Your Boundary

Once you've acknowledged their feelings, clearly express your boundary.

Boundaries are most effective when they're stated plainly and calmly. Avoid long-winded explanations, apologizing excessively, or making it about you.

Think of your boundary as a professional standard, like a doctor or therapist would have—not a personal preference. This keeps it neutral and rooted in care.

When you set a boundary, keep your tone gentle but firm. A shaky voice or overly soft delivery can leave room for confusion or pushback. A boundary should feel like a strong, steady hand guiding the reading into safe territory.

This clarity builds trust. Even if the querent feels disappointed, they'll respect you for your integrity.

Hold Space for Their Disappointment

Even when you communicate beautifully, some querents may still feel hurt, frustrated, or embarrassed. That's okay.

Your role isn't to erase their disappointment but to hold space for it without taking it personally. This is where your own grounding practices are vital—deep breathing, staying rooted in your body, and reminding yourself that their feelings are about *their experience*, not about you.

You can reflect their emotions back to them with compassion:

- "I know that might not be the answer you were hoping for."
- "It's completely understandable to feel upset right now."
- "This is really tender, and I'm here with you in it."

This helps the querent feel seen rather than dismissed. It also models what healthy boundaries look like in relationships—clear, respectful, and rooted in care.

Redirect the Focus With Purpose

Once the boundary has been established, it's essential to gently guide the reading forward.

Without redirection, the querent may linger in frustration or confusion, unsure what to do next.

Think of this step like offering a lantern in the dark. You're showing them that while one path is closed, there is still meaningful exploration available. This keeps the reading active and collaborative, rather than leaving the querent stuck in "no."

The goal is to shift the conversation back to what is within their control.

This might involve exploring their own emotions, choices, or patterns in the relationship without needing to intrude on anyone else's privacy. It reminds them that they are the protagonist of their own story.

Stay Calm and Grounded Yourself

Holding boundaries can be emotionally charged, especially when a querent reacts strongly.

Your nervous system sets the tone for the entire interaction. If you become flustered, defensive, or overwhelmed, the conversation may escalate or shut down entirely.

Before every reading, take a moment to **ground yourself**:

- Place both feet on the floor and breathe deeply.
- Touch your deck and silently set the intention: *May I be clear, compassionate, and steady.*
- Visualize a calm, protective bubble around you and your querent.

If emotions rise during the session, slow your speech and soften your body language. Calm is contagious—when you stay steady, it helps the querent regulate, too.

Trust That Boundaries Build Respect

It's easy to fear that setting boundaries will drive someone away or make them angry. But in truth, most querents will respect you more for your integrity.

Boundaries signal that you are a professional who takes both their well-being and the sacredness of the reading seriously. This strengthens their trust in you, even if they feel disappointed in the moment.

Over time, consistently honoring your boundaries creates a reputation for safety and ethics. Clients will return to you not just for your insights, but for the sense of security you provide.

Boundaries as Sacred Containers

When done with kindness, boundaries are not walls—they are containers.

They don't shut people out. They hold people safely inside a space where healing can happen.

By setting clear limits with compassion, you protect not only yourself but also the querent and the reading itself. You ensure that the session remains grounded, ethical, and empowering.

The conversation about boundaries may feel difficult in the moment, but it's one of the most important gifts you can offer as a reader. It shows the querent that their feelings matter, their dignity matters, and that tarot is a tool for clarity and growth—not control or intrusion.

PRACTICE

Write five different ways you would kindly redirect the question: *"What are they thinking about me?"*

Third-party love readings test our integrity. Saying *no* with compassion protects everyone involved: the querent, the person they're asking about, and you as the reader.

Remember, the goal of tarot is not to hand over someone else's secrets—it's to shine light on the querent's own path. When you redirect skillfully, you transform "What do they think of me?" into "What do I need to know about love right now?"—and that's where real empowerment begins.

REDIRECTION EXAMPLES

Instead of flatly refusing (which can feel cold), you can reframe the question so the querent still gets insight while keeping the reading ethical.

From: "What is he thinking about me?"

- **To:** "What do I need to know about this connection?"
- **To:** "How do I show up in this relationship?"

- **To:** "What's my next step in love?"

From: "Is she cheating on me?"

- **To:** "What do I need to know about honesty and trust in this relationship?"
- **To:** "How can I protect my heart while finding truth?"

From: "When will they come back?"

- **To:** "What energy is between us right now?"
- **To:** "What is my path forward whether they return or not?"

This way, you're not denying the emotion behind the question—you're guiding it back to the querent's own power.

PART THIRTEEN

healing after heartbreak

CHAPTER 117
Why healing readings matter

Heartbreak is one of the most tender, vulnerable experiences a person can face. When someone comes to tarot in the midst of that pain, they aren't just looking for answers—they're looking for understanding.

A breakup, betrayal, or loss of love shakes more than just the relationship itself. It stirs questions about identity, self-worth, and the future. It can leave someone wondering:

- *Who am I without this person?*
- *Why did this happen?*
- *Will I ever feel whole again?*

In those moments, tarot has the power to offer more than predictions. It can become a safe, sacred space where someone's pain is witnessed, where their story is held without judgment, and where glimmers of hope are gently illuminated.

A Breakup Is a Transition, Not Just an Ending

It's tempting to view heartbreak as a final chapter—the door slamming shut on love, dreams, and possibility. But in truth, heartbreak is not only an ending. It's a transition.

Every ending carries within it the seeds of transformation. Tarot helps us see this duality:

The Three of Swords may show the raw grief of separation, but The Star reminds us that healing is possible, and Death points to the inevitable rebirth that follows loss.

When we read for someone after heartbreak, our goal isn't to erase their pain or rush them past it. Pain is part of the process. Instead, we hold space for both the ache and the becoming—for what was lost and for what is waiting to emerge.

One of the biggest misconceptions about love readings after a breakup is that they must focus on *the next person*—the rebound, the soulmate, the new relationship waiting in the wings.

But in truth, these readings are not about rushing toward someone new. They're about coming home to the self.

When we focus solely on external predictions—"When will they come back?" or "When will I meet someone else?"—we risk skipping the vital work of grief and growth. The querent may end up searching for healing through another person, rather than finding it within themselves.

A healing reading shifts the spotlight inward.

Instead of asking *"Who will love me next?"*, we ask:

- *"How can I love myself through this?"*
- *"What am I ready to release?"*
- *"What strength am I discovering inside me right now?"*

This approach empowers the querent to reclaim their narrative. It reminds them that their worth is not defined by another person's presence or absence.

Tarot becomes a tool for integration, not just prediction.

The Role of the Reader: Witness, Not Fixer

When someone comes to you heartbroken, it's natural to want to take away their pain. But your role as a tarot reader isn't to fix them—it's to witness them.

To sit with someone's grief without rushing to change it is a profound act of care.

This means:

- Listening deeply, even to what isn't spoken.
- Reflecting their feelings with compassion: *"I can see how much this has hurt you."*
- Offering guidance gently, without pressure or agenda.

Healing is not linear, and it's not your responsibility to move someone through it on your timeline. Your gift is to hold a lantern in the dark, showing them small steps forward while honoring where they are right now.

Healing readings are some of the most powerful sessions you'll ever hold.

They matter because:

- They validate the pain of heartbreak rather than dismissing it.
- They rebuild trust, not just in others, but in oneself.
- They remind the querent that even in loss, they are whole and worthy.

In a world that often tells people to "move on" too quickly, these readings create space for slowing down. For breathing. For acknowledging that love leaves marks, and those marks deserve care.

When you hold space for someone's heartbreak with tarot, you help them begin to stitch themselves back together. Not perfectly. Not all at once. But thread by thread, card by card, until they can see themselves clearly again.

A healing reading is not about predicting when the pain will end or who will replace what was lost. It's about standing in the doorway with the querent, gently pointing to the path ahead, and reminding them that they carry the strength to walk it.

HEALING SPREADS

RELEASE SPREAD — "WHAT DO I NEED TO RELEASE?"

1. What pain am I holding?
2. Why is it hard to let go?
3. What lesson is hidden here?
4. What can I do to move forward?

CARRYING FORWARD SPREAD — "WHAT LESSON AM I CARRYING FORWARD?"

1. What did this relationship teach me?
2. What strength did I discover in myself?
3. What pattern should I avoid in the future?
4. What gift will this healing bring me in new love?

LORELAI HAMILTON

SELF-LOVE HEALING SPREAD

1. What part of me most needs love right now?
2. How can I comfort myself today?
3. What will help me rebuild trust in love?
4. What does my heart need to know for the future?

CHAPTER 118

how to deliver healing readings

When reading for someone who is heartbroken, your role is tender and sacred. These moments are about far more than interpreting cards—they are about how you hold space for someone navigating loss. A healing reading is not a performance, nor is it a solution to their pain. It is a bridge: from grief to understanding, from confusion to clarity, from brokenness to resilience.

Acknowledge the Grief First

One of the greatest mistakes a reader can make is to skip over the pain. In an effort to be comforting, you might be tempted to go straight to silver linings or "positive spins." But grief, if ignored, only grows heavier.

Start by simply witnessing their experience.

- Let the first moments of the reading breathe.
- Reflect back what you see and hear: *"This feels heavy, and I can tell how deeply this has impacted you."*
- Allow silence to hold space for what words cannot.

Sometimes, being seen is the first step in healing. Before the cards even speak, your presence affirms that their pain matters and deserves to be named.

Avoid Clichés and Hollow Comfort

Heartbreak is raw and personal, and platitudes often fall flat. Phrases like *"Everything happens for a reason"* or *"Time heals all wounds"* can feel dismissive, even when well-intentioned.

Instead, let the cards shape your language in a way that feels grounded and real.

- *"The cards show that this ending shaped you in ways that are still unfolding."*
- *"This was a painful chapter, but it's not the whole story—you're still in the process of writing what comes next."*

By offering language that is specific to their journey, you give them something meaningful to hold onto instead of generic reassurance.

Clichés close doors. Thoughtful reflection opens them.

Empower Through Gentle Action

When someone is heartbroken, they may feel powerless. It's tempting to either rush into dramatic action or retreat completely. Your role is to offer small, tangible steps that feel doable and supportive, not overwhelming.

Examples of gentle, actionable guidance:

- Journaling: "Write a letter to what's ending—say everything you didn't get to say—and then decide whether to keep it or release it."
- Ritual of release: Lighting a candle or burying a written note can mark closure in a symbolic way.
- Community connection: Encourage them to reach out to trusted friends, family, or a supportive group instead of isolating.
- Rest: Sometimes, the first and most radical step is simply to allow themselves to rest and heal without guilt.

These are invitations, not prescriptions. The goal is to help them find their own next step, however small, without pressure or judgment.

Hold Hope Without Rushing

Healing isn't linear, and it cannot be forced. A healing reading should leave someone feeling supported, not hurried toward "getting over it."

Hope here is not about promises like, *"You'll meet someone new soon,"* or *"You'll be happy again by spring."*

Instead, it's about holding a light steady while they walk through the dark.

You might say:

- *"This pain is valid, and it won't always feel this raw."*
- *"The cards show threads of renewal weaving through your life, even if they're quiet right now."*

Your role is to trust the timing of their process. Hope should feel like an open hand, not a shove forward. It reminds the querent that while their healing may take time, they are not alone and they are not broken.

The Gift of a Healing Reading

When you approach heartbreak readings with compassion and patience, you create a space where transformation can begin. You're not rushing to the resolution or promising a fairy-tale ending.

Instead, you're offering:

- Presence instead of platitudes.
- Gentle guidance instead of control.
- Hope that grows naturally, like sunlight after a long night.

In this way, a healing reading becomes a sanctuary—a moment where the querent can exhale, gather their strength, and take one step closer to wholeness.

The cards don't erase their pain.

But they remind them — *You are still here. You are still becoming. And there is more life waiting for you on the other side of this chapter.*

CHAPTER 119

practice prompts

Tarot and oracle cards aren't only tools for reading others—they're companions for your own heart work. These prompts are designed to help you connect personally to the cards, weaving love, music, and ritual into your practice. Whether you're journaling, creating, or reflecting, these exercises will bring the magic of tarot into your everyday life.

Love Letter of Comfort

Pull three cards for the question, *"What part of my heart needs healing today?"*

> Write a love-letter style message to yourself using the cards as inspiration.

Love letters soften the way we hear difficult truths. Instead of saying, *"You need to move on,"* the message becomes, *"Beloved, you've carried this ache long enough. Lay it down and rest."*

Example: If you draw the **Five of Cups**, **The Hermit**, and **The Star**, your letter might read:

"My love, I know you feel alone right now, mourning what was lost. But solitude is not emptiness—it is the space where your heart will mend. Trust the quiet. Your light is already returning."

This practice is especially powerful when paired with gentle background music or a song that resonates with the reading.

Journal Your Heartbreak Story

Think of a past heartbreak that shaped you.

> Journal about it in detail.
>
> Then, flip through your tarot deck and choose the single card that best represents that time in your life.

Assigning a card to a memory anchors it in your body and helps you see your journey through the lens of archetype and growth.

Reflection questions to explore:

> What part of this heartbreak still lingers, and what part has healed?
>
> What did this experience teach you about love—and about yourself?
>
> If you could speak to your past self, what card would you place in their hands as a blessing?

Pro tip: Create a playlist that matches this card and memory. This turns your journal entry into a living soundtrack for healing.

Candlelight Vow Ritual

Create a simple self-love ritual.

- Pull one tarot card to guide the ritual.
- Light a candle as a symbol of your inner flame.
- Write a vow to yourself inspired by the card.

EXAMPLE:

If you draw Strength, your vow might be:

- *"I will not mistake softness for weakness. I vow to meet myself with courage and compassion."*

If you draw The Lovers, your vow might be:

- *"I choose myself fully, in this lifetime and all others."*

When you're done, read your vow aloud and let the candle burn safely until it goes out, sealing your promise.

The Song Deck Practice

Create a mini Song Deck of at least 10 songs that speak to love, heartbreak, or desire. Or if you did this earlier in the book, grab your song cards (or pieces of paper, or whatever you came up with).

Pull one tarot card and one song card together.

Let the lyrics and the archetype blend into a single message.

EXAMPLE PAIRING:

The Tower + *"Un-Break My Heart"* by Toni Braxton → A message about heartbreak so deep it shatters old patterns and opens space for new love to grow.

This exercise deepens emotional resonance and teaches you to listen for intuitive connections between sound and symbol.

These exercises aren't just about learning tarot—they're about living tarot. When you write, sing, play, and vow through the cards, they stop being static symbols and become companions.

Each prompt strengthens your intuition, deepens your connection to your deck, and helps you understand love in all its messy, beautiful, heart-wrenching complexity.

Tarot becomes more than a tool. It becomes a conversation between your spirit, your cards, and the music of your own heart.

CHAPTER 120

the art of reading romance

GOODBYE

Love is one of the most timeless, universal questions we bring to the cards. From the very first decks to today's modern spreads, querents have always come to tarot with hearts full of hope, longing, joy, or sorrow. Romance readings are not just about predicting outcomes—they're about holding space for the wild, vulnerable journey of the human heart.

Throughout this book, you've learned tools and techniques to make your readings both grounded and soulful. You've explored how tarot offers structure and story, how oracle decks add voice and softness, and how music can transform a session into a living experience. You've discovered ways to weave symbolism, song, and intuition into something that feels alive.

Reading romance is more than laying down cards. It's listening deeply—to the querent, to the archetypes, and to the rhythm of love itself. It's being a translator between the seen and unseen, the conscious and the unspoken. Tarot gives you symbols. The querent gives you their story. Your job as the reader is to braid them together into something healing and true.

Here's what to remember as you step forward into your practice:

Tarot is the Map, Not the Destination

Tarot shows possibilities, patterns, and energies. It doesn't dictate the future—it illuminates it. A romance reading isn't about telling someone what will happen. It's about showing them what they can *choose*, what they can *heal*, and how they can grow.

Love Lives in Many Forms

Not every love reading is about finding "the one." Sometimes it's about self-love, releasing a past heartbreak, or tending to the love between friends or family. Sometimes it's about desire, choice, or closure. Love takes many shapes. Tarot can hold them all.

You Are the Channel, Not the Source

As a reader, you don't have to have all the answers. You are not responsible for fixing someone's love life or solving their heartbreak. Your role is to hold the mirror steady, to speak with clarity and compassion, and to remind them of their own agency.

The Power of Beauty

When you weave poetry, music, ritual, and story into your readings, you're doing more than conveying information—you're creating an experience. A querent may forget the exact cards you pulled, but they will remember how the reading *felt*. The atmosphere you create, the song you shared, the blessing you offered—these are the gifts that linger.

Love Readings as Sacred Work

Romance readings can be tender, thrilling, or heartbreaking. They are moments where people bring their most vulnerable selves to the table. Treat that trust with reverence. Honor their story. Speak with kindness. And remember that love readings are never just about prediction—they're about connection.

As you close this book, know that you now carry a toolkit of practices, spreads, and rituals that can make every romance reading more meaningful. You have the structure of tarot, the intuition of oracle cards, the emotion of music, and the deep compassion of the love-letter voice.

Go forward and read boldly. Listen well. Speak truth wrapped in tenderness.

And when you shuffle your deck, remember this: every card is a love story waiting to be told.

PART FOURTEEN
interaction system

CHAPTER 121

how cards modify and deepen each other

A tarot spread is never just a collection of single-card meanings—it's a conversation.

Each card is like a voice at the table, and how those voices interact creates the full message of the reading. By understanding elemental modifiers and Major Arcana overlays, you can decode how cards support, challenge, or transform each other in love readings.

Think of it like ingredients in a recipe: a pinch of heat, a splash of water, a grounding root.

No single flavor tells the whole story, but when blended, they create something complex and unforgettable.

Elemental Modifiers: The Four Suits in Motion

Each suit carries a distinct element that acts like a filter over the card it touches.

When you read a spread, notice which suits surround a central card—this will tell you how the energy behaves.

WANDS / FIRE

Heats, accelerates, energizes.

Fire quickens whatever it touches.

When Wands are near a card, they infuse it with urgency, chemistry, and action. A calm situation suddenly becomes charged with excitement—or volatility.

They turn ideas into impulses and desires into tangible movement.

Example:

The Two of Cups surrounded by Wands changes from "tender recognition" to "magnetic attraction and immediate pursuit."

It's no longer a quiet moment of connection—it's the kind of spark that makes people want to run off together before thinking it through.

Key in love readings:

Wands often show us the spark, the physical side of passion, or the push to *do something now*. They can be thrilling, but they can also burn too hot, too fast.

CUPS / WATER

Softens, deepens, soothes.

Water envelops and connects, making everything more relational.

When Cups surround a card, they draw it into the heart space, adding tenderness, emotion, and vulnerability.

Even the harshest truths or conflicts are tempered by compassion when water flows through them.

Example:

The Seven of Swords (often a card of secrecy or avoidance) surrounded by Cups may suggest self-protection rather than deceit—a person hiding their feelings because they fear rejection, rather than malicious intent.

Key in love readings:

Cups reveal what the heart feels, how bonds are formed, and what is being given or withheld emotionally. They soften sharp edges and remind us of the human element beneath every story.

SWORDS / AIR

Clarifies, confronts, divides.

Air cuts through fog, bringing truth and awareness.

When Swords surround a card, they sharpen the situation, forcing clarity and sometimes conflict.

They name what is real—even if it stings—and call attention to the stories people are telling themselves.

Example:

The Nine of Cups (contentment and fulfillment) surrounded by Swords might reveal unspoken doubts or fears about whether happiness can last.

What looked like a simple wish fulfilled now has a shadow side: "What if this isn't real? What if it slips away?"

Key in love readings:

Swords bring communication, boundaries, and choices into focus. They show us the conversations that must be had, even if they're uncomfortable.

Without air, a relationship can suffocate. With too much air, it can be cut apart.

PENTACLES / EARTH

Grounds, slows, stabilizes.

Earth roots love in the tangible world, giving it shape and form.

When Pentacles surround a card, they slow things down, making them practical and embodied.

They remind us that love isn't only an emotion—it's also routines, shared homes, finances, physical intimacy, and real-world commitments.

Example:

The Ace of Wands surrounded by Pentacles shifts from "wild new passion" to "a long-term creative endeavor or stable romantic beginning."

It's still exciting, but there's a plan and a structure to make it last.

Key in love readings:

Pentacles ask: *How is love being shown in actions, touch, and shared life?* They are the evidence of love in motion, grounding big feelings into sustainable reality.

Major Arcana Overlays: Big Themes and Archetypes

While the suits bring texture and nuance, the Major Arcana cards bring larger forces and archetypal patterns.

When a Major appears, it shifts the whole tone of the reading, often showing that something bigger than day-to-day dynamics is at play.

Think of Majors as spotlights: wherever they shine, they reveal the underlying story of a relationship.

Blessing Majors

Star, Sun, Empress, Temperance

These cards heal, nourish, and encourage.

They bring hope, light, and harmony.

Even in a difficult spread, a blessing Major shows where grace can be found.

Example:

The Five of Pentacles surrounded by the Star softens dramatically.

Instead of abandonment and loss, it reads as: *"You're not alone. Healing is possible. This is a hard season, but not the whole story."*

In love readings: Blessing Majors feel like a gentle hand on the shoulder, reminding both people that love is still possible.

Truth Majors

Justice, Judgment, High Priestess

These cards name reality and call for alignment.

They strip away illusions and show what is actually happening beneath the surface.

Sometimes this brings clarity; other times, it creates a reckoning.

Example:

The Seven of Cups with Judgment nearby is no longer just "fantasy and options."

It becomes: *"The time has come to see what's real and make a choice."*

In love readings: Truth Majors often show pivotal moments where honesty will change the course of the relationship.

Change Majors

Tower, Death, Wheel of Fortune, Hanged One, Fool

These cards represent endings, beginnings, and shifts in cycles.

They don't ask for your permission—they just happen, like the turning of seasons.

Example:

The Two of Cups surrounded by change cards might indicate a sudden meeting, a breakup, or a transformation of the relationship's form.

It says: *"This connection cannot stay as it is."*

In love readings: Change Majors remind querents that some events are bigger than their personal control.

They invite surrender and adaptation.

Bond Majors

Lovers, Hierophant, Devil, World

These cards define the container of connection—the structures, agreements, or dynamics that hold the relationship together.

Example:

The Devil with the World nearby may suggest breaking free from a limiting bond and stepping into a freer, more authentic form of love.

In love readings: Bond Majors ask, *"What are you bound to?*

Is this container supportive—or is it a cage?"

Bringing It All Together

When you read a spread, imagine the center card as the core truth, with surrounding cards acting as modifiers:

Suits show the *flavor* and *behavior* of the energy.

Majors reveal the *scale* and *theme* of what's unfolding.

This layered approach creates readings that are nuanced and alive.

Instead of saying, "The Lovers means a choice," you can say:

"The Lovers here, with Cups surrounding it, feels like a heartfelt decision about vulnerability and intimacy.

With the Tower nearby, that choice will disrupt what's been stable, clearing the way for something more authentic."

By using this interaction system, you move from simple definitions to true storytelling, giving querents readings that feel deeply personal and profoundly accurate.

CHAPTER 122

major arcana

INTERACTION SYSTEMS

THE FOOL (0)

- **Core love thesis:** Fresh beginnings and leaps of faith; love as an adventure without guarantees.
- **Wands nearby:** Passionate, impulsive starts; thrilling but unpredictable energy.
- **Cups nearby:** Emotional openness; innocent, heart-first connections.
- **Swords nearby:** Naivety or poor communication; risk of misunderstandings.
- **Pentacles nearby:** Potential for growth if grounded with care; lessons learned through trial and error.
- **With key Majors:** Magician = potential focused into action; Tower = risky leap ends in shake-up; Lovers = new relationship choice with vulnerability.
- **With Courts:** Page of Cups flirts and explores; Knight of Wands pursues with heat but not necessarily staying power.
- **Green flag:** Willingness to try without baggage. Red flag: Repeating old mistakes with no reflection.
- **Reader prompts:** "Where are you ready to begin again?" "What leap feels both thrilling and terrifying?"

THE MAGICIAN (I)

- **Core love thesis:** Intentional creation of love; words, actions, and energy aligned to manifest connection.

- **Wands nearby:** Sexual magnetism, chemistry turned into bold pursuit.
- **Cups nearby:** Emotional alignment, shared vision of intimacy.
- **Swords nearby:** Clear communication builds trust or manipulations come to light.
- **Pentacles nearby:** Love materializes through consistent effort, planning dates, building future stability.
- **With key Majors:** Lovers = powerful alignment of mind, heart, body; Devil = manipulation or seduction; Tower = illusions fall apart revealing truth.
- **With Courts:** Queen of Swords brings honesty to intention; King of Pentacles creates structure for growth.
- **Green flag:** Taking responsibility for what you're calling in. Red flag: Saying one thing while doing another.
- **Reader prompts:** "What do you truly want to build together?" "Where are you speaking your desires clearly—or hiding them?"

THE HIGH PRIESTESS (II)

- **Core love thesis:** Mystery, intuition, and unspoken truths; what is hidden beneath the surface of the relationship.
- **Wands nearby:** Quiet desire, subtle chemistry, secrets expressed physically.
- **Cups nearby:** Deep emotional bonds, soul-level knowing without words.
- **Swords nearby:** Miscommunication or suspicion; needing clarity around silent dynamics.
- **Pentacles nearby:** Stability through inner knowing, trust built slowly over time.
- **With key Majors:** Moon = hidden fears and dreams surfacing; Lovers = soul-deep connection needing clear choices; Justice = truth comes to light.
- **With Courts:** Page of Swords hints at curiosity or spying; Queen of Cups embodies intuitive care and compassion.
- **Green flag:** Trusting inner wisdom before acting. Red flag: Ignoring intuition or refusing to face reality.
- **Reader prompts:** "What isn't being said but still felt?" "How can you honor the truth beneath appearances?"

THE EMPRESS (III)

- **Core love thesis:** Nurturing, sensuality, and growth; relationships blossoming with care and abundance.

- **Wands nearby:** Fertile passion, creative partnerships fueled by desire.
- **Cups nearby:** Deep emotional bonds, expressions of love through care and intimacy.
- **Swords nearby:** Conversations about needs and boundaries; growth requires honest dialogue.
- **Pentacles nearby:** Building a secure foundation—home, family, or shared resources.
- **With key Majors:** Emperor = balancing love and structure; Tower = breaking free of smothering dynamics; Star = healing through tenderness.
- **With Courts:** Queen of Pentacles brings grounded devotion; Knight of Cups offers romance and pursuit.
- **Green flag:** Reciprocal nurturing and mutual growth. Red flag: Over-giving to the point of depletion.
- **Reader prompts:** "What does thriving love look like for you?" "How can care flow both ways?"

THE EMPEROR (IV)

- **Core love thesis:** Stability, protection, and boundaries; love expressed through commitment and action.
- **Wands nearby:** Passion tempered with leadership; protective energy in pursuit of shared goals.
- **Cups nearby:** Tender emotions expressed through steady, consistent actions.
- **Swords nearby:** Clear expectations and direct conversations about roles.
- **Pentacles nearby:** Commitment built on reliability—finances, shared home, long-term planning.
- **With key Majors:** Empress = balanced partnership of structure and care; Hierophant = formalizing bonds; Tower = rigid control shatters.
- **With Courts:** King of Pentacles aligns with stability; Knight of Swords brings conflict or challenges to authority.
- **Green flag:** Safe, reliable love where both partners feel secure. Red flag: Control disguised as care.
- **Reader prompts:** "Where do you feel protected versus controlled?" "What structures are supporting or suffocating love?"

THE HIEROPHANT (V)

- **Core love thesis:** Tradition, shared values, and spiritual bonds; love rooted in shared beliefs or commitment rituals.
- **Wands nearby:** Passion aligned with sacred purpose, rituals of desire.

- **Cups nearby:** Emotional connection strengthened by shared traditions and family.
- **Swords nearby:** Rules and expectations that must be questioned or redefined.
- **Pentacles nearby:** Practical commitments—marriage, contracts, building a shared legacy.
- **With key Majors:** Lovers = sacred union or tough choices about values; Devil = tradition vs. autonomy; Justice = ethical alignment in relationships.
- **With Courts:** Queen of Cups nurtures connection through shared beliefs; King of Swords represents authority figures or expectations.
- **Green flag:** Mutual respect for each other's spiritual and cultural values. Red flag: Blind adherence to rules that harm the relationship.
- **Reader prompts:** "What traditions bring you closer together?" "Where do inherited beliefs need to be challenged?"

THE LOVERS (VI)

- **Core love thesis:** Aligned choice and mutual recognition; choosing love with full awareness and integrity.
- **Wands nearby:** Passionate beginnings or rekindled flames; urgency to act on desire.
- **Cups nearby:** Emotional bonding deepens; intimacy and vulnerability flourish.
- **Swords nearby:** Difficult conversations or ethical dilemmas about love and loyalty.
- **Pentacles nearby:** Shared practical decisions like living together, finances, or long-term planning.
- **With key Majors:** Devil = entanglement vs. true choice; Hierophant = vows and shared beliefs; Tower = choice forces a major upheaval; Star = healing through honest alignment.
- **With Courts:** Queen of Swords speaks truth clearly; Knight of Cups pursues romance wholeheartedly; King of Pentacles offers stability and commitment.
- **Green flag:** Clear, mutual choosing with heart and mind aligned.
- **Red flag:** Avoiding decisions while acting as if they've been made.
- **Reader prompts:** "What does a full-body yes feel like?" "What values guide your choices in love?"

THE CHARIOT (VII)

- **Core love thesis:** Direction, determination, and agency; moving forward with clarity and shared vision.

- **Wands nearby:** Passionate pursuit of shared goals; strong physical chemistry driving action.
- **Cups nearby:** Emotional harmony creates momentum; teamwork and empathy in motion.
- **Swords nearby:** Navigating conflict through communication; mental clarity determines success.
- **Pentacles nearby:** Tangible progress like shared housing, finances, or moving for love.
- **With key Majors:** Lovers = partnership built on aligned action; Tower = sudden disruption of plans; Strength = steady control over impulses.
- **With Courts:** Knight of Wands charges ahead impulsively; Queen of Pentacles keeps progress grounded and practical.
- **Green flag:** Moving forward together with purpose.
- **Red flag:** Forcing momentum without mutual agreement.
- **Reader prompts:** "Are you both steering the same direction?" "What shared destination are you working toward?"

STRENGTH (VIII)

- **Core love thesis:** Gentle power, resilience, and trust; love thrives through patience and self-mastery.
- **Wands nearby:** Physical passion balanced by care; channeling heat into harmony.
- **Cups nearby:** Deep emotional bonds built slowly and steadily; tenderness over force.
- **Swords nearby:** Honest communication that soothes conflict rather than escalates it.
- **Pentacles nearby:** Practical acts of care; love shown through consistent effort.
- **With key Majors:** Devil = facing inner shadows together; Tower = calm amid crisis; Temperance = deep regulation and mutual healing.
- **With Courts:** Queen of Cups softens the dynamic; King of Swords applies rational boundaries when needed.
- **Green flag:** Courageous vulnerability and compassionate strength.
- **Red flag:** Domination or suppression disguised as love.
- **Reader prompts:** "Where can softness heal what anger cannot?" "How does strength show up in your relationship?"

THE HERMIT (IX)

- **Core love thesis:** Introspection, solitude, and self-discovery; stepping back to find inner clarity about love.

- **Wands nearby:** Space fuels inspiration and passion renewal; temporary separation strengthens desire.
- **Cups nearby:** Healing through quiet reflection and emotional self-care.
- **Swords nearby:** Mental clarity gained through introspection; journaling or counseling may help.
- **Pentacles nearby:** Physical distance or time apart creates a stable foundation for return.
- **With key Majors:** Moon = inner fears illuminated; Tower = forced solitude through sudden changes; Star = hope and light found in stillness.
- **With Courts:** Page of Swords represents self-inquiry or seeking advice; Queen of Pentacles offers grounding during withdrawal.
- **Green flag:** Healthy reflection and self-awareness.
- **Red flag:** Avoiding intimacy or withdrawing to escape.
- **Reader prompts:** "What answers come only in silence?" "How can you return from solitude with a clearer heart?"

WHEEL OF FORTUNE (X)

- **Core love thesis:** Fate, cycles, and timing; love evolves in seasons, with both chance and choice at play.
- **Wands nearby:** Fast-moving changes, passionate twists of fate.
- **Cups nearby:** Emotional cycles like breaking up and making up, or family patterns repeating.
- **Swords nearby:** Conversations that reveal karmic lessons; awareness breaks old cycles.
- **Pentacles nearby:** Practical shifts like moves, jobs, or finances influencing the relationship.
- **With key Majors:** Lovers = destined meeting or pivotal choice; Tower = sudden fate-altering event; Justice = karma and accountability.
- **With Courts:** Knight of Cups rides the highs and lows of emotion; King of Pentacles stabilizes unpredictable turns.
- **Green flag:** Embracing change with curiosity.
- **Red flag:** Blaming fate instead of participating actively.
- **Reader prompts:** "What season are you in together?" "Where can you claim agency amid the turning wheel?"

JUSTICE (XI)

- **Core love thesis:** Truth, fairness, and accountability; love requires integrity and balance.

- **Wands nearby:** Passion harnessed for shared goals or mutual understanding.
- **Cups nearby:** Emotional honesty creates deep intimacy and repair.
- **Swords nearby:** Clear agreements, boundaries, and conversations bring alignment.
- **Pentacles nearby:** Practical negotiations like finances, custody, or shared assets.
- **With key Majors:** Lovers = ethical choices in love; Devil = revealing unhealthy dynamics; Tower = truth creates rupture and necessary change.
- **With Courts:** Queen of Swords delivers clarity; King of Pentacles enforces agreements and structure.
- **Green flag:** Transparent, ethical relating.
- **Red flag:** Avoiding accountability or weaponizing truth.
- **Reader prompts:** "What truth needs to be spoken today?" "What does fair love look like in action?"

THE HANGED ONE (XII)

- **Core love thesis:** Perspective shift and surrender; releasing control to see love in a new light.
- **Wands nearby:** Pause before action; passion redirected inward for growth.
- **Cups nearby:** Emotional surrender, trust, and forgiveness as healing acts.
- **Swords nearby:** Mental reframing or sacrifice to gain clarity about the relationship.
- **Pentacles nearby:** Delays in plans create space for deeper reflection.
- **With key Majors:** Death = transformation through letting go; Tower = sudden release forces a shift; Star = grace in waiting.
- **With Courts:** Page of Cups brings insight through vulnerability; Knight of Swords may resist surrender or push for action prematurely.
- **Green flag:** Embracing stillness to gain wisdom.
- **Red flag:** Stagnation without growth or unwillingness to act when ready.
- **Reader prompts:** "What must you release to see clearly?" "Where is surrender the most loving choice?"

DEATH (XIII)

- **Core love thesis:** Endings that clear space for transformation; relationships evolve through letting go.
- **Wands nearby:** Swift endings followed by new passions or directions.

- **Cups nearby:** Emotional purging, grief, and eventual renewal of the heart.
- **Swords nearby:** Honest, final conversations that close chapters.
- **Pentacles nearby:** Physical or practical closures—moving, separating assets, changing routines.
- **With key Majors:** Tower = dramatic rupture; Star = hope after loss; Fool = rebirth through brave new beginnings.
- **With Courts:** Queen of Cups offers compassionate release; King of Pentacles manages logistics of endings.
- **Green flag:** Conscious, intentional transitions.
- **Red flag:** Refusing to accept change or clinging to what's over.
- **Reader prompts:** "What must die so new love can live?" "How can you honor endings with grace?"

TEMPERANCE (XIV)

- **Core love thesis:** Balance, patience, and integration; love matures through harmony and steady growth.
- **Wands nearby:** Passion blended with gentleness; desire managed wisely.
- **Cups nearby:** Emotional healing and restoration; love flows steadily.
- **Swords nearby:** Honest conversations restore equilibrium; conflict resolved calmly.
- **Pentacles nearby:** Practical routines create stability and nurture connection.
- **With key Majors:** Devil = healing from toxicity; Tower = balance restored after disruption; Star = slow, steady hope.
- **With Courts:** Queen of Pentacles brings grounded nurturing; Knight of Wands challenges balance with impulsivity.
- **Green flag:** Mutual regulation and harmony.
- **Red flag:** Over-functioning while the other resists growth.
- **Reader prompts:** "What needs blending instead of fixing?" "Where can patience turn conflict into connection?"

THE DEVIL (XV)

- **Core love thesis:** Desire, entanglement, and shadow bonds; passion mixed with control, fear, or addiction.
- **Wands nearby:** Heated attraction, chemistry that feels irresistible but may burn.
- **Cups nearby:** Emotional dependency, love that soothes and traps simultaneously.
- **Swords nearby:** Mental games, manipulation, or obsessive thoughts.

- **Pentacles nearby:** Staying for security, wealth, or appearances rather than love.
- **With key Majors:** Lovers = choice between devotion and bondage; Tower = liberation through upheaval; Star = healing the root of toxic patterns.
- **With Courts:** Knight of Wands fuels volatility; Queen of Pentacles stays out of loyalty or obligation.
- **Green flag:** Conscious passion with clear boundaries.
- **Red flag:** Control, secrecy, or staying where harm outweighs care.
- **Reader prompts:** "What does this connection cost you?" "Where can freedom and love coexist?"

THE TOWER (XVI)

- **Core love thesis:** Sudden change, shocking truth, or disruption; love built on false foundations comes undone.
- **Wands nearby:** Explosive fights or passionate exits; drastic shifts in dynamics.
- **Cups nearby:** Emotional storms, grief, or cathartic breakthroughs.
- **Swords nearby:** Truth revealed—words cut through illusion.
- **Pentacles nearby:** Home, finances, or routines shaken; life logistics impacted by love's upheaval.
- **With key Majors:** Star = healing follows the storm; Lovers = choice revealed through crisis; Death = permanent ending or rebirth after destruction.
- **With Courts:** Page of Swords brings unwelcome news; King of Cups steadies emotions in chaos.
- **Green flag:** Liberation through truth; false structures cleared away.
- **Red flag:** Rebuilding the same broken patterns.
- **Reader prompts:** "What truth just changed everything?" "What can be rebuilt with more honesty and care?"

THE STAR (XVII)

- **Core love thesis:** Healing, hope, and tenderness; love returns with honesty and renewal after loss or pain.
- **Wands nearby:** Inspiration to act on hope; creative reconnection and passion.
- **Cups nearby:** Emotional restoration; forgiveness and trust begin to grow.
- **Swords nearby:** Late-night talks and vulnerable truths rebuild intimacy.

- **Pentacles nearby:** Steady, practical efforts toward healing—small actions over time.
- **With key Majors:** Tower = post-shock healing arc; Moon = trust amid uncertainty; Temperance = long-term, patient repair.
- **With Courts:** Page of Cups offers apology; King of Cups holds safe emotional space.
- **Green flag:** Consistent, gentle steps toward closeness.
- **Red flag:** Clinging to hope without actual change or action.
- **Reader prompts:** "What would healing look like in practice?" "Where can trust slowly return?"

THE MOON (XVIII)

- **Core love thesis:** Mystery, dreams, and illusions; the heart wanders through fog before clarity arrives.
- **Wands nearby:** Romantic fantasy, desire mixed with confusion or secrecy.
- **Cups nearby:** Deep emotions, longing, or intuitive undercurrents not yet spoken aloud.
- **Swords nearby:** Misunderstandings, hidden truths, or unclear communication.
- **Pentacles nearby:** Physical circumstances remain uncertain—waiting for facts or stability.
- **With key Majors:** High Priestess = intuition sharpened; Tower = illusions shattered; Star = hope returns after confusion.
- **With Courts:** Page of Swords seeks answers; Queen of Cups navigates emotion with care.
- **Green flag:** Trusting intuition while seeking truth.
- **Red flag:** Projection, deception, or clinging to fantasy over reality.
- **Reader prompts:** "What's real versus imagined here?" "What truth hides beneath the surface?"

THE SUN (XIX)

- **Core love thesis:** Joy, clarity, and warmth; love thrives in openness and authenticity.
- **Wands nearby:** Playfulness, passion, and vitality light up the relationship.
- **Cups nearby:** Emotional safety and shared happiness deepen bonds.
- **Swords nearby:** Honest conversations bring relief and freedom.
- **Pentacles nearby:** Practical joy—shared adventures, children, home life in harmony.

- **With key Majors:** Star = pure optimism and trust; Tower = joy follows crisis; Lovers = wholehearted choice with clarity.
- **With Courts:** Page of Wands brings playful energy; King of Pentacles builds security under the sun's warmth.
- **Green flag:** Radical honesty and authentic love.
- **Red flag:** Ignoring shadows or pretending all is perfect.
- **Reader prompts:** "What truth sets your heart free?" "Where is joy ready to return?"

JUDGMENT (XX)

- **Core love thesis:** Awakening, reckoning, and renewal; relationships reborn through truth and accountability.
- **Wands nearby:** Passion reignites after clarity or reconciliation.
- **Cups nearby:** Emotional forgiveness, second chances, or deep release of the past.
- **Swords nearby:** Honest conversations bring closure or rebirth.
- **Pentacles nearby:** Practical changes align love with values or purpose.
- **With key Majors:** Death = rebirth after endings; Lovers = choices made with full awareness; Justice = ethical alignment.
- **With Courts:** Knight of Swords demands accountability; Queen of Cups offers emotional compassion during renewal.
- **Green flag:** Facing the past to create a conscious future.
- **Red flag:** Avoiding responsibility or repeating old mistakes.
- **Reader prompts:** "What chapter needs closing—or rewriting?" "What call to truth are you resisting or ready to embrace?"

THE WORLD (XXI)

- **Core love thesis:** Completion, fulfillment, and wholeness; relationships or cycles reach natural resolution or mastery.
- **Wands nearby:** Celebratory energy—marriage, milestones, adventures together.
- **Cups nearby:** Emotional closure, harmony, or long-term fulfillment.
- **Swords nearby:** Final conversations bring clarity, peace, or understanding.
- **Pentacles nearby:** Tangible legacies—shared homes, family, or life built together.
- **With key Majors:** Fool = cycles restart with new beginnings; Tower = ending clears the way for growth; Lovers = relationships evolve into new forms.

- **With Courts:** King of Pentacles secures the legacy; Page of Cups marks emotional softness even in closure.
- **Green flag:** Celebrating growth, milestones, or conscious endings.
- **Red flag:** Forcing completion before it's ready or resisting closure.
- **Reader prompts:** "What cycle is completing with grace?" "What new beginning waits beyond this ending?"

CHAPTER 123

minor arcana – swords

INTERACTION SYSTEMS

ACE OF SWORDS

- **Core love thesis:** A breakthrough of truth and clarity; honest communication begins or a decision is made.
- **Wands nearby:** Passion drives conversations, creating decisive forward motion.
- **Cups nearby:** Emotional truths are spoken aloud, deepening intimacy.
- **Swords nearby:** Sharp clarity—nothing is left unsaid.
- **Pentacles nearby:** Conversations focus on practical plans and shared stability.
- **With key Majors:** Justice = truth revealed with fairness; Lovers = clarity about choices; Tower = truth disrupts the relationship.
- **With Courts:** Queen of Swords delivers honesty with grace; Knight of Swords pushes for direct action.
- **Green flag:** Clear, transparent communication that builds trust.
- **Red flag:** Words used as weapons or truth spoken without care.
- **Reader prompts:** "What needs to be named today?" "How can honesty strengthen love?"

TWO OF SWORDS

- **Core love thesis:** Indecision and emotional stalemate; refusing to see or act creates tension.

- **Wands nearby:** Passionate desires clash, adding pressure to the choice.
- **Cups nearby:** Emotional uncertainty or fear of hurting someone by deciding.
- **Swords nearby:** Avoidance leads to mental overwhelm or dishonesty.
- **Pentacles nearby:** Practical matters like money or living arrangements stall progress.
- **With key Majors:** Lovers = pivotal choice between love paths; Moon = lack of clarity; Tower = decision made suddenly or by outside force.
- **With Courts:** Queen of Cups brings emotional perspective; Knight of Wands pushes for action too soon.
- **Green flag:** Taking time to reflect before making a decision.
- **Red flag:** Endless avoidance that leaves everyone stuck.
- **Reader prompts:** "What truth are you resisting?" "What decision needs to be faced with courage?"

THREE OF SWORDS

- **Core love thesis:** Heartbreak, separation, and painful truth; love is tested by loss or betrayal.
- **Wands nearby:** Anger and reactive actions deepen the wound.
- **Cups nearby:** Deep grief and sorrow surface for healing.
- **Swords nearby:** Words or secrets cut sharply, leaving scars.
- **Pentacles nearby:** Practical fallout—dividing homes, custody issues, shared responsibilities.
- **With key Majors:** Tower = shocking discovery; Star = hope after pain; Justice = accountability and fairness in endings.
- **With Courts:** Queen of Swords brings clean closure; Knight of Cups offers apology or reconciliation.
- **Green flag:** Honest acknowledgment of the hurt as part of healing.
- **Red flag:** Reopening wounds through drama or avoidance.
- **Reader prompts:** "What truth must be named to heal?" "What support do you need as you grieve?"

FOUR OF SWORDS

- **Core love thesis:** Rest, reflection, and pause; stepping back to heal or gain perspective.
- **Wands nearby:** Temporary separation restores passion and energy.
- **Cups nearby:** Quiet emotional processing creates safety.
- **Swords nearby:** Mental clarity grows through silence and retreat.
- **Pentacles nearby:** Time apart brings practical stability and perspective.

- **With key Majors:** Hermit = deep reflection; Temperance = slow, healing balance; Tower = forced rest after upheaval.
- **With Courts:** Page of Cups brings small gestures of care; Knight of Swords resists the pause and pushes for answers.
- **Green flag:** Healthy boundaries and space to recharge.
- **Red flag:** Silent treatment or withdrawal as punishment.
- **Reader prompts:** "What space is needed to heal?" "How can stillness strengthen connection?"

FIVE OF SWORDS

- **Core love thesis:** Conflict without resolution; power struggles leave emotional wreckage.
- **Wands nearby:** Heated arguments escalate quickly, fueled by ego.
- **Cups nearby:** Hurt feelings and resentment linger after fights.
- **Swords nearby:** Words weaponized, leaving lasting harm.
- **Pentacles nearby:** Arguments over money, home, or shared resources.
- **With key Majors:** Devil = toxic fighting patterns; Justice = accountability needed; Tower = rupture caused by destructive conflict.
- **With Courts:** Knight of Swords fans the flames; Queen of Cups brings calm and repair.
- **Green flag:** Naming conflict to stop harmful cycles.
- **Red flag:** Winning arguments at the expense of love and trust.
- **Reader prompts:** "What's the need beneath the fight?" "Where can compassion replace competition?"

SIX OF SWORDS

- **Core love thesis:** Moving forward after difficulty; love finds peace through transition and distance.
- **Wands nearby:** Action toward healing—new adventures or relocation.
- **Cups nearby:** Emotional processing leads to calm waters ahead.
- **Swords nearby:** Honest conversations create closure and understanding.
- **Pentacles nearby:** Physical moves or logistical changes support harmony.
- **With key Majors:** World = cycle completion and resolution; Tower = moving on after upheaval; Star = hope restored through change.
- **With Courts:** Queen of Pentacles provides stability during transition; Page of Cups softens with care.
- **Green flag:** Choosing peace and mutual growth.
- **Red flag:** Avoiding deeper issues by running away.

- **Reader prompts:** "What needs to be left behind?" "How can you move forward with grace?"

SEVEN OF SWORDS

- **Core love thesis:** Secrets, deception, and hidden motives; truth obscured in relationships.
- **Wands nearby:** Passion used to distract or conceal dishonesty.
- **Cups nearby:** Emotional manipulation or withheld feelings.
- **Swords nearby:** Lies and misunderstandings multiply without transparency.
- **Pentacles nearby:** Hidden financial or logistical matters strain trust.
- **With key Majors:** Moon = illusion deepened; Justice = truth revealed; Tower = sudden exposure of secrets.
- **With Courts:** Knight of Cups may romanticize deceit; Queen of Swords demands honesty.
- **Green flag:** Strategic privacy with consent and agreement.
- **Red flag:** Gaslighting, cheating, or intentional harm through secrecy.
- **Reader prompts:** "What truth is being hidden or denied?" "How can honesty restore safety?"

EIGHT OF SWORDS

- **Core love thesis:** Feeling trapped by fear or limiting beliefs; love hindered by self-imposed barriers.
- **Wands nearby:** Desire to escape but confusion about how to act.
- **Cups nearby:** Emotional patterns of shame or guilt create paralysis.
- **Swords nearby:** Overthinking and anxiety keep clarity out of reach.
- **Pentacles nearby:** Financial or practical limitations reinforce the sense of being stuck.
- **With key Majors:** Devil = toxic entrapment; Tower = sudden release; Star = hope and freedom through healing.
- **With Courts:** Queen of Cups offers emotional support; Knight of Swords pushes for action.
- **Green flag:** Recognizing self-limiting patterns and seeking help.
- **Red flag:** Staying trapped due to fear or external control.
- **Reader prompts:** "What fear keeps you bound?" "What step toward freedom feels possible today?"

NINE OF SWORDS

- **Core love thesis:** Anxiety, worry, and sleepless nights; fear consumes clarity and peace.
- **Wands nearby:** Passion twists into restless tension or jealousy.
- **Cups nearby:** Emotional overwhelm causes breakdown or tears.
- **Swords nearby:** Thoughts spiral without resolution or relief.
- **Pentacles nearby:** Stress about money, housing, or shared stability adds weight.
- **With key Majors:** Moon = heightened illusions and nightmares; Tower = crisis revealed; Star = light and healing are still possible.
- **With Courts:** Page of Swords represents restless mental energy; Queen of Cups soothes with compassion.
- **Green flag:** Naming fears and seeking comfort to move forward.
- **Red flag:** Letting anxiety run the relationship or block intimacy.
- **Reader prompts:** "What fear is loudest right now?" "Who can help you hold the worry so you don't hold it alone?"

TEN OF SWORDS

- **Core love thesis:** Final endings and deep hurt; love reaches a breaking point that clears the way for renewal.
- **Wands nearby:** Explosive closure or dramatic parting.
- **Cups nearby:** Heartbreak reaches its peak but releases space for healing.
- **Swords nearby:** Harsh words finalize the end, clarity through painful truth.
- **Pentacles nearby:** Tangible separation—dividing lives, homes, or resources.
- **With key Majors:** Death = ultimate transformation; Tower = collapse of what was false; Star = hope glimmers in the aftermath.
- **With Courts:** Knight of Swords may end things abruptly; Queen of Pentacles helps with practical rebuilding.
- **Green flag:** Clear closure and conscious endings.
- **Red flag:** Dragging out the pain through denial or cruelty.
- **Reader prompts:** "What must fully end for healing to begin?" "Where can you honor what was and release it?"

PAGE OF SWORDS

- **Core love thesis:** Curiosity, questions, and information-gathering; love explored through learning and awareness.

- **Wands nearby:** Playful, adventurous exploration in dating or intimacy.
- **Cups nearby:** Emotional growth sparked by curiosity about the other.
- **Swords nearby:** Clear, direct communication creates a safe learning space.
- **Pentacles nearby:** Conversations about shared goals, resources, or plans.
- **With key Majors:** Lovers = learning about each other; Moon = confusion needing clarity; Justice = truth-seeking strengthens trust.
- **With Courts:** Queen of Swords refines communication; Knight of Wands adds impulsivity.
- **Green flag:** Open curiosity and honest inquiry.
- **Red flag:** Gossip, spying, or unhealthy obsession.
- **Reader prompts:** "What do you need to ask or express?" "Where can learning deepen love?"

KNIGHT OF SWORDS

- **Core love thesis:** Swift action and bold truth-telling; rushing into conversations or decisions.
- **Wands nearby:** Passion intensifies speed and urgency.
- **Cups nearby:** Emotions may be dismissed in favor of action.
- **Swords nearby:** Clarity comes fast but may lack tact or sensitivity.
- **Pentacles nearby:** Practical matters are rushed without full planning.
- **With key Majors:** Chariot = unstoppable momentum; Tower = sudden conflict or change; Justice = truth delivered bluntly.
- **With Courts:** Queen of Swords provides balance; Knight of Wands adds to volatility.
- **Green flag:** Courageous communication and decisive action.
- **Red flag:** Impulsivity, recklessness, or careless words.
- **Reader prompts:** "What needs action now?" "Where can slowing down bring more care?"

QUEEN OF SWORDS

- **Core love thesis:** Loving truth, healthy boundaries, and clear communication; intimacy through honesty.
- **Wands nearby:** Assertive clarity brings passion into focus.
- **Cups nearby:** Compassion and logic blend to heal conflict.
- **Swords nearby:** Transparent dialogue creates stability and trust.
- **Pentacles nearby:** Boundaries applied to shared resources or life logistics.

- **With key Majors:** Justice = alignment through truth; Star = truth as healing balm; Devil = cutting cords to unhealthy attachments.
- **With Courts:** King of Pentacles provides grounding; Knight of Swords challenges balance.
- **Green flag:** Clear, honest love rooted in respect.
- **Red flag:** Using "honesty" to harm or control.
- **Reader prompts:** "What truth protects your heart?" "Where does clarity invite deeper connection?"

KING OF SWORDS

- **Core love thesis:** Wisdom, strategy, and clear vision; love thrives through fairness and perspective.
- **Wands nearby:** Passion tempered by logic and planning.
- **Cups nearby:** Emotional balance achieved through calm guidance.
- **Swords nearby:** Truth prioritized above confusion or illusion.
- **Pentacles nearby:** Practical structures stabilize the relationship long-term.
- **With key Majors:** Lovers = rational choices about love; Justice = ethical alignment; Tower = stability challenged by sudden truth.
- **With Courts:** Queen of Swords matches clarity and partnership; Knight of Cups softens rigidity.
- **Green flag:** Fair, rational leadership and accountability.
- **Red flag:** Coldness, emotional detachment, or controlling logic.
- **Reader prompts:** "Where can truth lead with compassion?" "What structure helps love thrive?"

CHAPTER 124

minor arcana - wands

INTERACTION SYSTEMS

ACE OF WANDS

- **Core love thesis:** A spark ignites—new passion, chemistry, or a bold beginning in love.
- **Wands nearby:** Energy surges; quick attraction leads to impulsive action.
- **Cups nearby:** Passion meets emotion; chemistry deepens into tenderness.
- **Swords nearby:** Decisions must be made quickly; words may lag behind desire.
- **Pentacles nearby:** Passion becomes grounded through intentional effort and stability.
- **With key Majors:** Lovers = passionate choice of new love; Tower = sudden spark disrupts old patterns; Fool = daring leap into romance.
- **With Courts:** Knight of Wands fuels the fire; Queen of Cups balances heat with emotional depth.
- **Green flag:** Embracing excitement and new beginnings.
- **Red flag:** Burning bright without considering long-term compatibility.
- **Reader prompts:** "What new energy is asking to be explored?" "How will you tend this spark so it lasts?"

TWO OF WANDS

- **Core love thesis:** Vision and planning; deciding what future you want to create together.
- **Wands nearby:** Excitement about shared adventures or possibilities.
- **Cups nearby:** Emotional considerations shape plans; love influences decisions.
- **Swords nearby:** Clarity needed before acting; conversations determine alignment.
- **Pentacles nearby:** Focus on logistics—finances, moves, practical next steps.
- **With key Majors:** Chariot = action toward shared goals; Lovers = choice between paths; Wheel of Fortune = fate plays a role in timing.
- **With Courts:** King of Pentacles grounds ideas in reality; Knight of Swords pushes for quick action.
- **Green flag:** Dreaming together with clear communication.
- **Red flag:** Planning without checking if both partners share the same vision.
- **Reader prompts:** "What future are you envisioning?" "Whose dream is driving this choice?"

THREE OF WANDS

- **Core love thesis:** Expansion and anticipation; love grows through shared goals and trust in what's coming.
- **Wands nearby:** High energy, excitement for the future, new adventures ahead.
- **Cups nearby:** Emotional connection strengthens as plans come to fruition.
- **Swords nearby:** Honest communication needed to navigate expectations.
- **Pentacles nearby:** Practical preparation supports growth—resources and stability must align.
- **With key Majors:** Chariot = successful forward motion; World = fulfillment of shared dreams; Tower = plans disrupted by surprise events.
- **With Courts:** Queen of Wands leads with confidence; Page of Cups adds emotional openness to growth.
- **Green flag:** Hopeful anticipation matched by action and trust.
- **Red flag:** Waiting passively for love without effort or clarity.
- **Reader prompts:** "What are you actively calling in?" "How can you prepare for the love you desire?"

FOUR OF WANDS

- **Core love thesis:** Celebration, harmony, and milestones; love reaches a joyful stage of stability or ritual.
- **Wands nearby:** Passion fuels celebration; playful, exciting shared energy.
- **Cups nearby:** Emotional fulfillment through connection, family, or chosen kin.
- **Swords nearby:** Clear agreements ensure harmony; conversations about commitments deepen trust.
- **Pentacles nearby:** Tangible steps toward shared home or stability.
- **With key Majors:** Hierophant = traditional ceremonies like marriage; Sun = joy and clarity; Tower = sudden changes to planned milestones.
- **With Courts:** Queen of Pentacles nurtures stability; Knight of Wands brings excitement and spontaneity.
- **Green flag:** Celebrating love authentically and publicly.
- **Red flag:** Performing happiness for others instead of living it genuinely.
- **Reader prompts:** "What milestone are you ready to honor?" "How can celebration deepen intimacy?"

FIVE OF WANDS

- **Core love thesis:** Conflict, competition, and misunderstandings; passion sparks friction that needs resolution.
- **Wands nearby:** Heated fights or power struggles without clear direction.
- **Cups nearby:** Emotional hurt stemming from misaligned desires or jealousy.
- **Swords nearby:** Arguments sharpen; words become weapons.
- **Pentacles nearby:** Conflicts about resources, routines, or physical space.
- **With key Majors:** Devil = destructive conflict patterns; Justice = fair resolution through accountability; Temperance = healing through balance.
- **With Courts:** Knight of Swords escalates fights; Queen of Cups soothes tension.
- **Green flag:** Healthy debate that strengthens understanding.
- **Red flag:** Competition eroding trust and intimacy.
- **Reader prompts:** "What's the real need beneath the argument?" "Where can collaboration replace conflict?"

SIX OF WANDS

- **Core love thesis:** Recognition and validation; love thrives when effort is seen and celebrated.
- **Wands nearby:** Shared victories, public displays of affection, joyful progress.
- **Cups nearby:** Emotional pride in each other; tender acknowledgment of growth.
- **Swords nearby:** Honest communication solidifies achievements and trust.
- **Pentacles nearby:** Practical progress celebrated—financial wins, moves, shared accomplishments.
- **With key Majors:** Sun = radiant joy and harmony; Lovers = partnership triumphs through mutual effort; Tower = sudden disruptions to success.
- **With Courts:** Queen of Wands radiates confidence; Page of Swords seeks to understand and share in the win.
- **Green flag:** Mutual recognition and appreciation.
- **Red flag:** Ego overshadowing partnership or love used for performance.
- **Reader prompts:** "Where do you feel most seen and valued?" "How can you celebrate each other more openly?"

SEVEN OF WANDS

- **Core love thesis:** Defensiveness and boundaries; love tested by external pressures or internal doubts.
- **Wands nearby:** Fierce protection of the relationship; standing up for love.
- **Cups nearby:** Emotional triggers fuel protective or reactive behavior.
- **Swords nearby:** Conflicts escalate; clarity is needed about what's worth defending.
- **Pentacles nearby:** Fighting over practical matters—finances, commitments, shared spaces.
- **With key Majors:** Justice = holding boundaries ethically; Devil = defensiveness rooted in fear or control; Star = healing through vulnerability.
- **With Courts:** Knight of Wands may fight impulsively; Queen of Swords clarifies what is truly being defended.
- **Green flag:** Clear, loving boundaries that protect the relationship.
- **Red flag:** Defensiveness masking deeper fears or insecurities.
- **Reader prompts:** "What are you really protecting?" "Where can softness create safety?"

EIGHT OF WANDS

- **Core love thesis:** Swift movement, messages, and breakthroughs; love accelerates quickly.
- **Wands nearby:** Passion surges; events move at exhilarating speed.
- **Cups nearby:** Emotional connection deepens rapidly—falling in love fast.
- **Swords nearby:** Clarity is essential to avoid miscommunication amidst rapid change.
- **Pentacles nearby:** Plans manifest physically—travel, moves, or tangible next steps.
- **With key Majors:** Chariot = unstoppable forward motion; Tower = sudden, shocking developments; World = journey reaches fulfillment.
- **With Courts:** Knight of Swords intensifies speed and urgency; Queen of Pentacles helps slow down and stabilize.
- **Green flag:** Exciting momentum fueled by clear mutual desire.
- **Red flag:** Moving too quickly without grounding or consent.
- **Reader prompts:** "What is rushing forward right now?" "Where do you need clarity before continuing?"

NINE OF WANDS

- **Core love thesis:** Resilience and persistence; love weathering challenges through endurance and trust.
- **Wands nearby:** Passion fuels determination; the relationship pushes through tough times.
- **Cups nearby:** Emotional fatigue needs tenderness and rest to continue.
- **Swords nearby:** Mental stress and overthinking may lead to burnout or withdrawal.
- **Pentacles nearby:** Practical stability supports survival during rough patches.
- **With key Majors:** Strength = inner courage to keep going; Tower = navigating crisis without losing faith; Star = hope for renewal.
- **With Courts:** Queen of Wands provides inspiration; Knight of Cups offers emotional care and encouragement.
- **Green flag:** Standing together through adversity with love intact.
- **Red flag:** Staying out of fear or obligation without joy.
- **Reader prompts:** "What's worth fighting for?" "How can you rest while staying committed?"

TEN OF WANDS

- **Core love thesis:** Burdens and overwhelm; love feels heavy under responsibilities or unspoken expectations.
- **Wands nearby:** Too much passion without balance creates burnout.
- **Cups nearby:** Emotional labor unbalanced; one person carries the weight.
- **Swords nearby:** Miscommunication adds stress; resentment builds silently.
- **Pentacles nearby:** Financial, household, or practical pressures take a toll.
- **With key Majors:** Devil = toxic obligation; Tower = collapse under strain; Temperance = rebalancing through shared effort.
- **With Courts:** Queen of Pentacles offers grounding support; Knight of Swords may escalate pressure through conflict.
- **Green flag:** Shared responsibility and mutual care.
- **Red flag:** Carrying it all alone or enabling imbalance.
- **Reader prompts:** "What weight isn't yours to carry?" "Where can you ask for help?"

PAGE OF WANDS

- **Core love thesis:** Playful curiosity and exploration; love expressed through flirtation and discovery.
- **Wands nearby:** Exciting new adventures, romantic sparks, and fun dates.
- **Cups nearby:** Emotional openness softens playful energy into intimacy.
- **Swords nearby:** Clear communication helps prevent misunderstandings.
- **Pentacles nearby:** Fun remains sustainable when supported by stability.
- **With key Majors:** Fool = joyful beginnings; Lovers = exploring connection openly; Tower = youthful recklessness leads to surprises.
- **With Courts:** Knight of Wands intensifies playfulness; Queen of Cups brings emotional depth.
- **Green flag:** Staying open-hearted and curious about love.
- **Red flag:** Avoiding depth or accountability while chasing fun.
- **Reader prompts:** "What feels exciting to explore?" "Where does play create deeper connection?"

KNIGHT OF WANDS

- **Core love thesis:** Pursuit and passion; chasing love with heat and intensity, often impulsively.
- **Wands nearby:** Fiery romance, thrilling chemistry, adventurous dates.
- **Cups nearby:** Deep emotion may stabilize wild energy—or get swept up in it.
- **Swords nearby:** Bluntness or impatience may cause conflict or misunderstandings.
- **Pentacles nearby:** Struggles with routine or long-term stability.
- **With key Majors:** Chariot = unstoppable pursuit; Temperance = need to slow down and balance; Lovers = passion tested by choice.
- **With Courts:** Queen of Wands matches intensity; King of Pentacles demands reliability.
- **Green flag:** Mutual desire for fun, adventure, and freedom.
- **Red flag:** Future-faking or hot-and-cold commitment.
- **Reader prompts:** "Where is the fire sustainable?" "What happens when the chase ends?"

QUEEN OF WANDS

- **Core love thesis:** Confidence, magnetism, and radiant passion; love thrives through bold authenticity.
- **Wands nearby:** Fiery, empowered energy sparks excitement and mutual attraction.
- **Cups nearby:** Warmth and care balance charisma with tenderness.
- **Swords nearby:** Clarity of communication ensures passion doesn't turn to conflict.
- **Pentacles nearby:** Desire grounded by practicality and shared stability.
- **With key Majors:** Sun = radiant self-expression; Lovers = magnetic partnership; Devil = power dynamics need balance.
- **With Courts:** Knight of Cups brings romance to passion; King of Pentacles supports ambition with grounding energy.
- **Green flag:** Authentic, empowered love without fear of visibility.
- **Red flag:** Ego-driven competition or domination.
- **Reader prompts:** "Where can confidence deepen intimacy?" "How do you shine without overshadowing others?"

KING OF WANDS

- **Core love thesis:** Leadership and vision; love thrives through action, inspiration, and shared purpose.
- **Wands nearby:** Dynamic energy for pursuing shared goals and adventures.
- **Cups nearby:** Emotional wisdom softens ambition into partnership.
- **Swords nearby:** Clear strategy and honest dialogue maintain harmony.
- **Pentacles nearby:** Practicality ensures that passion becomes sustainable long-term.
- **With key Majors:** Chariot = unified leadership and direction; Emperor = strong structure in love; Tower = sudden shifts in control or plans.
- **With Courts:** Queen of Wands is an equal partner; Page of Cups brings innocence and playfulness to balance intensity.
- **Green flag:** Inspiring and supportive leadership within love.
- **Red flag:** Controlling or domineering behaviors disguised as guidance.
- **Reader prompts:** "What shared vision are you leading together?" "Where can leadership become collaboration?"

CHAPTER 125

minor arcana - cups

INTERACTION SYSTEMS

ACE OF CUPS

- **Core love thesis:** A new emotional beginning; love blooms, bringing openness and deep feeling.
- **Wands nearby:** Passion fuels romance, exciting beginnings full of chemistry.
- **Cups nearby:** Overflowing tenderness, intimacy, and devotion.
- **Swords nearby:** Words of love or vulnerability spoken aloud for the first time.
- **Pentacles nearby:** Love expressed through practical care and physical gestures.
- **With key Majors:** Lovers = mutual recognition and devotion; Star = healing through new love; Tower = sudden emotional awakening.
- **With Courts:** Knight of Cups arrives with a romantic offer; Queen of Pentacles nurtures this new beginning.
- **Green flag:** Willingness to open the heart and receive love.
- **Red flag:** Projection or fantasy mistaken for true connection.
- **Reader prompts:** "What love is ready to flow into your life?" "How can you soften to receive what's offered?"

TWO OF CUPS

- **Core love thesis:** Mutual recognition, connection, and partnership; the moment of being truly seen.
- **Wands nearby:** Chemistry and attraction surge, sparking passion.

- **Cups nearby:** Emotional safety and vulnerability deepen trust.
- **Swords nearby:** Clear conversations define boundaries and intentions.
- **Pentacles nearby:** Building shared routines, home life, and stability.
- **With key Majors:** Hierophant = formalizing commitment; Devil = over-attachment or enmeshment; Temperance = balanced, reciprocal love.
- **With Courts:** Page of Cups represents early exploration; Queen of Pentacles brings nurturing harmony.
- **Green flag:** Mutual giving and equal emotional investment.
- **Red flag:** One-sided connection or unspoken imbalance.
- **Reader prompts:** "How do you both show up for each other?" "What makes you feel truly chosen?"

THREE OF CUPS

- **Core love thesis:** Celebration, friendship, and joy; community supports and enriches love.
- **Wands nearby:** Exciting social events and lively gatherings that spark connection.
- **Cups nearby:** Emotional fulfillment through shared joy and laughter.
- **Swords nearby:** Conversations about boundaries with friends, exes, or third parties.
- **Pentacles nearby:** Financial or household gatherings like weddings or shared ventures.
- **With key Majors:** Lovers = love celebrated openly; Devil = interference or unhealthy triangles; Tower = friendships tested by love challenges.
- **With Courts:** Knight of Cups brings romantic gestures; Page of Swords may stir curiosity or jealousy.
- **Green flag:** Community involvement that enriches the relationship.
- **Red flag:** Gossip, triangulation, or competing loyalties.
- **Reader prompts:** "Who supports your love journey?" "Where do friendships strengthen or strain your relationship?"

FOUR OF CUPS

- **Core love thesis:** Emotional apathy or disconnection; longing for what's missing while ignoring what's present.
- **Wands nearby:** Restlessness sparks desire for change or adventure.
- **Cups nearby:** Withdrawal or numbness blocks intimacy.
- **Swords nearby:** Honest reflection needed to break free of discontent.

- **Pentacles nearby:** Relationship stagnates due to routine or external stressors.
- **With key Majors:** Moon = confusion or emotional fog; Star = hope rekindled through self-care; Tower = wake-up call to action.
- **With Courts:** Page of Cups offers renewal; Knight of Wands challenges apathy with bold gestures.
- **Green flag:** Pausing to reflect and realign with needs.
- **Red flag:** Taking love for granted or ignoring growth opportunities.
- **Reader prompts:** "What's being overlooked in this connection?" "Where can gratitude reopen your heart?"

FIVE OF CUPS

- **Core love thesis:** Grief, regret, and loss; mourning what has ended while forgetting what remains.
- **Wands nearby:** Anger or impulsive actions during heartbreak.
- **Cups nearby:** Deep emotional pain, yearning for what cannot return.
- **Swords nearby:** Clarity through difficult conversations or closure.
- **Pentacles nearby:** Tangible losses—home, money, or shared responsibilities.
- **With key Majors:** Death = transformative endings; Star = healing after grief; Judgment = reconciliation or forgiveness possible.
- **With Courts:** Queen of Cups offers compassion; Knight of Swords may trigger further conflict.
- **Green flag:** Honoring grief while staying open to future love.
- **Red flag:** Becoming stuck in sorrow or guilt.
- **Reader prompts:** "What grief needs acknowledgment?" "Where can love still grow, even amid loss?"

SIX OF CUPS

- **Core love thesis:** Nostalgia, innocence, and sweet reconnection; the past resurfaces tenderly.
- **Wands nearby:** Rekindling old passion or playful adventures.
- **Cups nearby:** Emotional safety and cherished memories flow easily.
- **Swords nearby:** Honest conversations about past wounds or unfinished business.
- **Pentacles nearby:** Returning to old places, shared homes, or childhood ties.
- **With key Majors:** Lovers = reunion or soul recognition; Moon = confusion about past vs. present; Tower = old patterns break open.
- **With Courts:** Page of Cups reconnects playfully; Queen of Pentacles helps ground nostalgia into reality.

- **Green flag:** Healing and growth through revisiting shared history.
- **Red flag:** Romanticizing the past instead of engaging with the present.
- **Reader prompts:** "What from the past still needs closure or celebration?" "How do old memories shape current love?"

SEVEN OF CUPS

- **Core love thesis:** Fantasy, choices, and confusion; love clouded by dreams or illusions.
- **Wands nearby:** Passion overwhelms clarity; impulsive decisions fueled by desire.
- **Cups nearby:** Deep longing creates projection or idealization.
- **Swords nearby:** Clarity needed to separate truth from fantasy.
- **Pentacles nearby:** Real-world consequences of choices must be addressed.
- **With key Majors:** Moon = heightened illusion; Lovers = vital choice point; Tower = reality disrupts fantasy.
- **With Courts:** Page of Swords asks questions; Knight of Cups pursues dreams with emotion but not practicality.
- **Green flag:** Imagination fueling possibility with healthy awareness.
- **Red flag:** Escaping into fantasy to avoid reality.
- **Reader prompts:** "What is real versus imagined?" "Which option reflects your heart's truth?"

EIGHT OF CUPS

- **Core love thesis:** Sacred leaving; walking away from what no longer nourishes the heart.
- **Wands nearby:** Quick, decisive action toward new horizons.
- **Cups nearby:** Gentle, bittersweet goodbyes rooted in self-respect.
- **Swords nearby:** Clarity and boundary-setting guide departure.
- **Pentacles nearby:** Practical logistics of leaving—moving, separation, or tangible shifts.
- **With key Majors:** World = graduation from old cycles; Death = complete transformation; Fool = brave new beginnings.
- **With Courts:** King of Pentacles supports the transition; Page of Wands brings inspiration for the next step.
- **Green flag:** Choosing growth and self-love even when it's hard.
- **Red flag:** Leaving with resentment or manipulation instead of clarity.
- **Reader prompts:** "What can't thrive in this space?" "What blessing can you offer as you walk away?"

NINE OF CUPS

- **Core love thesis:** Emotional fulfillment, wishes granted, and self-satisfaction; love flourishes when aligned with joy.
- **Wands nearby:** Passion paired with deep contentment and playfulness.
- **Cups nearby:** Overflowing emotional abundance; love feels complete.
- **Swords nearby:** Clarity about desires ensures they are sustainable.
- **Pentacles nearby:** Pleasure shared through shared resources or stability.
- **With key Majors:** Sun = joy illuminated; Star = hope realized; Devil = indulgence or selfishness unchecked.
- **With Courts:** Queen of Cups offers nurturing abundance; Knight of Wands adds excitement and spontaneity.
- **Green flag:** Healthy self-celebration and gratitude in love.
- **Red flag:** Complacency or hoarding happiness without sharing.
- **Reader prompts:** "What joy are you ready to savor?" "How can gratitude deepen intimacy?"

TEN OF CUPS

- **Core love thesis:** Harmony, family, and emotional completion; love expressed as shared joy and unity.
- **Wands nearby:** Playful, active family or chosen family life.
- **Cups nearby:** Deep bonds of care and belonging overflow.
- **Swords nearby:** Communication keeps harmony clear and sustainable.
- **Pentacles nearby:** Tangible investments in home, legacy, or shared future.
- **With key Majors:** World = completion and fulfillment; Hierophant = formal vows or ceremonies; Tower = family structures challenged.
- **With Courts:** King of Pentacles anchors stability; Page of Cups represents children or innocence.
- **Green flag:** Mutual love and emotional safety for all involved.
- **Red flag:** Projecting perfection while ignoring real issues.
- **Reader prompts:** "What does a loving legacy mean to you?" "How can harmony be nurtured daily?"

PAGE OF CUPS

- **Core love thesis:** Innocence, vulnerability, and emotional curiosity; love begins softly.

- **Wands nearby:** Playful flirtation and fun exploration of feelings.
- **Cups nearby:** Sweetness, tenderness, and gentle emotional growth.
- **Swords nearby:** Clear words help translate vulnerable feelings into understanding.
- **Pentacles nearby:** Small, consistent acts of care nurture emotional safety.
- **With key Majors:** Lovers = first love or tender choices; Moon = intuitive exploration; Star = hopeful new beginnings.
- **With Courts:** Knight of Cups deepens romance; Queen of Pentacles offers steady emotional grounding.
- **Green flag:** Honest emotional openness and willingness to learn.
- **Red flag:** Naivety or avoidance of deeper conversations.
- **Reader prompts:** "Where can you express love simply?" "What small vulnerability might open the door to deeper connection?"

KNIGHT OF CUPS

- **Core love thesis:** Romantic pursuit; love expressed through passion, creativity, and devotion.
- **Wands nearby:** Bold, passionate gestures and thrilling romance.
- **Cups nearby:** Deep emotional investment and vulnerability.
- **Swords nearby:** Need for clarity to balance dreams and reality.
- **Pentacles nearby:** Romance sustained through tangible effort and grounded presence.
- **With key Majors:** Lovers = wholehearted romantic pursuit; Moon = navigating illusions in love; Tower = dramatic declarations or surprises.
- **With Courts:** Queen of Cups receives and matches romance; Knight of Wands competes for attention.
- **Green flag:** Pursuing love with sincerity and emotional bravery.
- **Red flag:** Over-promising or future-faking.
- **Reader prompts:** "What is being offered to you emotionally?" "Where does romance need action to match words?"

QUEEN OF CUPS

- **Core love thesis:** Compassion, intuition, and emotional mastery; love expressed through care and deep listening.
- **Wands nearby:** Passion softened by emotional depth and nurturing.
- **Cups nearby:** Mutual vulnerability creates profound intimacy.
- **Swords nearby:** Gentle truth-telling heals old wounds.
- **Pentacles nearby:** Practical actions ground emotional care into stability.

- **With key Majors:** High Priestess = intuitive connection; Star = deep emotional healing; Justice = emotional truth meets accountability.
- **With Courts:** Knight of Cups brings romance to her steadiness; King of Pentacles offers protective stability.
- **Green flag:** Safe space for feelings to thrive.
- **Red flag:** Over-giving to the point of depletion.
- **Reader prompts:** "Where can love be softer and more intuitive?" "How do you nourish both yourself and others?"

KING OF CUPS

- **Core love thesis:** Emotional leadership and stability; love thrives through safety and wise compassion.
- **Wands nearby:** Warmth and enthusiasm expressed with control and care.
- **Cups nearby:** Depth of emotion, empathy, and harmony.
- **Swords nearby:** Clear, calm communication during conflict or crisis.
- **Pentacles nearby:** Tangible stability and reliable acts of care.
- **With key Majors:** Lovers = wise, stable choice in love; Tower = emotional strength during upheaval; Temperance = harmony and balance.
- **With Courts:** Queen of Cups offers deep connection; Knight of Wands challenges stability with wildness.
- **Green flag:** Mature, secure emotional connection.
- **Red flag:** Emotional suppression or avoidance of vulnerability.
- **Reader prompts:** "What does emotional safety look like here?" "Where can love be expressed with steadiness and depth?"

CHAPTER 126

minor arcana – pentacles

INTERACTION SYSTEMS

ACE OF PENTACLES

- **Core love thesis:** A tangible beginning; love takes root through action, commitment, or shared goals.
- **Wands nearby:** Passion drives practical steps forward.
- **Cups nearby:** Emotional vulnerability meets tangible care.
- **Swords nearby:** Honest conversations define what's being built.
- **Pentacles nearby:** Strong foundation for a long-term relationship.
- **With key Majors:** Lovers = choosing to build love with intention; World = new chapter begins; Tower = unexpected opportunity or disruption sparks growth.
- **With Courts:** Queen of Pentacles nurtures stability; Knight of Cups brings romance to the foundation.
- **Green flag:** Love supported by consistent, tangible actions.
- **Red flag:** Commitment in words but not in deeds.
- **Reader prompts:** "What small action will grow love today?" "Where is the soil ready for planting?"

TWO OF PENTACLES

- **Core love thesis:** Balance and juggling; managing priorities, relationships, and responsibilities in love.
- **Wands nearby:** Exciting but chaotic energy, easily unbalanced.
- **Cups nearby:** Emotional highs and lows create waves in the connection.

- **Swords nearby:** Clear communication helps manage overwhelm.
- **Pentacles nearby:** Practical challenges—finances, time management, long-distance love.
- **With key Majors:** Justice = equilibrium restored through fairness; Lovers = juggling choices in love; Wheel of Fortune = cycles of change.
- **With Courts:** Knight of Wands adds passion but instability; Queen of Cups brings soothing balance.
- **Green flag:** Flexibility and playfulness amid life's demands.
- **Red flag:** Avoiding hard conversations about priorities.
- **Reader prompts:** "Where is balance being lost?" "What really matters most to you both?"

THREE OF PENTACLES

- **Core love thesis:** Teamwork and collaboration; love grows through mutual effort and shared building.
- **Wands nearby:** Passion fuels joint projects and creativity.
- **Cups nearby:** Emotional investment deepens teamwork and harmony.
- **Swords nearby:** Honest feedback and communication strengthen bonds.
- **Pentacles nearby:** Practical plans—home, family, finances—come together.
- **With key Majors:** Hierophant = shared traditions or marriage; Lovers = conscious co-creation of a future; Tower = structural changes needed.
- **With Courts:** Queen of Pentacles brings steady care; Knight of Swords may challenge harmony with impatience.
- **Green flag:** Collaborative partnership where each voice is valued.
- **Red flag:** One-sided effort or lack of appreciation.
- **Reader prompts:** "How can we build together today?" "Whose voice is missing from this plan?"

FOUR OF PENTACLES

- **Core love thesis:** Holding on too tightly or guarding one's heart; stability vs. possessiveness in love.
- **Wands nearby:** Passion is contained or controlled out of fear.
- **Cups nearby:** Emotional withholding blocks intimacy.
- **Swords nearby:** Fear-driven communication creates tension.
- **Pentacles nearby:** Focus on material stability overshadows emotional connection.

- **With key Majors:** Devil = attachment rooted in fear or control; Lovers = choice between freedom and clinging; Tower = sudden loss challenges security.
- **With Courts:** Knight of Pentacles offers steady care; Queen of Swords challenges possessiveness with clarity.
- **Green flag:** Healthy boundaries protect both partners.
- **Red flag:** Control, jealousy, or fear masquerading as love.
- **Reader prompts:** "What are you afraid to lose?" "Where can letting go bring closeness?"

FIVE OF PENTACLES

- **Core love thesis:** Hardship and exclusion; feeling abandoned or unsupported in love.
- **Wands nearby:** Struggles lead to reactive conflict or burnout.
- **Cups nearby:** Emotional despair and loneliness deepen pain.
- **Swords nearby:** Communication breakdown creates further isolation.
- **Pentacles nearby:** Financial or logistical stress impacts the relationship.
- **With key Majors:** Tower = external crisis disrupts love; Star = hope in dark times; Judgment = awareness of what can be rebuilt.
- **With Courts:** Queen of Cups brings compassion; King of Pentacles offers tangible support.
- **Green flag:** Facing challenges together, hand in hand.
- **Red flag:** Abandonment or unwillingness to weather storms as a team.
- **Reader prompts:** "Where do you feel left out in the cold?" "Who or what can help bring warmth back?"

SIX OF PENTACLES

- **Core love thesis:** Giving and receiving; love thrives through mutual generosity and balance.
- **Wands nearby:** Exciting shared experiences fueled by passion.
- **Cups nearby:** Emotional reciprocity strengthens bonds.
- **Swords nearby:** Honest conversations about what's fair and equitable.
- **Pentacles nearby:** Tangible generosity through gifts, support, or shared resources.
- **With key Majors:** Justice = equality and fairness in love; Lovers = conscious sharing and mutual care; Devil = imbalance revealed.
- **With Courts:** Knight of Pentacles offers steady support; Queen of Cups provides emotional giving.

- **Green flag:** Reciprocal care and mutual investment.
- **Red flag:** Power dynamics or conditional giving.
- **Reader prompts:** "Where does giving feel joyful?" "What needs to be rebalanced between you?"

SEVEN OF PENTACLES

- **Core love thesis:** Patience and long-term growth; love is cultivated over time.
- **Wands nearby:** Passion must be sustained through consistent effort.
- **Cups nearby:** Emotional investments deepen slowly, like roots growing beneath the surface.
- **Swords nearby:** Conversations clarify whether the growth is mutual.
- **Pentacles nearby:** Physical and practical structures strengthen over time.
- **With key Majors:** Temperance = steady progress; Star = hope sustained through trust; Death = re-evaluation of what is worth keeping.
- **With Courts:** Knight of Pentacles represents long-term commitment; Page of Swords questions the process.
- **Green flag:** Slow, intentional building of love and stability.
- **Red flag:** Waiting forever without meaningful growth or change.
- **Reader prompts:** "What seeds are you nurturing?" "Where might it be time to replant?"

EIGHT OF PENTACLES

- **Core love thesis:** Dedication and effort; love strengthened through skillful attention and daily acts.
- **Wands nearby:** Passion drives the work needed to grow love.
- **Cups nearby:** Emotional labor done with care and joy.
- **Swords nearby:** Clear communication ensures efforts align with needs.
- **Pentacles nearby:** Strong focus on shared routines, financial health, and tangible growth.
- **With key Majors:** Hierophant = disciplined commitment; Lovers = shared goals achieved through work; Tower = disruption demands adaptation.
- **With Courts:** Queen of Pentacles excels at nurturing effort; Knight of Swords pushes for rapid progress.
- **Green flag:** Intentional care shown through actions, not just words.
- **Red flag:** Burnout from one-sided labor or unspoken expectations.

- **Reader prompts:** "What daily effort makes love stronger?" "Where are actions out of alignment with intentions?"

NINE OF PENTACLES

- **Core love thesis:** Independence and self-worth; thriving alone or within a relationship through strong personal grounding.
- **Wands nearby:** Passion pursued freely, honoring personal autonomy.
- **Cups nearby:** Emotional fulfillment found within self and shared with others.
- **Swords nearby:** Clear boundaries protect independence.
- **Pentacles nearby:** Financial stability and personal success strengthen love.
- **With key Majors:** Empress = flourishing growth; Lovers = interdependence without losing self; Tower = independence challenged or tested.
- **With Courts:** Queen of Pentacles embodies self-sufficiency; Knight of Wands respects freedom while adding excitement.
- **Green flag:** Healthy balance between self and partnership.
- **Red flag:** Isolation or walls built too high to let love in.
- **Reader prompts:** "How do you thrive as your own person?" "Where can independence and intimacy coexist?"

TEN OF PENTACLES

- **Core love thesis:** Legacy, stability, and shared future; love expressed through family, home, and lasting commitments.
- **Wands nearby:** Passion integrated into daily life and family structures.
- **Cups nearby:** Deep emotional safety and generational connection.
- **Swords nearby:** Honest conversations about long-term vision.
- **Pentacles nearby:** Financial health, home life, and shared responsibilities flourish.
- **With key Majors:** Hierophant = traditional family or vows; World = completion of a cycle; Tower = unexpected disruptions to stability.
- **With Courts:** King of Pentacles oversees legacy building; Queen of Cups brings warmth and care to stability.
- **Green flag:** Building a loving, supportive future together.
- **Red flag:** Prioritizing appearances or wealth over love.
- **Reader prompts:** "What legacy are you creating together?" "How do you define long-term love?"

PAGE OF PENTACLES

- **Core love thesis:** Learning and beginnings; love grows through curiosity and steady effort.
- **Wands nearby:** Excitement to act, with careful pacing.
- **Cups nearby:** Emotional openness supports steady growth.
- **Swords nearby:** Communication clarifies intentions early on.
- **Pentacles nearby:** Tangible actions and learning create security.
- **With key Majors:** Fool = starting fresh with practical hope; Lovers = learning how to love well; Temperance = patience during early stages.
- **With Courts:** Knight of Pentacles brings consistency; Queen of Swords adds clarity.
- **Green flag:** Willingness to grow and learn together.
- **Red flag:** Refusing to engage in the work of building love.
- **Reader prompts:** "What lesson is love teaching you now?" "Where can small steps make a big difference?"

KNIGHT OF PENTACLES

- **Core love thesis:** Reliability, steadiness, and devotion; love grows slowly through consistent action.
- **Wands nearby:** Passion balanced by thoughtful planning.
- **Cups nearby:** Deep emotional loyalty expressed through presence.
- **Swords nearby:** Clear, direct conversations about future intentions.
- **Pentacles nearby:** Practical plans for stability, family, and shared resources.
- **With key Majors:** Hierophant = vows and traditions honored; World = steady progress to long-term success; Tower = disruption tests dedication.
- **With Courts:** Queen of Pentacles is the perfect match for devotion; Knight of Wands challenges stability with impulsivity.
- **Green flag:** Dependable, sustainable love.
- **Red flag:** Stagnation or resistance to needed change.
- **Reader prompts:** "How is love showing up in tangible ways?" "What pace serves both partners best?"

QUEEN OF PENTACLES

- **Core love thesis:** Nurturing, grounded care; love expressed through comfort, stability, and abundance.
- **Wands nearby:** Passion integrated into steady devotion.
- **Cups nearby:** Emotional safety flourishes through thoughtful actions.

- **Swords nearby:** Honest conversations about needs and responsibilities.
- **Pentacles nearby:** Strong home life, finances, and physical intimacy are prioritized.
- **With key Majors:** Empress = nurturing love expanded; Lovers = harmonious connection rooted in care; Tower = stability challenged by outside forces.
- **With Courts:** King of Pentacles equals her in devotion; Page of Cups softens and inspires.
- **Green flag:** Love expressed through generous, tangible acts of care.
- **Red flag:** Over-functioning while others take without giving.
- **Reader prompts:** "Where can love be shown through everyday gestures?" "How do you nurture yourself as well as others?"

KING OF PENTACLES

- **Core love thesis:** Provider, protector, and builder; love expressed through reliability and legacy creation.
- **Wands nearby:** Passion directed into long-term visions and actions.
- **Cups nearby:** Warmth and deep emotional loyalty beneath steady exterior.
- **Swords nearby:** Clear, strategic decisions for the relationship's future.
- **Pentacles nearby:** Financial security, home, and shared growth thrive.
- **With key Majors:** Emperor = strong structure and protection; World = lasting legacy fulfilled; Tower = sudden changes test stability.
- **With Courts:** Queen of Pentacles is his perfect partner; Knight of Cups brings romance to his grounded energy.
- **Green flag:** Reliable, protective love built on devotion.
- **Red flag:** Control through money, resources, or rigid traditions.
- **Reader prompts:** "What foundations support this love?" "Where does stability need to evolve?"

acknowledgments

May every card you draw be a mirror,
showing the love that already lives within you.
May your readings be gentle and true,
guiding others not just to answers,
but to themselves.
May the stories you tell through tarot
heal hearts, open doors,
and honor the messy, beautiful dance of desire.
And when the final card is laid down,
may you remember,
you are not only a reader of love stories—
you are also living one.
Shuffle bravely.
Read tenderly.
Love endlessly.

about the author

Lorelai Hamilton is a seasoned tarot reader with over 15 years of professional experience in the field. Based in the Pacific Northwest, Lorelai has honed her craft and established herself as a trusted guide in the realm of tarot.

Alongside her tarot practice, Lorelai shares her expertise with a global audience. Having conducted readings for individuals across 25 countries, she has cultivated a deep understanding of the universal human experience and the interconnectedness of souls around the world.

Despite her worldly reach, Lorelai remains dedicated to providing personal and insightful readings for clients, offering virtual consultations that resonate with authenticity and compassion. In her journey as a tarot reader, she has been accompanied by her familiar, Ham, whose quiet presence adds an element of magic to her practice.

www.ingramcontent.com/pod-product-compliance
Lightning Source LLC
Chambersburg PA
CBHW050059170426
43198CB00014B/2394